HEALTH INSURANCE
AND
PUBLIC POLICY

Recent Titles in
Contributions in Political Science

Israeli Politics in the 1990s: Key Domestic and Foreign Policy Factors
Bernard Reich and Gershon R. Kieval, editors

John Marshall: International Statesman, 1793–1801
Frances Howell Rudko

Plans for Peace: Negotiation and the Arab–Israeli Conflict
Karen A. Feste

The President as Party Leader
James W. Davis

Spain and Central America: Democracy and Foreign Policy
Robin L. Rosenberg

Armed Forces and Political Power in Eastern Europe: The Soviet/Communist Control System
Bradley R. Gitz

Youth's Battle for the Ballot: A History of Voting Age in America
Wendell W. Cultice

Using Theory to Improve Program and Policy Evaluations
Huey-tysh Chen and Peter H. Rossi, editors

East Central Europe after the Warsaw Pact: Security Dilemmas in the 1990s
Andrew A. Michta

Public Management in an Interconnected World: Essays in the Minnowbrook Tradition
Mary Timney Bailey and Richard T. Mayer, editors

United Germany: The Past, Politics, Prospects
H. G. Peter Wallach and Ronald A. Francisco

Watergate and Afterward: The Legacy of Richard M. Nixon
Leon Friedman and William F. Levantrosser, editors

HEALTH INSURANCE AND PUBLIC POLICY

Risk, Allocation, and Equity

EDITED BY

Miriam K. Mills

AND

Robert H. Blank

PREPARED UNDER THE AUSPICES OF THE
POLICY STUDIES ORGANIZATION
Stuart S. Nagel, *Publications Coordinator*

CONTRIBUTIONS IN POLITICAL SCIENCE,
NUMBER 299

Greenwood Press
Westport, Connecticut • London

Library of Congress Cataloging-in-Publication Data

Health insurance and public policy : risk, allocation, and equity /
    edited by Miriam K. Mills and Robert H. Blank ; prepared under the
    auspices of the Policy Studies Organization.
        p.   cm. — (Contributions in political science, ISSN 0147–1066
    ; no. 299.)
        Includes bibliographical references and index.
        ISBN 0–313–28465–2 (alk. paper)
        1. Insurance. Health—Government policy—United States.
    I. Mills, Miriam K.   II. Blank, Robert H.   III. Policy Studies
    Organization.   IV. Series.
    HD7102.U4H412   1992
    368.3'82'00973—dc20   91–43370

British Library Cataloguing in Publication Data is available.

Library of Congress Catalog Card Number: 91–43370
ISBN: 0–313–28465–2
ISSN: 0147–1066

First published in 1992

Greenwood Press, 88 Post Road West, Westport, CT 06881
An imprint of Greenwood Publishing Group, Inc.

Printed in the United States of America

The paper used in this book complies with the
Permanent Paper Standard issued by the National
Information Standards Organization (Z39.48–1984).

10 9 8 7 6 5 4 3 2 1

In grateful memory of
Dr. John Peter Minton, physician, researcher, surgeon, and healer.

Contents

Tables and Figures

TABLES

FIGURES

Introduction

Miriam K. Mills

In the United States, we are faced with steadily accelerating costs for health care, high medical fees, and the exclusion of significant segments of the population from access to care. Among most industrialized nations, only in the United States are millions uninsured or remain in employment positions solely to preserve coverage. In no other country must the elderly become impoverished to qualify for public assistance. While there are many contributing factors to the high cost of care, one element is the payment system, which fails to reward constraint. Patients frequently do not know the cost of services provided and, more significantly, those with insurance do not express concern for cost. Further, too many insurance policies are artfully constructed to avoid high-risk individuals.

Although medical care costs have been steadily escalating at 20 percent annually, nearly one in every seven Americans lack insurance. Not only do lawmakers press for change, but so do taxpayers, insurance agencies, health providers, and patients. At present, almost 60 percent of health care is sponsored by employers. Private coverage accounts for 7 percent, Medicaid 6 percent, Medicare 8.6 percent, military 2 percent, combined benefits 3.7 percent. This leaves a dangerously undercovered group of 13.1 percent of the population (*New York Times*, May 27, 1991).

Who are those most at risk? For many, serious illness such as AIDS, cancer, or significant heart damage is grounds for exclusion. The rural poor, young workers without full-time jobs, the suddenly unemployed, the mentally ill, and the homeless are united in their exclusion from coverage (Gold, 1989). Thus, daily, millions of people fail to receive necessary medical care.

The public wants a health care system that will preserve freedom of choice for the patient but allows the physician to make medical decisions without fear of economic sanctions.

Some observers are suggesting managed care, which ultimately creates a conflict of interest for physicians because they will be rewarded for deliberately limiting care. While we all stress the importance of quality care, the greater emphasis today has been one of concentration on cost containment and the elimination of abuse. Neither of these concerns, however, are likely to improve the overall provision of care. Some of the suggestions to be noted later may, in fact, help contain runaway costs, but considerable questions remain as to the implications for quality and responsive care. Prior to an understanding of health and the security provided by insurance, it may be wise to consider a definition of well-being. The three most generally used terms are life situation, morale, and happiness. Implicit within these constructs are concepts of life embracing purposeful progress toward goals, goodness of fit between the individual and the environment, as well as satisfaction with one's attributes (Antonovsky, 1987). We now turn to a consideration of health within a social context.

SOCIAL ASPECTS OF HEALTH

We are beginning to evolve a system of health service based on the social value that everybody should have relatively equal access to health care, regardless of ability to pay (Anderson, 1968). As a nation, we recognize that the well-being of the general population is a necessary starting point for productivity and an edifying sense of purpose. Too frequently, however, it is the poor who are excluded from health insurance and diminished by the lack of medical sophistication, even where marginal insurance is provided. The question of access is a complex one that includes within it questions of equity, cost, and consideration of patient compliance.

There are some who call for a changing model of health that would lay the emphasis upon individual responsibility. Here the emphasis is on reducing those expenses linked to variations in voluntary life-style. Thus, illness or disability resulting from smoking, alcoholism, drug abuse, and obesity would not be cared for in the same way as what may be termed accidental fate. (It may be that more of the illnesses and disabilities that occur are linked to life-style, but the nature of the link has not yet been determined.)

It could be argued that in order to claim societal health resources, a person should be expected to act responsibly and not unduly contribute to the risk of ill health. Although people have a right to design their own life style, if they choose to engage in practices and behaviors that put them at high risk, they should be prepared to relinquish their claim on societal health care resources (Blank 1986:195).

As a society, we would like to be protected from calamities that people bring on themselves (Wikler, 1978). The underlying view of the worthy and unworthy ill poses some ethical issues. Is health insurance a right or a privilege? Are only the deserving to be spared excessive costs? While some may conclude that each individual life-style choice is irrevocably or genetically determined, the emphasis should be more on outcome than inputs. Health insurance needs to encompass the idea of prevention and education. For all those felled by serious disease who have not had the benefit of preventive guidance, they are nonetheless owed a measure of care.

Physical illness may demand technical intervention, but illnesses deriving from social problems require political organization. "This distinction, often blurred by the undeniable impact of social conditions on physical health, is nonetheless essential to maintain, if therapy is to include both physical and social elements" (Waitzkin, 1983).

CONFLICT OF PERSONAL VERSUS SOCIETAL GOALS

As a people, we are terribly alarmed by the medical care crisis, despite the fact that most individuals are satisfied with the quality of their own medical care. Cost, availability, and quality are not the only concerns. Any sensible health insurance plan needs to balance conflicting purposes made up partially by the exaggeration of medical care problems, coupled with unrealistic expectations for a comprehensive national health insurance program. We require a plan that would balance many contradictory and conflicting purposes, including fiscal constraints, political feasibility, administrative flexibility, and improved care without inflationary cost. Marmor (1983) suggests that resolving all these problems simultaneously is extremely difficult, if not impossible. Cost control, administrative simplicity, and medical efficacy can not easily be reconciled.

We operate on the hopeful assumption that each person has the right to receive unlimited medical care. Yet this assumption is disastrous societally when resources are limited. When we consider the financing delivery of health care, we must consider the ethical problems caused by constraints. Problems will be encountered at all levels of health providers, including physicians, hospitals, the community, and the nation. A delicate balance must be maintained between responsive care and cost containment. Up to now, limited use has been made of incentives to individual physicians to provide more limited services. Many are uneasy with the notion that physicians receive incentives to provide less care. Ultimately, our past experience has made it easier for us to tolerate excessive services rather than to limit their provision (Daniels, 1985).

Underlying concepts of equality is the conviction that equality of opportunity in access to personal medical services is a significant goal. This rosy view, however, is severely limited by the painful realities of expense. We are generally unwilling to permit unequal income distributions to dominate the choice of who does and does not receive necessary care. "We fear the unpredictability of illness and know we (and others) may require help in meeting the costs of care" (Fein, 1986:172). We maintain some caution that in our enthusiasm to contain costs for society-at-large, we as individuals may be harmed by such choices. The insistence of reformers is that reimbursement formulations are motivated solely by the desire to make the health care system more responsive and cost-effective. Unhappily, the consequence may well be that the poor will receive less care because it is easier to contain the costs of specially targeted programs. The poor, and the unhealthy poor, stand to face the greatest deprivation under programs purportedly designed to improve cost-effectiveness.

Rational people, in considering issues of physical and mental well-being are concerned also for related benefits in the social, economic, and educational spheres. Maximizing the good in any one of these areas will, of necessity, diminish costs in others. Veatch (1990) suggests that rational individuals will be willing to trade off benefits in different spheres until the aggregate total is maximized. There will be occasions where the physicians' commitment to patients' well-being may contradict or confront other activities or concerns of the patient. The physician, by entering into a specific relationship, is obliged to act in the best interests of the patient. Yet the cost of an ideal regimen of care may be beyond the physical capacity of the patient. There is also the problem of demanding patient compliance with programs that may be difficult to complete.

INCREASING COSTS

We all deplore the rapidly increasing costs of health care and search for means of containment. While there is general agreement that all citizens should indeed be provided with basic health care, rising costs have limited governmental efforts to increase such access. As the cost of providing care has risen, sacrifices in terms of higher taxes and high employment contributions have made it harder to achieve support for increased access (Ginsburg, 1990).

What are the key factors that explain hospital expenditures? They include rising incomes, the growth of third-party coverage, technological progress, and the graying of the population. There has also been a relative lack of concern about cost at the time of care, partially because of increased insurance in the private sector, as well as more extensive public programs. The single most critical factor in costs has been technology. Hip replacements, chronic dialysis, coronary bypass, and CT scanners are all new weapons in the arsenal of care that become more costly (Aaron and Schwartz, 1984). In 1970, health care costs were roughly $369 per American. By 1986 the cost had climbed to $1,896, with medical technology the primary contributing factor ("Innovation Imperiled," 1988).

As more Americans live longer, there are increasing costs relevant to chronic illness and relative slowness in the recuperation process. Many of the frail elderly of today have limited resources their pensions and other coverage were based on lower income. The high costs and steady expansion of care for the elderly, especially through the Medicare program, has led to a relatively jaundiced view by government of further expansion of Medicare. Another equally compelling factor relating to rising medical costs is the prevailing fee-for-service system. Physicians are rewarded for providing many services to patients who do not object because those with coverage pay but a small portion of the total bill. In some instances, the fact that services are available means that they will be used even if the utility is questionable (*New York Times*, June 15, 1991). Because care is essentially free when demanded, "incentives encourage the provision of all care that produces positive benefits whatever the cost" (Aaron and Schwartz, 1984:113). Although there are internal auditing services within hospitals and programs like Diagnosis Related Groups (DRG) aim at conserving costs, nonetheless, charges steadily accelerate.

While many are concerned for the costs of catastrophic care, this is not a substitute for first-dollar insurance. Even noncatastrophic care can, over time, be exceedingly costly. One approach that is being considered is prior approval of nonemergency admissions. Whereas in 1984 only 5 percent of workers covered by insurance required prior approval, today one-half to three-fourths are in programs requiring that review. Observers of this approach suggest that despite initial savings, due in large part to outpatient treatment and shorter in-hospital confinements, the programs do not continue to reduce increasing costs (National Academy of Sciences, 1989).

In years past, the idealistic health professional always put the interest of the patient foremost. This view has become modified to assuring patient benefits, but only within fiscally superscribed constraints. Is the question here one of reducing costs for existing services or increasing the utility of services provided for cost containment? If the consequence of financial straits is to limit services, this may be an unfortunate consequence. Many insurers are unwilling to pay the costs of experimental treatment that, though very costly, may have the promise of ultimately preserving health. Just as more attention must be paid to preventive measures, it would be shortsighted to willfully reduce the level of technology or innovative interventions in the misguided attempt to contain runaway costs.

LIMITS OF PREVENTION

While the insurance companies are increasing attention to preventive medicine, it should be recognized that prevention as such is neither risk-free nor inexpensive. Sometimes the risk cannot be fully measured until there has been large-scale application. One example was the debate over smallpox vaccine. As new information became available, as changes in the vaccine developed, and as the disease revealed itself, there was a shifting balance of costs and benefits (Russell, 1986).

One looks to prevention as a way of minimizing medical costs, to providing added years of life, to minimizing institutionalization expenses, and to permitting greater productivity. Yet for all that, there are still times where prevention buys more health for the expenditure areas. In other occasions, cure is more economical. As Russell (p. 111) points out, many medical choices will include both prevention and attempted cure, with an important issue being what is the best mix of prevention and treatment. "Curative care remains necessary for those who suffer the disease, despite reasonable efforts to avoid it, as well as for those for whom prevention was introduced too late."

Where prevention can show greater benefits is by earlier health education to minimize or eradicate patterns of drug abuse, tobacco dependency, and improper nutrition. Since violence is also an all-too-frequent cause of injury and death, perhaps some early preventive education should be undertaken to help guide individuals into better coping mechanisms for countering fury and disappointment.

ORGANIZED CARE

Thus far, consideration has been given to existing mechanisms for insurance, as well as options for preventive care. Another track now being considered is organized care wherein increasing numbers of people enroll within entities such as Health Maintenance Organizations (HMOs) and Preferred Payer Organizations. The intent is that these groups will energetically compete with each other to provide the patient-consumer with increasing value for the health dollar. Among the mechanisms used in contrast to the traditional fee-for-service would be those for quality assurance, peer review pressure, and joint development of standards of care (Ginsburg, 1990).

The general public, legislators, physicians, and hospitals are all too aware of the problems involved in any systematic change of approach. There is no system of control or oversight that is so artful that methods for subverting goals are not possible. Those who argue for competitive independent systems assume that there are greater benefits to responsive systems, rather than to more significant economies of scale.

Some may press for a governmental system of widespread insurance, but this would presuppose even tighter regulation and administrative substructure. "This alternative implies that controls can be imposed equitably when the gross expenditure for personal health care service is beyond that which the country feels it can afford for all people in either voluntary or governmental systems" (Anderson, 1968:208). All would agree that patients need protection against catastrophic costs of illness, and that ideally programs should aim at simplicity, with minimal regulation and administrative paperwork. In the case of drug coverage, the elderly, the disabled, and the poor all urgently require expansion of existing programs so as to achieve adequate drug coverage. Under Medicaid, poor patients can receive drugs at no cost, both in and out of the hospital. For the elderly and disabled qualifying for Medicare, there is coverage only for in-hospital prescription drugs. Those with expensive pharmaceutical needs may have to forego food or clothing in order to meet medical drug needs (Silverman, Lee, and Lydecker, 1981).

As noted earlier, there is an implicit assumption that too much medical service, which may be neither effective nor appropriate, is recklessly delivered. All efforts at cost containment have to consider that there is still the capacity for harm in the overassessment of suitability of care. As Jerome Grossman noted, the potential for harm may be "to discourage appropriate care, mishandle confidential patient information, and interfere with physician-patient relationships" (National Academy of Sciences, 1989:12). He has also noted the importance of making provision for due process so that patients and physicians can appeal review decisions.

IMPACT OF CONTROLS

Even the best-designed system for equalizing medical care costs is likely to cause changes in operation. Some observers speculate that limiting expenditures would not really generate significant changes within medical practice. The most likely first containment targets would be cutbacks on purchase and replacement of equipment. Overhead in heating and lighting might occur. One could also expect delayed replacement of linens, reduced quality and range of food, and deferral of maintenance expenditures (Aaron and Schwartz, 1984). Whereas some hospitals under DRG have had surpluses, now deficits would be more likely, which might compel them to draw from endowment funds. It is also reasonable to expect that general staff vacancies would be left open longer, with the result that work loads would increase and morale might suffer. This might indeed be shortsighted. Georgeopolous (1972) has argued that one of the single best contributors to shorter hospital stay is the ratio of registered nurses to patients. Professional nurses, if permitted to provide quality care, can serve the important secondary functions of patient education and motivation.

If one increases the costs to certain beneficiaries, there is a greater likelihood that they will increase voluntary premiums rather than participate directly in cost sharing (Ginzburg, 1990). Generally labor unions have strongly rejected patient cost sharing with the conviction that establishing further financial obstacles would diminish access to care. If the cost sharing is increased to too high a level, the consequence will be that individuals will, of necessity, forego care at earlier stages. They will become sicker and the ultimate burden will be still greater.

Just as the physician is the catalyst for the dimensions of care, it may not be entirely proper to urge physicians to "become societal agents to eliminate marginally beneficial care" (Veatch, 1990:466). Driving the physician further away from the concept of patient loyalty can be destructive to expert opinion and to the single-minded patient concern so essential to patient recovery and compliance. It may indeed be quite proper to exempt the physician from the "social duty of limiting health resource expenditures" (Veatch, 1990:467). Yet, on the other end, if the physician foregoes any role within cost containment, he or she then has unwittingly transferred that power to nonmedical control agents.

Additional impacts of controls include factors relating to overall access and equity. Given the many sunk costs in facilities and equipment, it is foolhardy to expect that resource distribution will ever be totally equitable. Geographic and socioeconomic factors also limit even-handed adjustments to the existing systems.

There will continue to be class differences in the quality of care due to different deductibles, tax allowances, as well as deterrents to unnecessary care. Too much emphasis on eliminating such "unnecessary" care can also limit the application of required care.

Indeed cutting unnecessary care by fiat rather than by reforming the incentives of the system may keep such unnecessary care while severely hitting more necessary care for the poor, since the government funded care is the most likely to be cut, since private care cannot so easily be judged unnecessary and correspondingly cut (Paton, 1990:167).

The designer's dream of sharply curtailing unnecessary care may not come to pass because of the limit of flat-fee HMOs, as well as consumer ignorance. As costs for insurance are passed on to employers, there may be an additional unintended consequence of hurting the poor as employers hold back on positions or lower salaries in order to cover the costs of additional insurance.

To look at cost containment in another way, perhaps the key lies within shared decision-making. As patients are made more cost conscious, with perhaps a limit on tax-deductible insurance premiums, this might be the incentive for patients to choose more cost-effective care systems over the traditional fee-for-service. At the same time, costs can be contained by cutting back on excessive defensive testing used to protect practitioners against malpractice suits. Since physician charges must cover their out-of-pocket malpractice insurance, perhaps some tinkering with the system of penalties and deterrents should be considered. Another approach would be to permit smaller businesses to collaborate in the negotiation and purchase of insurance contracts. If greater market power can be given to smaller employers, they may, in fact, pay to negotiate more favorable premiums.

POLITICAL WILL

Ultimately, it is our desire to maintain competition but minimize undesirable side effects. Many agree that resources can be allocated more wisely and that care should be delivered fairly and efficiently. Clearly, we are no longer able to afford a health sector governed by an uncontrolled insurance system. With all the limits and obstacles, nonetheless, new approaches must be sought.

If we lack the political will to begin to move toward a system of universal coverage coupled with budget controls of hospitals and physicians, it is time to stop the charade that there is a real support for effective cost control or for a more equitable distribution of care.... The fact that access is allocated by an impersonal market and invisible hand may make it more acceptable. It hardly makes it virtuous. (Fein, 1986:215)

Blank (1986) has emphasized the need for difficult rationing decisions. He suggests that this could be done best within a framework of clear goals and priorities. He notes that such a shift will call for greater emphasis on broad preventive approaches, rather than on high-technology curative goals. Making the trade-offs explicit is also essential.

Whatever resulting programs are undertaken, certain inherent inequities will be hard to eliminate, such as between states, between professionals, and between insurance companies. Thus far, the greatest emphasis has been on physicians' charges. A more realistic approach will include a broad reexamination of hospital and outpatient structures as well.

While a government program could provide almost total enrollment in a short time compared with voluntary enrollment, there is still a question as to which is the preferable route. How long would it take voluntary health insurance to cover all the population, even if it is able to do so (Anderson, 1968)?

We are also struck by the differences between members of the population seeing themselves as taxpayers as contrasted to consumers. Each can take the role of the other. "Modern scientific medicine emerged when the political, social, and economic values of this country were not congenial to the concept of government-supported health and welfare programs for the self-supporting segment of the population" (Anderson, 1968:194).

We sometimes examine the performance of other countries. While the National Health Service in England provides care at little or no charge, one cannot therefore conclude that England guarantees an unqualified right to health care. In Canada as well, patients frequently wait many months for diagnostic procedures and surgery. In addition, there is a question whether Canadian treatment lags behind the United States in technological sophistication.

Clearly the lack of information that individuals have about the cost of their insurance may make them less interested in cost containment. It is, however, improper to extrapolate to say that individuals unerringly choose the most costly and wasteful mechanism. It would be better to concentrate on the analysis of cost-benefit results, with the bulk paid by insurance for those procedures that have some reasonable likelihood of impact, with a steadily accelerating portion of the costs to be paid partially by the individual and partially from a high-risk pool. There is always the major inequity caused by prosperity and education, as well as medical sophistication. The United States needs to reevaluate the criticality of widespread health insurance so as to increase the health, well-being, and productivity of its populace. We are one of the few industrial nations that does not provide health care for all. The question comes down to one of right or privilege. Is health care a necessary right and, if so, at what level and up to what point is there entitlement? One may see statistical outcomes, but there is still considerable imprecision. The person faced with serious illness will understandably balk at any possible limitation.

Hope is a necessary correlate of a nation's well-being. The concept of triage is odious because of choices. Whereas we try to stress the value of preparing for a rainy day, sometimes families can be overwhelmed by cost. While other nations provide a basic safety net of health care, this is not really available in the United States. We seem more geared to heroic and high-tech measures. Commercial insurers pushed their premiums over 20 percent in 1989 and further increases are on the way. Whereas cost is never a constraint in individual circumstances, it is difficult to abstract from that to societal taxpayer costs. There are also differences in personal capacity for overcoming bureaucracy. Is it fair that the intelligent and industrious necessarily get better health care, or should it occur easily and naturally without special effort?

We must reluctantly come to the conclusion that large expenditures are no longer associated only with rare and catastrophic events. As Fein has noted, few families could finance an average hospital stay out of current income. Further insurance covering expenditures beyond a defined amount would be of no benefit to those unable to meet expenses below the limit. "At the same time, catastrophic insurance and the guaranteed payment of large bills could lead to unnecessary duplication of costly facilities and stimulate the purchase and use of high technology. The result could be both increased cost and misallocation of resources" (Fein, 1986:147).

This book's contributors examine many aspects of health insurance, providing a full understanding of the disparate operating forces. Discussions of the findings precede each section. It is our hope that this book will contribute to full review and consideration of the complexity of health insurance coverage and financing.

REFERENCES

Aaron, Henry J. and William B. Schwartz. 1984. *The Painful Prescription: Rationing Hospital Care.* Washington, DC: The Brookings Institution.

Anderson, Odin W. 1968. *The Uneasy Equilibrium: Private and Public Financing of Health Services in the United States, 1875–1965.* New Haven, CT: College & University Press.

Antonovsky, Aaron. 1987. *Unraveling the Mystery of Health: How People Manage Stress and Stay Well.* San Francisco: Jossey-Bass.

Blank, Robert H. 1986. *Rationing Medicine.* New York: Columbia University Press.

Daniels, Norman. 1985. *Just Health Care.* New York: Cambridge University Press.

Fein, Rashi. 1986. *Medical Costs: The Search for a Health Insurance Policy.* Cambridge, MA: Harvard University Press.

Georgopolous, Basil. 1972. *Organization Research in Health Institutions.* Ann Arbor: University of Michigan.

Ginsburg, Paul B. 1990. "Alternative Approaches to Health Care Cost Containment." *Jurimetrics Journal* 30(4):447–52, 459.

Gold, Allan R. 1989. "Living with No Medical Insurance: The Struggle to Make Do." *New York Times*, July 30.

"Innovation Imperiled? Medical Technology in an Era of Cost Containment." A conference sponsored by the American Medical Association and the Health Policy Agenda for the American People. October 27–28, 1988. Chicago.

Marmor, Theodore R. 1983. *Political Analysis and American Medical Care: Essays.* New York: Cambridge University Press.

National Academy of Sciences. "Balancing Cost Control and Quality in Health Care." 1989. *National Research Council News Report* 39:10.

New York Times. 1991. "Half a Medical Plan is Better..." (Editorial). June 15.

New York Times. 1991. "The Right Medicine." (Editorial). May 27.

Paton, Calum S. 1990. *U.S. Health Politics.* Brookfield, VT: Gower.

Russell, Louise B. 1986. *Is Prevention Better Than Cure?* Washington, DC: The Brookings Institution.

Silverman, Milton, Philip R. Lee, and Mia Lydecker. 1981. *Pills & the Public Purse: The Routes to National Drug Insurance.* Berkeley: University of California Press.

Veatch, Robert M. 1990. "Physicians and Cost Containment: The Ethical Conflict." *Jurimetrics Journal* 30(4):464, 466–67, 471, 481.

Waitzkin, Howard. 1983. *The Second Sickness: Contradictions of Capitalist Health Care.* New York: The Free Press.

Wikler, Daniel I. 1978. "Persuasion and Coercion for Health: Ethical Issues in Government Efforts to Change Life Styles." *Milbank Memorial Fund Quarterly* 56(3):303–338.

PART I
OVERVIEW OF HEALTH POLICY IMPACTS

Part I of this volume considers health policy broadly by examining the congressional setting and competing proposals. Chapter 1 examines alternative approaches to the finance of health care. Given the huge numbers of uninsured and underinsured individuals, great pressures are placed on society to provide equitable care. Broyles, Reilly, and Jones provide a thorough assessment of eight proposals for cost containment, each of which offers a varied approach to administrative structure and design. Some emphasize prospective payment mechanisms, whereas others consider compensating providers.

Broyles, Reilly, and Jones indicate that market pressures encourage providers to compete for patients as well as for physicians. Attracting these groups can result in significant increased costs for equipment and technicians. Broyles et al. suggest the advantages of a prepayment program, as well as cost containment of annual salaries. While nationalized health insurance is a feasible option, there is currently still much opposition.

Chapter 2 by Hinckley and Hill suggests that while it is difficult enough to predict the actions of individual congressional members, the collective behavior is even more difficult to predict. Several alternative descriptive frameworks have received wide currency, and the authors examine those developed by Davis, Dempster, and Rodolfsky; the issue of typology originated by Lowi; and the closely related cost-benefit assignment approaches expressed by Wilson in 1973. Practical events, however, expose the weaknesses in theory. Incrementalism has suffered from changes within the budget environment of the 1980s. These events raise serious questions about the redistribution and cost assignment hypotheses stemming from the Lowi and Wilson approaches. This chapter by Hinckley and Hill is an effort to identify and overcome some of the predictable weaknesses of these theoretical approaches. All too frequently, Congress does not act as the theories predict. The authors point out that no policy is a self-sufficient entity and that all policies are in some way affected by provisions within other legislation.

Armstrong in Chapter 3 observes that the goals of a national health insurance policy are to improve the health of the population by providing access to services and to operate efficiently in terms of costs and management. This suggests that the major tasks of evaluation are to monitor the health status of the public, evaluate different models of providing health care, and analyze the interaction between consumers and providers of health care services so as to determine what contributes to effectiveness, consumers' satisfaction, and awareness of available services. National health insurance policy evaluation must also determine and measure the effectiveness of alternative health insurance options. This chapter presents a social policy analysis framework to examine the interaction between health care, health insurance, and health status.

1

National Health Insurance:
A Qualitative Assessment
of Several Proposals

Robert W. Broyles, Bernard J. Reilly, and Walter J. Jones

The American health industry is in a state of disarray. Despite efforts to control inflationary pressures, spending on health care consumes 11.5 percent of the gross national product (GNP) and, if present trends continue, it is estimated that 15 percent of our output will be committed to health care by the year 2000. Adjusted for inflation, the amount of spending per person increased at an annual rate of 4.0 percent during 1970–80 and 4.6 percent per year during 1980–86 (U.S. Department of Commerce, 1990; Division of National Cost Estimates, 1987; Schieber and Poullier, 1987). Confronted with the deficit and foreign competition, the growth in health spending represents an increasingly intolerable burden to the federal government and the business community.

Concurrently, recent estimates indicate that approximately 37 million Americans are uninsured and that many others are underinsured. The growing reluctance of employers to offer coverage to employees or their dependents, the emphasis by insurance carriers on enrolling those who are least likely to require care, and the emphasis on provisions that exclude preexisting conditions have contributed to an expanding pool of uninsured and underinsured Americans (Sulvetta and Swartz, 1986; Wilensky, 1988; Farley, 1985b). Further, inadequacies in coverage and a growing reliance on cost-sharing arrangements not only reduce access to care by those who are in greatest need but also exacerbate inequities in the distribution of service (Manga and Weller, 1980).

Recently, policy deliberations focused on national health insurance as a mechanism that might control spending, improve access, and reduce inequities in the distribution of care. Among the most prominent of these proposals are:

1. A National Health Program for the United States, proposed by Himmelstein et al. (1989)
2. A National Medical Care System, suggested by Terris et al. (1991)
3. The U.S. Health Act, recommended by Roybal (1991)
4. A Blue Print for Health Care Reform, developed by the Pepper Commission (Rockefeller, 1991)
5. Restructuring Health Care in the United States, recommended by Nutter et al. (1991)
6. The Health Security Partnership, proposed by the Committee for National Health Insurance (Fein, 1991)
7. For the Health of a Nation, developed by the National Leadership Commission on Health Care (1989)
8. A Consumer-Choice Health Plan, recommended by Enthoven and Kronick (1991)

The basic features of these proposals are by no means uniform and, if adopted, each would create a set of incentives that materially influence the potential for controlling inflationary pressures and ensuring distributional equity.

Summarized in Table 1.1 are the basic features and administrative arrangements recommended by each of the proposals. It is possible to classify the national health plans into two broad categories. The first consists of proposals advanced by Himmelstein et al., Terris et al., and the Committee for National Health Insurance (NHI). As indicated in the table, these proposals recommend a national health plan that is administered by a public agency and financed by a single source of funding. In addition, this first group recommends a reliance on prospective payment mechanisms to compensate providers and the elimination of direct charges as a mechanism of financing or rationing health care.

The second set of proposals is comprised of the plans recommended by Enthoven and Kronick, the National Leadership Commission, the Pepper Commission, and Nutter et al. If adopted, these proposals would require employers to sponsor private insurance coverage for employees and depend on a public subsidy to finance the premiums of unemployed members of society. The plans comprising the second group also rely, in varying degrees, on current methods of compensating providers and an increased dependence on direct charges to ration health care. Predicated on the assumption that the goals of a national health plan and related financial arrangements are to control spending, improve access, and ensure that the use of service is determined by medical need, the purpose of this chapter is twofold. The first purpose is to assess the potential of the proposals to control inflationary

Table 1.1
Basic Features and Administration

AUTHOR	BASIC FEATURES	ADMINISTRATION
Himmelstein	National Public Insurance Program	Public Agencies
Terris	National Medical Care System	Health Departments
Roybal	National Insurance Program	Public Agency
Committee for NHI	Federal-State Program of Health Insurance Through Qualified Plans	Public Agency; Private Insurers
National Leadership Commission	Excluding Medicare All Persons or Firms Required to Purchase Insurance or Pay Tax to Support Care Used by the Uninsured	Private Insurance Based on Employment Status; Residual Administered by State Agency
Nutter	Employer-Sponsored Coverage for Employees and Dependents. Expanded Medicaid and Risk Pool for Others	Public Agency Private Insurers
Pepper Commission	Employee-Sponsored Coverage; Federal Program to Insure Use by Unemployed	Public Agency Private Insurers
Enthoven Kronick	Employers Required to Provide Coverage for Employees and Dependents Medicare, Medicaid Voluntary Insurance for Others, Subsidized by States	Employers Contract with Private Carrier for Employees; States Contract with Insurers for All Others

pressures in the hospital industry and the market for physician services. The second purpose is to evaluate the potential of the proposed plans to improve access and redress inequities in the distribution of care.

THE FOUNDATIONS

The debate concerning inflationary pressures in the health industry resulted in essentially two policy options that are embodied in the proposals (Reilly and Broyles, 1986). Based on normative economic theory, proponents of the first contend that an increased reliance on market mechanisms will control costs and expenditures on health care. The market solution consists of policies designed to stimulate the cost consciousness of providers, thereby altering supply decisions, improving efficiency, lowering costs, and reducing prices (Enthoven, 1981; Greenberg, 1985; Havighurst, 1983; Brecher, 1984; Prottas and Handler, 1987).

Proponents of the competitive approach also contend that the insurance mechanism protects consumers from the financial risks of illness or injury, lowers the effective price of care, and reduces the cost consciousness of consumers. Designed to attenuate the effects of insurance coverage, proponents of the market solution recommend several policy options. The first involves the traditional tax treatment of premiums financed by the employer. It is contended that, by eliminating the practice of excluding the employer's contribution to premium payments from the taxable income of the employee, the demand for health insurance and health care might be reduced. Also designed to reduce the demand for health insurance and health care are proposals to transfer the responsibility for financing premium payments from the employer to the employee (Butler, 1991; Chernick et al., 1987; Pauly, 1986; Jensen et al., 1984). Further, recognizing that health insurance reduces effective prices, proponents of the market solution also recommend a greater reliance on cost-sharing arrangements to depress use and costs (M. Feldstein, 1971; Pauly, 1971; Seidman, 1977).

The second of the two policy options involves an increased dependence on regulatory intervention and, in particular, the adoption of prospective payment to control inflationary pressures. Prospective payment is a generic term that refers to financing mechanisms in which the rate or level of compensation is predetermined and the provider receives the amount irrespective of the costs that are incurred. Proponents of prospective payment argue that providers are induced to ensure that costs are less than or equal to the predetermined rate or level of compensation.

CONTROL OF COSTS AND EXPENDITURES: A FOCUS ON PROVIDERS

The assessment of the potential of the national health plans to control costs and expenditures is predicated on the assumption that the method of compensation is a primary determinant of the provider's performance. The evaluation of the various proposals focuses on expenditures, operating costs or expenses, and spending on capital. For the purposes of this chapter, operating costs or expenses refer to the monetary value of direct resources, comprised of labor and consumable supplies, that are used to provide patient care. Accordingly, the potential of national health insurance to control operating costs depends on the differential effects of the proposals on the mix of patients, the composition of care, the efficiency of resource use, and factor prices. Excluded as an item of operating costs are those expenses that are related to the plant and equipment of the provider, a source of inflationary pressure that is considered separately. Finally, the term "expendi-

Table 1.2
Provisions That Induce Providers to Control Costs and Expenditures

AUTHOR	HOSPITALS	PHYSICIANS
Himmelstein	Prospective Payment Based on Global Budget	Salary or Negotiated Fee Schedule
Terris	Prospective Payment Based on Budget	Compensation from Budget of Provider Organization
Committee for NHI	Prepayment Based Negotiated Budget	Capitation or Fee Schedule
Roybal	Universal System of Prospective Prices, Based on DRGs	Fees, Based on RBRVS
Nutter	Universal System of Prospective Prices, Based on DRGs	Fees, Based on RBRVS
Pepper Commission	Public: Prospective Prices, Based on DRGs Private: Payment Mechanisms Unchanged Managed Care, ADS	Fees, Based on RBRVS
Enthoven Kronick	Managed Care, ADS	Managed Care, ADS
National Leadership Commission	Not specified	Not specified

ture" will refer to the actual or anticipated payments from patients or public and private insurers to providers of care.

This section considers the potential of the proposals to control expenditures and the operating costs in the markets for hospital and physician care. The assessment concludes with an evaluation of potential effects of the two groups of proposals on the costs of capital.

Control of Operating Costs and Expenditures in the Hospital Industry

Summarized in Table 1.2 are the provisions of each proposal that are likely to exert a direct effect on expenditures and operating costs in the market for hospital care. The descriptions of the various funding mechanisms reveal that Enthoven and Kronick and, to a lesser extent, the Pepper Commission recommend an increased dependence on the pricing system and the market mechanism as approaches to the problem of controlling hospital costs and expenditures. Conversely, the other proposals recommend a re-

liance on regulatory intervention and prospective payment to control inflationary pressures.

Among the desirable attributes of the proposals advanced by Himmelstein
et al., the Committee for NHI, Terris et al., and Nutter et al. are a universal
application of rate regulation, the elimination of multiple sources of funding,
and the recommendation to adopt a uniform method of determining rates
or levels of compensation. It is common to argue that the concurrent dependence on multiple sources of funding and several payment mechanisms
contribute to the inflationary pressures in the hospital sector (Evans, 1983;
Manga and Broyles, 1986; Iglehart, 1986; Detsky et al., 1983). That costs,
charges, and profitability differ among multiple sources of funding has been
demonstrated previously (Miller and Byrne, 1977; Lewin and Associates,
1981; Danzon, 1982; Sloan and Becker, 1984). These findings suggest that
the dependence on multiple payers and financial arrangements induces the
hospital to transfer costs from one group of patients or payers to another
and thereby reduce the fiscal pressure to control operating expenses. By
eliminating the fragmentation in responsibility for controlling expenses and
expenditures inherent in the current system of financing care, it is probable
that the adoption of a universal system of prospective payment would exert
uncompromised fiscal pressure to reduce spending in the hospital industry.

The relative effects of a partial and universal application of prospective
payment have been explored previously (Rosko, 1989b). Compared to the
rate of inflation that would occur in the absence of prospective payment,
Hadley and Swartz (1989) concluded that the universal application of rate
regulation lowered costs by 13 to 15 percent, while a partial application
reduced expenses by 11 percent. Similarly, results reported by Broyles (1990)
and Rosko and Broyles (1986, 1987) indicate that a universal application
of prospective payment exerts greater fiscal pressure on hospitals to control
operating costs than a partial application of rate regulation. That a universal
application of prospective payment reduces price differentials and thereby
increases the imperative to control operating costs has also been documented
by Rosko (1989a), Blair (1987), and Thorpe (1987). Accordingly, the proposals advanced by Himmelstein et al., Terris et al., the Committee for NHI,
and Nutter et al. would eliminate the potential to transfer costs and engage
in differential pricing practices, a feature that would exert an uncompromised fiscal pressure on hospitals to improve the efficiency of resource use,
lower factor prices, and control operating costs.

Although not specified by the proposals, the incentive to control expenses
is enhanced by a provision that requires the hospital to absorb the net loss
of the period or enables the institution to retain all or a portion of the net
surplus for discretionary use. Conversely, the incentive to control operating
costs is reduced or eliminated if the payment mechanism finances all or a
portion of the net loss or if the institution is required to return a portion
or all of the net savings to the funding agent.

In addition to the scope of regulatory authority and the disposition of the net surplus or loss, the likely effects of prospective payment on expenditures and operating costs also depend on the unit of payment. Essentially two approaches are suggested by the proposals that recommend a reliance on rate regulation to finance hospital care. Excluding the costs of capital, the first involves the adoption of the global budget as the basis for determining the rate or level of compensation. Based on the Canadian approach, Himmelstein et al., Terris et al., and the Committee for NHI suggest that operating expenses should be financed by a system of prepayment in which the annual level of compensation is determined by the anticipated operating expenses reported in the global budget of the hospital. Once approved, the institution would receive the authorized amount of funding in the form of periodic installments that are intended to finance operating activity on a current basis.

The proposal to adopt a system of prepayment, based on the budget, is accompanied by several advantages. First, the fiscal responsibility of the funding agent is limited to the authorized level of compensation, a feature that is expected to control expenditures on hospital care. Further, the proposal to restrict funding to the set of periodic installments induces the hospital to ensure that operating expenses are less than the predetermined rate or level of prepayment. Recognizing that the proposals advanced by Himmelstein et al., Terris et al., and the Committee for NHI are similar to the Canadian system, previous research indicates that an adoption of the prepayment mechanism and the budget to determine the rate of compensation would control operating costs, improve the distribution of service, restrain administrative expenses, and maintain or improve the quality of care (Fuchs and Hahn, 1990; Barer and Evans, 1986; Iglehart, 1986; Detsky et al., 1983; Evans, 1983).

Even though a system of prepayment induces the hospital to improve operational efficiency and acquire resources at lower factor prices, a system similar to the Canadian method of financing hospital care might result in unintended and undesired outcomes. To ensure that operating costs are less than or equal to the periodic installment, the hospital may reduce the volume of care by lowering admissions, treating less severe cases, compressing the length of stay, and minimizing the amount of ancillary care provided to the patient population. Accordingly without modification, the fiscal incentives that accompany a system of prepayment based on the global budget may adversely influence access or compromise the quality of care.

The potentially undesirable outcomes might be avoided by supplementing the periodic installments with an end-of-period adjustment that compensates the hospital for all or a portion of the difference between actual operating costs and the predetermined amount of payment. As demonstrated elsewhere (Broyles and Rosko, 1987, 1990; Broyles and Reilly, 1984) it is possible to partition the difference between actual and expected costs into portions that are attributable to:

1. the provision of more or less required care than planned;
2. the provision of unnecessary services;
3. the use of resources more or less efficiently than anticipated;
4. a set of factor prices that were higher or lower than expected; and
5. a set of joint effects resulting from differences in volume, efficiency, and factor prices.

Assuming that actual operating costs exceed the annual amount of payment, the end-of-period adjustment should compensate the hospital for unanticipated increases in factor prices that are attributable to market forces and for additional units of care required to satisfy the health needs of the patient population. On the other hand, the additional costs resulting from the provision of unnecessary care and foregone discounts that result from a failure to honor obligations on a timely basis should be excluded from the expenses that are recovered as an end-of-period adjustment.

The end-of-period adjustment also represents a mechanism that induces the hospital to improve operational efficiency. For example, the institution should be permitted to retain, for discretionary use, all or a portion of the cost savings that are attributable to the employment of resources more efficiently than planned. Conversely, the additional costs that result from the relatively inefficient use of resources should be excluded from the expenses that are recovered as an end-of-period adjustment. Accordingly, the set of periodic installments and the end-of-period adjustment might be used as instruments that encourage the hospital to benefit from discounts offered by vendors, to improve operational efficiency, to avoid the provision of unnecessary service, and to provide the mix of care required by the health needs of the patient population.

Similar to the proposals advanced by Himmelstein et al., Terris et al., and the Committee for NHI, the plans developed by Roybal and Nutter et al. recommend a universal application of prospective payment to finance the costs of hospital care. Although a universal application of rate regulation induces the hospital to improve efficiency and acquire resources at lower prices, the recommendation to rely on case mix to determine rates of prospective payment may jeopardize quality, exacerbate the problem of distributional equity, and dilute the potential to control costs or expenditures. As indicated by assessments of the Medicare pricing system and other similar payment mechanisms, hospitals would be induced to ensure that operating costs per case are less than or equal to the predetermined rate of payment. In this regard, operating expenses per case might be controlled by improving operational efficiency, acquiring resources at lower prices, compressing the length of stay, and reducing the amount of ancillary care per patient (Broyles and Rosko, 1985; Rosko, 1989a; Broyles, 1990; Rosko and Broyles, 1986 and 1987).

In addition to the potentially adverse effects on quality that might result from a decline in the length of stay and the use of ancillary care, the flow of admissions may be influenced by incentives that induce the hospital to increase the number of admissions and thereby stimulate expenditures. An increase in the number of cases to which fixed costs are allocated lowers the cost per patient and, holding price constant, improves profitability or lowers the net loss. That a reduction in the cost per case is offset by an increase in volume has been documented previously. For example, findings reported by Rosko and Broyles (1986, 1987) and Salkever et al. (1986) suggest that the savings associated with a decline in the cost per case are attenuated by an increase in admissions.

It is also possible that the mix of admissions, costs, and expenditures would be influenced by the next surplus or loss per case. If rates of payment include a uniform profit margin per case, hospitals are induced to improve profitability by stimulating the admission of patients assigned to all diagnostic conditions, resulting in an improvement in access but an increase in both costs and expenditures. On the other hand, if the profit margin per case differs among the diagnostic categories, the institution is induced to increase the portion of the patient population for which a relatively high net surplus is anticipated and to reduce the number of cases that are expected to yield a low net surplus or result in a net loss. Similarly, the adoption of a stringent set of prospective prices may reduce costs and expenditures by lowering admissions, an outcome that would exacerbate inequities in the distribution of service.

It is also possible to argue that a reliance on case mix to establish rates of payment induces the hospital to admit patients who present less severe conditions and require a less intensive course of treatment, resulting in the control of cost but little, if any, effect on expenditures in the short term. Accordingly, if adopted, proposals to rely on Diagnosis Related Groups to establish prospective prices would enhance the dependence of the admission decision, access to care, and the course of treatment on financial incentives that are specific to the hospital rather than on the health needs of the patient.

The proposal advanced by the Pepper Commission recommends a reliance on a variety of payment mechanisms that might be developed and implemented by private insurers. In addition to costs, charges, and prospective pricing systems based on the patient, grouped by diagnostic nomenclature, insurers might employ the day of care, ancillary services, and operative procedures to establish predetermined rates of compensation.

The regulation of per diem rates or charges may result in desirable and unintended consequences. Depending on the unit of payment, it is reasonable to expect hospitals to reduce the cost per day or the cost per service by improving the efficiency of operations or acquiring resources at lower factor prices. Unfortunately, however, the regulation of per diem rates or charges induces the hospital to stimulate revenues and expenditures by increasing the volume of care (Rosko and Broyles, 1988). An increase in the number of units to which fixed costs are assigned lowers the expense per unit and, holding price constant, improves profitability. Further, most analysts recognize that the costs per day are higher during the early phases of the hospital episode than during the later phase or prior to discharge. Since a regulated per diem rate is constant, the hospital is encouraged to extend the length of stay and employ net surpluses earned during the latter phase of the hospital episode to subsidize losses that are incurred during the early stage. These observations suggest that the regulation of charges or per diem rates would probably stimulate volume, revenues, and expenditures.

Although most of the proposals summarized in Table 1.2 recommend prospective payment as a funding mechanism, Enthoven and Kronick and, to a lesser extent, the Pepper Commission propose market structures and competition among providers as the preferred solution to the problem of reducing inflationary pressures. These proposals are characterized by a dependence on multiple sources of funding and several methods of compensating hospitals. For reasons cited previously, these provisions encourage hospitals to engage in differential pricing practices, to transfer costs from one group of patients or payers to another, and to avoid the fiscal pressure to control costs and expenditures.

The health plans proposed by the Pepper Commission and by Enthoven and Kronick are predicated on the assumption that competitive pressures force providers to improve the efficiency of operations, acquire resources at lower factor prices, and control the costs of care. The proposals also assume that a growing number of providers increases supply, lowers price, and, if demand is inelastic in the relevant range, reduces expenditures. Enthoven and Kronick also contend that a growth in the number of providers who are associated with alternate delivery systems (ADSs) and, in particular, HMOs constitute the most effective approach to the problem of controlling use, costs, and expenditures.

Reviews by Luft (1981) and Rosko and Broyles (1988) suggest that the costs and use of care are lower among members of HMOs than their counterparts enrolled in traditional plans. Previous findings also indicate that expenditures per subscriber in traditional plans are 15 to 30 percent more than those of the typical member of an HMO. Further, the relative effectiveness of HMOs is attributable to a reduced use of hospital care as measured by the admission rate and the days of care per prescriber.

It is possible that the performance of HMOs is attributable to favorable selection, a dimension that has been the subject of extensive investigation. Although the evidence is mixed, recent studies reviewed by Rosko and Broyles (1988) indicate that HMOs benefitted from a favorable selection bias, a finding that may explain the lower utilization rates and costs achieved by HMOs. However, in an examination of expenditures and use, the Rand Health Insurance Experiment avoided the bias resulting from the treatment of insurance coverage as an exogenous variable. Based on 20 characteristics, the finite selection model was used to assign subjects to one of 14 insurance plans and a prepaid group practice. As a consequence, it is unlikely that favorable selection bias contributed to the 25 percent lower expenditure per HMO enrollee (Manning, Liebowitz et al., 1984).

Even though HMOs appear to control costs, the potential effectiveness of these systems depends on several factors. Proponents of the market solution contend that competitive pressures induce providers to improve efficiency, lower costs, and attract patients from inefficient sources of care by offering a more comprehensive range of benefits or reducing premiums, deductibles, and coinsurance rates. Among the more questionable aspects of the proposals that recommend the competitive solution to the problem of controlling costs and expenditures is the role of consumers in evaluating sources of care and selecting the provider that offers the "desired" mix of benefits at least cost.

An assessment of alternate sources of care requires consumers to evaluate their current and future health status in relation to the potential use of service, the benefit structure, the effectiveness of care, and relative costliness. The ability of the individual to evaluate current health status is impaired by several factors. With the exception of trivial conditions, episodes of illness are usually unique to the individual, a feature that reduces the ability of the individual to rely on previous experience as the basis for evaluating current health needs and alternate sources of care. The individual might consult with others but the experiences of laypersons are limited and their homeostatic processes are different. Alternatively, the individual might seek multiple opinions from health professionals but, since medicine is an inexact science, professional opinions may differ. Further, the individual must be aware of the benefits derived from several opinions and possess the ability to evaluate differences in professional judgments (Evans, 1983). Since it seems unreasonable to ascribe these attributes to the typical patient, the paucity of information available to most consumers represents an impediment to the rational assessment of current health needs in relation to relative costliness and effectiveness.

In addition to the factors that impede an evaluation of current health status, the assessment of future needs in relation to alternate sources of care, benefit structure, and relative costs is complicated by other considerations. As suggested by Arrow (1963), the need for medical services is irregular and unpredictable. Arrow also contends that uncertainty concerning quality and outcome is more pervasive in the health industry than in other sectors of the economy, and that "recovery from disease is as unpredictable as its incidence." Accordingly, uncertainties surrounding the inci-

dence of disease or injury, the potential need for service, and the efficacy
of treatment also impair the ability of the consumer to evaluate alternatives,
select the provider that offers the preferred benefit structure at least cost,
and ensure that only efficient plans will survive and flourish.

In addition to those specified above, other considerations appear to reduce
the potential effectiveness of proposals to rely on competitive pressures as
a mechanism to control costs. A growing body of evidence indicates that
greater market pressures induce providers to engage in nonprice competition
for patients, based on quality amenities. Similarly, hospitals may compete
for physicians by offering more amenities or acquiring sophisticated equipment, practices that increase costs (Robinson and Luft, 1987; Farley 1985a).
In this regard, results reported by Hadley and Swartz (1989) suggest that,
as competitive pressures grow, the costs of hospital care increase. Finally,
even if a reliance on market mechanisms results in lower prices and costs,
many service areas are unable to support the number of providers required
to ensure competition. Viewed from the perspective of incentives designed
to influence supply decisions, these observations indicate that the competitive solution is simply inappropriate for small or isolated markets and may
result in higher rather than lower costs.

Controlling Expenditures on Physician Care

The problem of controlling expenditures on physician care is perhaps the
most difficult issue confronting the policy analyst. As summarized in Table
1.2, fee-for-service, capitation, and salaries are recommended as mechanisms
for compensating physicians. In addition to the potential effects on expenditures, the proposed methods of financing physician care might exert
a differential influence on the prescribing patterns and productivity of the
provider.

The fee-for-service mechanism is characterized by several serious defi-
ciencies. First, most analysts recognize that the fee-for-service mechanism
induces the physician to augment professional income and increase expenditures by prescribing additional units of service (Langwell and Nelson,
1986; Wilensky and Rossiter, 1986). Further, since profit margins differ
among components of physician care, the provider is induced to prescribe
those services for which the net surplus is greatest, an incentive that distorts
the course of treatment in relation to the medical needs of the patient.
Proposals that recommend a reliance on the fee-for-service mechanism may
create incentives that result in an incongruence between prescribing patterns
and the medical needs of the patient population and are unlikely to control
expenditures or redress the problem of distributional equity.

The Committee for NHI, Roybal, Nutter et al., and the Pepper Commission recommend a reliance on the fee-for-service mechanism, modified
to reflect a relative value scale based on the resource consumption associated

with each procedure. The proposal to rely on time requirements, complexity, and practice costs to develop the relative value scale might establish a congruence between the cost per unit of each component of physician care and the corresponding fee. As a consequence, a reliance on relative resource costs to develop the fee schedule may reduce or eliminate the dependence of prescribing patterns on differential profit margins and redress inequities in the charges for cognitive and technical procedures (Hsaio et al., 1988).

Recognizing that a reliance on a relative value scale based on resource consumption to establish prices reduces several difficulties inherent in usual and customary charges, an important deficiency in the approach is worthy of note. In the absence of legislation that imposes a limit on expenditures or volume, the reliance on the fee-for-service mechanism, based on relative values and resource costs, induces the physician to augment professional income by providing additional units of all services, rather than conditioning clinical decisions on differential profit margins. As a consequence, the adoption of policies that ensure a congruence between the cost of resource consumption and the corresponding fee may reduce the dependence of prescribing patterns on differential profit margins but are unlikely to control spending on physician care (Lee et al., 1990).

In addition to the adoption of a modified fee-for-service mechanism, several of the proposals recommend salaries and per capita rates to finance physician care. A reliance on per capita rates is accompanied by several benefits. First, depending on the method of adjusting payment rates, the adoption of a capitation system may reduce financial incentives to augment professional income by increasing the volume of service. If adjustments in the rate of compensation are independent of previous prescribing patterns, the physician is induced to reduce the amount of care per case, a practice that would reduce costs, exacerbate inequities in the distribution of care, and exert little, if any, effect on expenditures in the short term. In addition, a reliance on per capita rates to compensate physicians transfers fiscal risk from the insurer to the provider. As a result, the adoption of a capitation scheme to compensate physicians induces the provider to increase net income by improving operational efficiency or acquiring resources at lower factor prices.

Although accompanied by several benefits, a reliance on per capita rates to compensate physicians might result in undesirable outcomes. If adjustments to the rate of payment per patient reflect prior prescribing patterns, the physician is induced to prescribe additional units so as to increase the capitation rate in a future period, resulting in inflationary pressures similar to those stimulated by the reliance on costs to compensate hospitals. Further, in the absence of provisions that reduce or eliminate the effects of favorable selection bias, physicians would be induced to augment net income by enrolling patients who are expected to require relatively few diagnostic and therapeutic services, a practice that might jeopardize the access of those in greatest need of care (Hornbrook et al., 1989; Rossiter et al., 1988; Thomas et al., 1983). As suggested by findings reported by Anderson et. al (1990), the effects of these outcomes might be reduced by basing per capita rates on the input costs of the provider and health status, as measured by age, sex, and disability.

A reliance on annual salaries to compensate physicians also severs the dependence of professional income on not only the volume of prescribed care but also the caseload of the physician—features that are likely to restrict spending more than those associated with capitation methods. For obvious reasons, however, a reliance on annual salaries induces physicians to restrict caseload, commit less time to market activity, and lower the volume of service per hour or per patient (Rosko and Broyles, 1988). In addition to the potentially adverse effects on quality, access, and productivity, a reliance on salaries to compensate physicians is accompanied by the imperative to develop an acceptable approach to the politically sensitive problem of establishing an income structure that depicts the relative value of the services provided by the various specialties. In addition, the salary structure should reflect differences in a variety of factors, to include not only the relative risks of malpractice litigation, but also the location, training, and experience of the physician.

To compensate for the potentially perverse incentives inherent in using per capita rates or annual salaries to finance physician care, Broyles and Reilly (1984) argue that the cash receipts of the provider should consist of two components. The first is comprised of a set of nonrandom payments that reflect a prospective fee schedule, based on relative values, and the mix of care that a typical physician practicing in a given specialty is expected to provide during the planning period. The second is an end-of-period adjustment that compensates the provider for additional units of service that are justifiable in clinical terms and were required to satisfy legitimate medical needs. On the other hand, the end-of-period adjustment should be reduced by the portion of the physician's professional income that was generated by providing unnecessary units of care and by charging fees that exceed predetermined rates of payment. Similar to the discussion of financing hospital care, the end-of-period adjustment might be employed as an instrument that induces the physician to provide units of required care and discourages the provider from prescribing unnecessary services or charging excessive fees, thereby controlling expenditures and ensuring that the mix of care is congruent with medical needs.

ACCESS AND DISTRIBUTIONAL EQUITY: THE EFFECTS OF COST SHARING

Proposals to rely on cost sharing may also reduce access and exacerbate the problem of distributional equity. As indicated previously, the theory of consumer behavior is based on the notion that, subject to the budget constraint, consumers purchase the commodity bundle that maximizes utility. However, the consumption of health services results in little, if any, direct utility. Rather, medical services are normally demanded to restore or maintain health status, suggesting that medical need is and ought to be a more important determinant of utilization behavior than price or ability to pay. Further, health needs are inversely related to income and positively associated with age, suggesting that the poor and elderly should consume more health services than wealthier and younger members of society. Recognizing that an increase in out-of-pocket expenditures reduces the financial liability of publicly funded programs and private insurers, the increased reliance on higher effective prices to ration health services diminishes the extent to which the health system addresses the medical needs of the poor and the elderly.

A growing body of theoretical considerations also indicates that a reliance on higher effective prices exacerbates the problem of distributional equity. For example, in an assessment of the policy implications of the benefits derived from health, Wagstaff (1986) and Muurinen and Le Grand (1985) suggest that the demand for health inputs—such as housing, nutrition, and medical care—is derived from a need to restore, maintain, or improve health status. The analysis also indicates that an increase in the effective price of health care diminishes health status and that the deleterious effects on health that are precipitated by higher prices are more pronounced among the poor than their wealthier counterparts.

That variation in deductibles and coinsurance rates affects access and the use of service has been documented previously (Anderson et al., 1990). In perhaps the most extensive investigation of the effects exerted by cost sharing on utilization behavior, results derived from the Rand Health Experiment revealed that higher deductibles and coinsurance rates significantly lower the probability of using hospital and physician care. In addition, reported coefficients support the contention that demand is inelastic and that higher deductibles or coinsurance rates reduced expenditures on physician and hospital care. Of particular concern, however, are findings that indicate that effects of reduced use are most pronounced among the poor and the children of the poor (Lohr et al., 1986; Manning, Wells et al., 1984; Brook et al., 1983; Beck, 1974). Accordingly, when combined with theoretical considerations, these findings seem to imply that the adoption of proposals to rely on cost sharing and the pricing system to ration care are likely to exacerbate the problem of distributional equity.

In contrast to those that propose a dependence of insurance coverage on employment status and a reliance on cost-sharing arrangements to ration care, the provisions of several plans that are summarized in Table 1.3 would probably reduce or eliminate inequities in access and the distribution of service. Essentially four features are common to the proposals advanced by

Table 1.3
Provisions That Influence Patients to Control Spending and Influence the
Distribution of Service

AUTHOR	EXTENT OF COVERAGE	RANGE OF BENEFITS	CHARGE RELATED METHODS
Himmelstein	Universal	All Necessary Services	Limited to Uninsured Services
Terris	Universal	All Necessary Services	None
Roybal	Universal	Benefit Structure of Medicare, LTC Psychiatric, and Rehabilitation	Market Mechanism: Deductible, Coinsurance, 20-25%; Maximum Limit
Committee for NHI	Universal	Qualified Plans Provide Basic Coverage: Medicare Medicaid	Below Poverty: None; Others Family Maximum; Deductible Coinsurance
Pepper Commission	Universal	Hospital, Surgical and Physician Care; Outpatient Rehabilitation	Market Mechanism Deductible Coinsurance 20-25%
National Leadership Commission	Excluding Medicare Depends on Employment Status	Depends on Plan; Minimum Structure Mandated by Government	Market Mechanism Deductible Coinsurance Limits Depend on Income
Nutter	Depends on Employment Status Medicaid and Risk Pool for Others	Depends on Plan	Market Mechanism Deductible Coinsurance No Maximum Limit
Enthoven Kronick	Depends on Employment Status Subsidies to Encourage Enrollment of Others	Plan Specific	Poverty: No Premium Sliding Scale for 100-150% of Poverty Cost Sharing Limited to 100% of Premium

Himmelstein et al. and Terris et al. Among the most important of these are
universal coverage, accessibility, and a comprehensive range of benefits.

Based on the Canadian system, the plans would eliminate the traditional
dependence of insurance coverage on employment status and extend protection from the financial risks of illness or injury to all Americans. These
proposals also recommend that all residents should be entitled to a com-

prehensive range of benefits, to include inpatient, outpatient, and long-term care (LTC). Also contributing to achieving the goal of distributional equity are provisions that, with the exception of uninsured services, eliminate direct patient charges as a factor that might influence utilization behavior. As expected of a national health plan, the second group of proposals would ensure unimpeded access when members of the insured population are absent from their residence and require health services.

The effects of a national health plan characterized by features similar to those proposed by Himmelstein et al. and Terris et al. have been documented previously. The weight of evidence clearly indicates that universal coverage, a comprehensive range of benefits, and the elimination of direct patient charges reduce not only unmet need in the insured population but also the dependence of utilization behavior on the socioeconomic status of the individual (Manga et al., 1987; Broyles et al., 1983; Barer et al., 1982; Gass and Venn, 1978; McDonald et al., 1973; Enterline et al., 1973; Siemiatycki et al., 1980; Beck, 1973). When combined with a system of prepayment and the end-of-period adjustment, these findings suggest that the national health plans recommended by Himmelstein et al. and Terris et al. would reduce or eliminate the dependence of use or access on financial considerations that are specific to the patient or the provider and ensure that utilization behavior is dependent on the medical needs or the health status of the individual.

CONCLUSIONS

The evaluation presented in this chapter suggests that, when combined with an end-of-period adjustment, the system of prepayment recommended by Himmelstein et al. and Terris et al. is the most effective approach to the problem of controlling operating expenses, capital costs, and, hence, expenditures on health care. Further, a reliance on annual salaries and an end-of-period adjustment is conducive to resolving the problem of controlling expenditures on physician care. The discussion also suggests that universal coverage, a comprehensive range of benefits, and the elimination of direct patient charges are options that ensure a congruence between utilization behavior and the medical needs of the patient. Even though the economic assessment suggests a reasonably clear structure for a national health plan, formidable opposition expressed by powerful interest groups may dilute the political commitment to resolve the problems of controlling cost, improving access, and ensuring that use is determined by medical need. However, in the absence of dramatic changes in the financial environment of the American health industry, inflationary pressures and inequities in the distribution of care will probably increase without abatement.

REFERENCES

Anderson, G., E. Steinberg, N. Powe et al. 1990. "Setting Payment Rates for Cap-
    itated Systems: A Comparison of Various Alternatives." *Inquiry* 27:225.
Arrow, K. 1963. "Uncertainty and the Welfare Economics of Medical Care." *Amer-
    ican Economic Review* 53:941.
Barer M. and R. Evans. 1986. "Riding North on a South-Bound Horse? Expendi-
    tures, Prices, Utilization and Incomes in the Canadian Health Care System."
    In *Medicare at Maturity: Achievements, Lessons and Challenges*, R. Evans
    and G. Stoddard, eds. Calgary: University of Alberta Press.
Barer, M., P. Manga, R. Shillington et al. 1982. *Income Class and Hospital Use in
    Ontario*. Toronto: OEC.
Beck, R. 1973. "Economic Class and Access to Physician Services Under Public
    Medical Care Insurance." *International Journal of Health Services* 3:341.
———. 1974. "The Effects of Copayment on the Poor." *Journal of Human Re-
    sources* 9:129.
Blair, B. 1987. *Maryland Hospital Financial Trends: 1977 Through 1986*. Baltimore:
    Maryland Chapter of The Hospital Financial Association.
Brecher, C. 1984. "Medicaid Comes to Arizona: A First Year Report on AHCCCS."
    Journal of Health Politics, Policy and Law 9:411
Brook, R., J. Ware, W. Rogers et al. 1983. "Does Free Care Improve Adults' Health?"
    New England Journal of Medicine 309:1426.
Broyles, R. 1990. "Efficiency, Costs and Quality: The New Jersey Experience Re-
    visited." *Inquiry* 27:86.
Broyles, R., P. Manga, D. Binder et al. 1983. "Use of Physician Care Under a National
    Health Insurance Scheme: An Examination of the Canada Health Survey."
    Medical Care 21:1037.
Broyles, R. and B. Reilly. 1984. "National Health Care Insurance: A New Imper-
    ative." *Journal of Medical Systems* 8:331.
———. 1985. "A Qualitative Assessment of the Medicare Prospective Payment
    System." *Social Science and Medicine* 10:1185.
———. 1987. "The Medicare Payment System: A Conceptual Approach to the
    Problem of Controlling Profitability." *Health Care Management Review*
    12:35.
———. 1990. *Fiscal Management of Healthcare Institutions*. Owings Mills, MD:
    National Health Publishing.
Butler, S. 1991. "A Tax Reform Strategy to Deal with the Uninsured." *Journal of
    the American Medical Association* 265:241.
Chernick, H., M. Homer, and D. Weinberg. 1987. "Tax Policy Toward Health
    Insurance and the Demand for Medical Services." *Journal of Health Eco-
    nomics* 6:1.
Danzon, P. 1982. "Hospital Profits: The Effects of Reimbursement Policy." *Journal
    of Health Economics* 1:29.
Detsky, A., S. Stacey, and C. Bombardier. 1983. "The Effectiveness of a Regulatory
    Strategy in Containing Hospital Costs." *New England Journal of Medicine*
    309:151.
Division of National Cost Estimates, Office of the Actuary, Health Care Financing

Administration (HCFA). 1987. "National Health Expenditures." *Health Care Financing Review* 8:1.

Enterline, P., V. Salter, A. McDonald et al. 1973. "The Distribution of Medical Services Before and After Free Medical Care: The Quebec Experience." *New England Journal of Medicine* 289:1174.

Enthoven, A. 1981. *Health Plan*. Reading, MA: Addison-Wesley.

Enthoven, A. and R. Kronick. 1991. "Universal Health Insurance Through Incentives Reform." *Journal of the American Medical Association* 19:2532.

Evans, R. 1983. *Strained Mercy: The Economics of Canadian Health Care*. Toronto: Butterworth.

Farley, P. 1985a. "Competition among Hospitals: Market Structure and its Relation to Utilization, Costs and Financial Position." DHHS No. PHS 85–3353. Washington, DC: Department of Health and Human Services.

———. 1985b. "Who Are the Uninsured?" *Milbank Memorial Fund Quarterly* 63:476.

Fein, R. 1991. "The Health Security Partnership." *Journal of the American Medical Association* 19:2555.

Feldstein, M. 1971. "A New Approach to National Health Insurance." *Public Interest* 23:93.

Gass, J.V.D. and W.V.D. Ven. 1978. "The Demand for Medical Care." *Medical Care* 16:299.

Greenberg, W. 1985. "Demand, Supply and Information in Health Care and Other Industries." In *Market Reforms in Health Care*, J. Meyer, ed. Washington, DC: American Enterprise Institute.

Hadley, J. and K. Swartz. 1989. "The Impact on Hospital Costs Between 1980 and 1984 of Hospital Rate Regulation, Competition and Changes in Health Insurance Coverage." *Inquiry* 26:35.

Havighurst, C. 1983. "The Contributions of Antitrust Law to a Pro-competitive Health Policy." In *Market Reforms in Health Care*, J. Meyer, ed. Washington, DC: American Enterprise Institute.

Himmelstein, D., S. Woolhandler et al. 1989. "A National Health Program for the United States: A Physician's Proposal." *New England Journal of Medicine* 320:102.

Hornbrook, M., M. Sennet, and M. Greenlick. 1989. "Adjusting the AAPCC for Selectivity and Selection Bias under Medicare Risk Contracts." In *Advances in Health Economics and Health Services Research*, R. Scheffler and L. Rossiter, eds. Greenwich, CT: JAI Press.

Hsaio, W., P. Braun, D. Yntema, and E. Becker. 1989. "Estimating Physicians' Work for a Resource-Based Relative Value Scale." *New England Journal of Medicine* 319:835.

Iglehart, J. 1986. "Canada's Health Care System." *New England Journal of Medicine* 315:202–8, 778–84.

Jensen, G., R. Feldman, and B. Dowd. 1984. "Corporate Benefit Policies and Health Insurance Costs." *Journal of Health Economics* 3:275.

Langwell, K. and L. Nelson. 1986. "Physician Payment Systems: A Review of History, Alternatives and Evidence." *Medical Care* 43:5.

Lee, P., L. Le Roy, P. Ginsberg, and G. Hammons. 1990. "Physician Payment Reform: An Idea Whose Time Has Come." *Medical Care Review* 47:137.

Lewin and Associates, Inc. 1981. "Differential Reimbursement of Hospitals." Final Report to HCFA, contract no. 60077–0073. Washington, DC: HCFA.

Lohr, K., R. Brook, C. Kamberg et al. 1986. "Use of Medical Care in the Rand Health Insurance Experiment: Diagnosis and Service Specific Analysis in a Randomized Control Trial." *Medical Care* 24 (Supplement).

Luft, H. 1981. *Health Maintenance Organizations; Dimensions of Performance.* New York: John Wiley.

Manga, P. and R. Broyles. 1986. "Evaluating and Explaining U.S.-Canada Health Policy." In *Public Policy Analysis and Management*, Stuart Nagel, ed. Greenwich, CT: JAI Press.

Manga, P., R. Broyles, and D. Angus. 1987. "The Determinants of Hospital Utilization under a Universal Public Insurance Program in Canada." *Medical Care* 27:658.

Manga, P. and G.Weller. 1980. "The Failure of the Equity Objective in Health: A Comparative Analysis of Canada, Britain and the United States." *Comparative Social Research* 3:229.

Manning, W., A. Liebowitz, G. Goldberg et al. 1984. "A Controlled Trial of the Effect of a Prepaid Group Practice on the Use of Services." *New England Journal of Medicine* 310:1503.

Manning, W., K. Wells, N. Dunn et al. 1984. "Cost Sharing and the Use of Ambulatory Mental Health Services." *American Psychologist* 39:1077.

McDonald, A., J. McDonald, N. Steinmetz et al. 1973. "Physician Services in Montreal before Universal Health Insurance." *Medical Care* 11:269.

Miller and Byrne, Inc. 1977. *Cost Differential Study: State of Connecticut.* Final report to the Connecticut Hospital Association.

Muurinen, J. and J. LeGrand, 1985. "The Economic Analysis of Inequalities in Health." *Social Science and Medicine* 20:1029.

National Leadership Commission on Health Care. 1989. *For the Health of a Nation.* Ann Arbor: MI: Health Administration Press.

Nutter, D., C. Helms et al. 1991. "Restructuring Health Care in the United States." *Journal of the American Medical Association* 19:2516.

Pauly, M. 1971. *Analysis of National Insurance Proposals.* Washington, DC: American Enterprise Institute.

———. 1986. "Taxation, Health Insurance and Market Failure in the Medical Economy." *Journal of Economic Literature* 24:629.

Prottas, J. and E. Handler. 1987. "The Complexities of Managed Care: Operating under a Voluntary System." *Journal of Health Politics, Policy and Law* 12:253.

Reilly, B. and R. Broyles. 1986. "The Reemergence of Regulatory Intervention in American Health Policy." *Hospital and Health Services Administration* 35:53.

Robinson, J. and H. Luft. 1987. "Competition and the Cost of Hospital Care." *Journal of the American Medical Association* June 19:3241.

Rockefeller, J. 1991. "The Pepper Commission's Blueprint for Health Care Reform." *Journal of the American Medical Association* 19:2507.

Rosko, J. 1989a. "A Comparison of Hospital Performance under the Partial Medicade PPS and State All-Payer Rate Setting Systems." *Inquiry* 26:48.

———— 1989b. "Impact of the New Jersey All-Payer Rate Setting System: An Analysis of Financial Ratios." *Hospital and Health Services Administration* 34:53.

Rosko, M. and R. Broyles. 1986. "Impact of the New Jersey All-Payer DRG System." *Inquiry* 23:67.

————. 1987. "Short-Term Responses to the DRG Prospective Pricing Mechanism in New Jersey." *Medical Care* 25:88.

————. 1988. *The Economics of Health Care: A Reference Handbook*. Westport, CT: Greenwood Press.

Rossiter, L., M. Nelson, and K. Adamache. 1988. "Service Use and Costs for Medicare Beneficiaries in Risk-Based HMOs and CMPs." *American Journal of Public Health* 78:937.

Roybal, E. 1991. "The US Health Act." *Journal of the American Medical Association* 19:2545.

Salkever, D., D. Steinwachs, and A. Rupp. 1986. "Hospital Cost and Efficiency under Per Service and Per Case Payment in Maryland." *Inquiry* 23:56.

Schieber, G. and J. Poullier. 1987. "Recent Trends in International Health Care Spending." *Health Affairs* 6:105.

Seidman, L. 1977. "Medical Loans and Major Risk National Health Insurance." *Health Services Research* 12:123.

Siemiatycki, J., L. Richardson, and I. Pless. 1980. "Equality in Medical Care under National Health Insurance in Montreal." *New England Journal of Medicine* 303:10.

Sloan, F. and E. Becker. 1984. "Cross Subsidies and Payment for Hospital Care." *Journal of Health Politics, Policy and Law* 8:660.

Sulvetta, J. and K. Swartz. 1986. "The Uninsured and Uncompensated Care." In *National Health Policy Forum*. Washington, DC: George Washington University.

Terris, M. and the Council on Medical Care. 1991. Summarized in "The Health Agenda for the 1990s: Medical Care." *Journal of Public Health Policy* 12:31.

Thomas, J., R. Lichenstein, L. Wyszewianski, and S. Berki. 1983. "Increasing Medicare Enrollment in HMOs: The Need for Capitation Rates Adjusted for Health Status." *Inquiry* 20:227.

Thorpe, K. 1987. "Does All-Payer Rate Setting Work: The Case of the New York Prospective Reimbursement Methodology." *Journal of Health Politics, Policy and Law* 12:391.

U.S. Department of Commerce. 1990. "Health and Medical Services." *U.S. Industrial Outlook*. Washington, DC.

Wagstaff, A. 1986. "The Demand for Health: Home Empirical Evidence." *Journal of Health Economics* 5:195.

Wilensky, G. 1988. "Filling the Gaps in Health Insurance: Impact on Competition." *Health Affairs* 7:133.

Wilensky, G. and L. Rossiter. 1986. "Alternative Units of Payment for Physician Services." *Medical Care Review* 43:133.

2

Biting the Bullet? Post-1980 Congressional Processes and Medicare Decisions

Katherine A. Hinckley and Bette S. Hill

It has been conventional wisdom in political science that Congress is more likely to allocate benefits to narrow interests than diffuse ones. Generally speaking, its decisions will tend to offer concentrated benefits to narrow interests, while spreading the costs broadly among taxpayers (Lowi, 1963; Wilson, 1973; Mayhew, 1974). This occurs primarily because narrow interests tend to be more attentive and better organized than the general public, and hence more willing and able to reward or punish legislators for their actions.

This conventional wisdom has important implications for health policy, as it suggests that provider interests will be able to block action that imposes severe costs on them, even though the more general public might thereby benefit (Marmor, Wittman, and Heagy, 1983). The success of groups like the American Medical Association (AMA) in preventing enactment of national health insurance, and in forcing significant concessions on Medicare policy, would appear to substantiate the basic argument. For that matter, Medicare itself, which provides health insurance for only the elderly portion of the population, yet is paid for by the whole, might be seen as evidence of the power of special interests.

In recent years, however, studies have emerged showing that Congress does *not* always favor the "special interests" (Derthick and Quirk, 1985; Birnbaum and Murray, 1987; Arnold, 1990). Under some conditions, legislators will grant benefits to more diffuse, general interests, even simultaneously imposing sizable costs on narrower groups. This work squares much better with the fact that over the period from 1980 through 1986, Congress pared back the Medicare program in a variety of ways, to the presumed benefit of the broad taxpaying public.

Our aim here is to examine that sequence of decisions. We will begin by offering a brief theoretical explanation for why such cuts might take place, and then proceed to delineate both the decisions themselves and the ways Congress made them. The conclusions we draw from the experience will simultaneously confirm and fill in the newer approach to congressional allocation of costs and benefits.

COSTS, BENEFITS, AND VISIBILITY

As stated earlier, the belief that diffuse interests are not well served by congressional decisions rests on the assumption that both costs and benefits are relatively invisible to the broad public. And yet, concern with the *visibility* of action underlies a great deal of behavior on Capitol Hill. What Congress is *seen* to do is at least as important to members as what is actually done. Members of Congress themselves certainly recognize the rewards of putting a proper appearance on their actions and the dangers of being "exposed" on issues, even though they do not frame them in explicit theoretical terms. If, as strong evidence indicates, most of the public *is* inattentive to most policy decisions, why do congresspersons worry so much about how their actions look?

R. Douglas Arnold, in *The Logic of Congressional Action* (1990), explains why. He argues that Congress must consider not only the existing policy preferences of narrow, organized groups, but also potential preferences of currently inattentive and unorganized publics, should the latter learn of what has been done. And those publics may well learn, especially if the effects are large and immediate and an "instigator," such as the media or an election challenger, is there to help things along. If, in addition, effects can plausibly be traced to government action, and a legislator's own part in the action can be located, then constituents may punish (or reward) the legislator retrospectively, even though they were paying no attention earlier. So Congress, in allocating costs and benefits, must estimate not just what narrow groups make of its actions today, but what larger publics might see and make of it later. Hence its concern about visibility and traceability— how noticeable the actions (and the effects of those actions) are, how they look, and to whom.

Arnold's incorporation of potential preferences into the logic of congressional action strikes us as a major theoretical contribution, for it provides the missing connection that allows—indeed, sometimes forces—Congress to choose general interests over special ones. Of almost equal importance is his delineation of the ways in which congressional action can be structured so as to either weaken or reinforce that connection. Though we cannot do justice to the fine points of Arnold's argument here, he provides rich evidence that congressional procedures can be used either to force members to stand up and be counted or, alternatively, to allow them to cover their tracks, with important results for voting outcomes. Furthermore, Arnold's case studies clearly point up the importance of the ways coalition leaders attempt to "frame" the issue at hand to emphasize the incidence of costs or benefits; in fact, his case study of economic policy provides an excellent line of reasoning for why cuts were made in Medicare throughout the 1980s.

However, no one book can do everything. None of Arnold's three cases concerns an entitlement program; nor do any of them consider what we might call the "suballocation" of costs and benefits within the category of more narrow interests. Finally, despite the richness of detail in the book, we think he inevitably missed a congressional trick or two. The examination of Medicare can help further develop theory in all these respects.

MEDICARE COSTS AND BENEFITS

The very establishment of Medicare is an excellent example of how intricate the assignment of costs and benefits can become. In fact, it suggests that even *identifying* the winners and losers of congressional action is not necessarily a simple matter.

Congress had long refused to pass any kind of health insurance because of the strong opposition of the American Medical Association, which, as Wilson observes (1973:334), felt it would be bearing important costs. However, in 1965, with a huge Democratic majority and pressure from the White House, Congress did pass both Medicare (for the elderly) and Medicaid (for the poor)—a considerably narrower set of beneficiaries than some had wanted. Beyond this, estimation of what Congress "really" did depends on one's perceptions. It overrode the objections of narrow provider groups, but also allayed opposition by allowing providers to be reimbursed on the basis of costs and "reasonable and customary charges." In fact, both hospitals and physicians profited handsomely under the act, gradually drawing a larger and larger share of their income from Medicare. One might almost say they were among the prime beneficiaries.

As to costs, Medicare made the elderly pay at least something for medical care in premiums, deductibles, and copayments; yet the bulk of financing for Part B (physician services) was obtained from general revenues, and Part A (hospital services) was financed through extension of the Social Security payroll tax system. While Congress thus in fact put the bulk of costs on taxpayers, it did so with the assurance that ultimately these "losers" would be beneficiaries by right to similar services. In addition, they enjoyed whatever benefits might obtain from adequate health care for the elderly generally.

Table 2.1
Medicare Growth, 1970–80

Year	Total Part A+B Expend (in mil)	Per cent Change Prev. Yr Total	Per cent Change Prev. Yr Part A	Per cent Change Prev. Yr Part B	Part A as Per cent Total
1970	$7,099	7.5	8.1	5.9	72.2
1971	$7,868	10.8	12.2	7.2	73.1
1972	$8,643	9.9	9.9	9.8	73.1
1973	$9,583	10.9	11.7	8.6	73.6
1974	$12,418	30.2	28.9	31.4	73.3
1975	$15,588	24.9	24.4	28.8	72.6
1976	$18,420	18.2	17.9	18.9	72.4
1977	$21,774	18.2	18.0	18.9	72.3
1978	$24,934	14.5	12.4	20.1	70.9
1979	$29,331	17.6	16.6	20.1	70.3
1980	$35,699	21.7	21.5	22.1	70.2
	$191,357 Sum	16.8 Avg	16.5 Avg	17.4 Avg	72.2 Avg

Source: Health Care Financing Administration (1983)

RISING MEDICARE COSTS

One really is forced to admire the way in which the costs of the original Medicare program were finessed. But by the late 1970s the opportunities for finesse had largely evaporated. In general, the costs of government programs were rising faster than could be supported by the economy's rather anemic growth rate. Specifically, the cost of entitlements was skyrocketing; and among entitlements, Medicare was particularly outstanding. Indeed, it was the fastest-growing element in the domestic budget. Table 2.1, which details the growth of the program from 1970 through 1980, shows an average growth rate of 16.8 percent in costs per year, amounting to a 400 percent increase over the decade. Admittedly the growth rate was somewhat uneven, both by year and by program sector. Overall costs started with a rate of less than 10 percent annually, jumped to 27.6 percent after the removal of wage and price controls in 1974–75, and then fell to 18 percent per year for the remainder of the decade. Part A costs rose at a yearly rate of about 16.5 percent, reflecting galloping inflation in hospital costs. In 1977, when President Carter proposed a stringent cost freeze for hospitals, the AMA and hospital associations instituted a voluntary cost containment program; this no doubt accounts for the sharply reduced rate of increase for Part A between 1977 and 1978. However, after the failure of the Carter initiative in Congress, Part A costs rose sharply again in the last two years of the decade.

Part B costs, almost all of which go to physician reimbursements, grew even faster. Though Part B increases were lower than those for Part A until 1973, they were considerably higher thereafter, for an average yearly growth of 17.4 percent over the decade.

The largest part of the Medicare cost increase—41 percent, according to an Urban Institute Report—stemmed from general inflation (*Public Policy and Aging Report*, 1988:2). But about 12.8 percent came from the increase of enrollees from 10.5 million to 28.5 million, and another third from increased services per enrollee, as technology improved and the proportion of very old enrollees increased. The remaining 12 percent was due to price rises exceeding inflation; health care inflation was significantly above general inflation throughout this period.

Nor was this all. The inexorable workings of demography promised even greater increases, for as time went on there would be more and more elderly and proportionately fewer to support them. The Hospital Insurance (HI) trust fund for Part A would sooner or later (probably sooner) simply go broke under these conditions, which in turn weakened the "losers as future winners" assurance to taxpayers. Meanwhile, the income of the elderly was rising faster than that of the average worker; talk of "intergenerational equity" began to arise.

RISING COSTS AND UNPLEASANT OPTIONS

Increases in government costs that outrun general economic and revenue growth can be handled in three ways—none of them particularly attractive from the visibility point of view. The "usual" way is to raise taxes, as the conventional wisdom about the power of narrow interests would suggest. With an income tax this can often be done rather invisibly, allowing "bracket creep" to take larger proportions of taxpayers' rising income. But the situation for Congress in the late 1970s and early 1980s was not that simple. The 1978 approval of California's Proposition 13 to roll back property taxes was widely interpreted as the first shot in a major tax revolt against existing tax levels. In fact, spurred by the interpretation of the Reagan election as a mandate to "get government off our backs," Congress even felt compelled to enact major tax cuts beginning in 1981.

A second option is simply to run a deficit. This has the advantage of transferring many costs to generations not yet on the scene and thus incapable of retaliating. Nonetheless, there are some costs to current citizens inherent in deficit financing; they may not be as visible as a tax increase, but they can become salient under constant reiteration. Particularly after the combination of the Reagan tax cuts and defense buildup began to produce huge deficits in the early 1980s, Congress became very much concerned about appearing indifferent to such costs. Reducing the deficit became a major aim for many members of Congress.

This concern leads directly to the third option—cutting back programs. But program cuts of course activate all the defensive mechanisms of the benefiting groups. In the case of Medicare, which because of its sheer size would inevitably be a likely target for cuts, those groups were quite formidable. Providers were well-organized and vocal, but increasingly so were the elderly. What is more, the elderly had come to see Medicare benefits as theirs by right. Any reductions in level would therefore be seen as losses— and highly visible losses, too. Psychological evidence indicates that losses are generally more salient than gains anyway; for the elderly, there was no mistaking increases in premiums, deductibles, or copayments.

Faced with this set of Hobson's choices, Congress predictably fuzzed matters as much as possible. Taxes *were* raised, as we shall see, but not directly. Deficit financing continued on an unprecedented scale; by the end of the 1980s interest payments on the federal debt were consuming 14.7 percent of federal outlays, in contrast with 8.9 percent in 1980 (*Congressional Quarterly [CQ] Weekly Report*, January 26, 1991:234).

At the same time, however, Congress also bit the bullet of program reduction. In a series of budget reconciliation acts from 1980 through 1986, they pursued (or were forced into) a series of "heroic" efforts at budget reduction, with Medicare expenditures as one of the prime targets.

The remainder of this chapter will examine the exact extent and allocation of the existing Medicare cuts. Our basic contention is that concerns with visibility and traceability deeply influenced both the content and the handling of these actions; but we will see, too, that cost allocation is often influenced by technical and administrative, as well as political, considerations. We will conclude with a series of lessons about cost allocation that can be derived from the Medicare experience.

The primary source of our allocative data is a July 1988 General Accounting Office (GAO) report, *Medicare and Medicaid: Updated Effects of Recent Legislation on Program and Beneficiary Costs*, which estimates the savings and increases for each Medicare-related provision of six major reconciliation acts of the 1980s: ORA (1980), OBRA (1981), TEFRA (1982), DEFRA (1984), COBRA (1985), and OBRA (1986). Their estimates were based on "economic assumptions in use at the time of enactment" (p. 19). The six laws, along with the Social Security Amendments of 1983, include almost all the important Medicare legislation of the period. Accounts of congressional handling of the legislation are derived from a variety of sources, but particularly *Congressional Quarterly* publications. Together the data provide important insights on how Congress handled a very difficult cost allocation problem.

OMNIBUS RECONCILIATION ACT (ORA), 1980

Before we begin discussion of the specific acts, a brief explanation of the budget process generally and as it relates to Medicare would be useful. The Budget and Impoundment Control Act of 1974 added new layers of activity to the old authorizing and appropriating processes by establishing budget committees in each chamber. The function of these committees was to develop concurrent resolutions setting general targets for revenues, expenditures, and the deficit each year. Originally there were to be two resolutions—one in April to guide the authorizing and appropriations committees, and a second before the start of the new fiscal year on October 1. There was also a process to bring into agreement, or "reconcile," the general budget targets and the specific committee actions. In the early years of the act, however, targets tended to be adjusted to fit committee actions, rather than the other way around, because the budget committees really lacked the power to force program cuts (Copeland, 1984).

The Medicare program has a somewhat unusual place in this budget process because, as part of Social Security, it is not under the jurisdiction of an ordinary authorizing committee. Instead, it is in the hands of the "tax" committees, Senate Finance and House Ways and Means (though the latter must now share jurisdiction over Part B with Energy and Commerce). In consequence, Medicare suffers a kind of "double exposure" to cost paring— once from program reduction pressures, and second, from revenue pressures. The committee can to some extent balance these out in its own way; but the point to note is that the tax committees cannot be as strongly focused on protecting "their" programs as other committees are. In fact, Copeland (1984) points out that Ways and Means was responsible for between one-quarter and one-half of all domestic cuts in the early 1980s.

In 1980 both budget committees managed to get reconciliation instructions attached to the *first* budget resolution. These instructions directed the various committees to produce specified amounts of savings in programs under their jurisdictions; the changes were then packaged into a single bill for floor consideration. ORA was the result. It represented a serious attempt to redeem President Carter's promise of a balanced budget; but in fact it missed the target by a sizable margin, actually *reducing* taxes and not clearing Congress until December 6, when its economic assumptions had already been undercut by rising unemployment.

That ORA passed at all reflects the increasing pressure for keeping program costs and taxes down; that it took so long reflects the difficulties Congress experiences in cutting established programs. The House had particular trouble. It actually rejected the first conference agreement on the budget resolution, and passed its reconciliation package largely with the aid of a rule strictly limiting amendments. This modified closed rule and the up-or-down vote on the package as a whole tend to protect members from traceable votes against popular programs; but even at that, ORA did not pass until safely after the 1980 elections.

Thought fights were plentiful on ORA, they were not particularly centered on Medicare, but rather on general defense versus domestic expenditures. Curiously, it appears that health groups were not fully aware of the potential impact on their interests until fall (CQ Weekly Report, September 20, 1980:2782). Yet ORA did result in some $1.7 billion in cuts for the Medicare program. Many of the provisions initiated a trend of more in-depth examination of how providers charges were calculated. How the cuts were allocated is shown in Table 2.2.

A first glance at the cuts might suggest that physicians received the bulk of the $1.725 billion in Medicare cuts. In a sense they did; but the savings shown for community-based doctors simply prevented physicians from delaying filing their claims until the end of the year when the rates were raised. Hospital-based radiologists and pathologists, who alone among physicians had been reimbursed at 100 percent of Medicare-approved charges, were now to receive such reimbursement only if they accepted "assignment"— that is, accepted Medicare reimbursement as payment in full for services. Thus the cuts to physicians were really adjustments to very lenient prior policies. Similarly, some hospitals' prior reimbursements were considered inappropriate because acute-care rates were charged when subacute services were provided. Also, less expensive outpatient surgery for certain procedures was encouraged by authorizing full payment for facilities accepting assignment. The only other providers targeted specifically were clinical laboratories. As the first action in an ongoing theme, insurance companies were required to act as first payers for elderly beneficiaries involved in accidents.

No direct costs were imposed on the elderly, although some cuts might be shifted to them (for instance, through higher accident premiums or additional charges from nonassignment physicians). Finally, Congress produced some "savings" through administrative changes that postponed fiscal year 1981 (FY81) payments to hospitals to FY82. As we shall see, however, they rearranged matters the next year.

The $1.725 billion in cuts were partially offset by *increases* in services estimated at $958 million. To encourage less expensive home health services, the previous 100-visit limit was removed, as was a requirement for prior

Table 2.2
Summary of Six Bills' Effects: Medicare Cost Cuts (in millions)

Target	OBR 80 FY81-85 sum all yrs. % of total	OBRA 81 FY81-86 sum all yrs. % of total	TEFRA 82 FY83-87 sum all yrs. % of total	DEFRA 84 FY84-87 sum all yrs. % of total	COBRA 85 FY86-87 sum all yrs. % of total	OBRA 86 FY87 sum all yrs. % of total	TOTALS ALL ACTS Sum all yrs. % of total
Hospitals	$215	$870	15,367	615	845	200	18,112
	12.5%	28.7%	69.6%	11.5%	48.7%	28.6%	52.3%
Physicians							
Hosp.base	90	0	2,415	0	50	0	2,555
Comm.base	1,143	0	0	1,025	575	200	2,943
Subtotal	1,233	0	2,415	1,025	625	200	5,498
	71.5%	0.0%	10.9%	19.2%	36.0%	28.6%	15.9%
Other providers							
Part A	125	520	190	0	0	0	835
Part B	0	232	880	660	0	0	1,772
Both	43	0	0	0	5	0	48
Subtotal	168	752	1,070	660	5	0	2,655
	9.7%	24.8%	4.8%	12.4%	0.3%	0.0%	7.7%
Employers/	109	0	1,725	865	225	300	3,224
Insur. co.	6.3%	0.0%	7.8%	16.2%	13.0%	42.9%	9.3%
Elderly	0	1,406	1,505	2,165	35	0	5,111
	0.0%	46.4%	6.8%	40.6%	2.0%	0.0%	14.8%
Totals	$1,725	$3,028	$22,082	$5,330	$1,735	$700	34,600
	100.0%	100.0%	100.0%	100.0%	100.0%	100.0%	100.0%

Source: GAO (1988).

hospitalization. Some new benefits were also added, such as occupational therapy, outpatient rehabilitation, and alcohol detoxification services.

Several proposals for both cuts and increases were dropped before final enactment, however. The most important, long advocated by Senator Herman Talmadge (D-Ga), was for a new system of hospital reimbursements based on average hospital rates rather than each hospital's own rate schedule. Though the American Hospital Association had a year earlier loudly preferred this Talmadge plan to Carter's cost freeze, it now objected strongly, and the proposal was finally dropped in conference. However, the same basic concepts underlay the prospective payment reform enacted three years later.

Also dropped were a proposal to reduce the nursing differential provided hospitals for the presumed extra costs of care to the elderly, and a moderate expansion of Medicare's mental health benefits. In a pattern to be repeated in later years, both the cost-cutting proposals were in the Senate version of reconciliation, while the additional benefits originated in the House bill.

OMNIBUS BUDGET RECONCILIATION ACT (OBRA), 1981

Promptly on entering office, the new Reagan administration proposed an exceedingly large package of cuts in domestic programs, replacing Carter's more modest budget proposals. In the past, Congress had been highly unresponsive to such suggestions; but 1981 was different. As Arnold (1990:178) says:

The principal innovation was to combine all spending cuts into a single package, to label the package as the president's economic recovery program, and then to force legislators to vote on the entire package without permitting amendments. This strategy transformed the usual programmatic votes into votes on explicit economic policy. It increased the likelihood that citizens would, at the time of the next election, connect the state of the economy with legislators' positions on the president's program. It decreased the chances that citizens might blame legislators for the loss of specific benefits.

The newly Republican-controlled Senate quickly passed a budget resolution with reconciliation instructions providing for some $36.9 billion in additional cuts for FY82 alone (*CQ Weekly Report*, April 11, 1981:622). In the House, a coalition of Republicans and conservative Democrats succeeded in substituting a similarly large budget-cutting resolution ("Gramm-Latta I") for the House Budget Committee proposal. But the key vote occurred in June, when the actual reconciliation package was brought to the House floor. Republicans had again prepared a substitute ("Gramm-Latta II") for the Budget Committee's weaker package. The Democratic-dominated Rules Committee attempted to force six separate votes on the various portions of that substitute, which would have made it a series of highly traceable votes against popular programs. In a rare procedural victory, however, the Republicans managed the defeat of that rule, and Gramm-Latta II passed. As in 1980, therefore, Medicare cuts were buried in the overall reconciliation package, and no separate vote outside the committees of jurisdiction was necessary.

The OBRA 1981 projected savings for FY82–FY86 (in millions of dollars) are shown in Table 2.2. The overall size of cuts was increased slightly from 1980 but the targets were significantly shifted in comparison. The total estimated Medicare cuts of $3.03 billion through FY86 did not even count the single largest FY82 reduction, which was not a cut at all but accounting sleight-of-hand. It shifted back to FY81 outlays in hospital payments that Congress had shifted ahead to the FY82 budget under ORA. The $522 million thus "saved" amounted to 36 percent of the total Medicare cuts for FY82.

As for real cuts, Table 2.2 shows that Medicare enrollees constituted OBRA's largest target (46 percent of the total savings). Three provisions affected them; the most important was an increase in Part B deductible from $60 to $75 (a 25 percent rise). In addition to the provisions listed above, the Part A hospital deductible increased 12 percent "through a technical change in the formula" that was permanently incorporated into the Part A deductible and coinsurance calculations according to Moon (1988:324).

The increase in the Part B deductible, along with a provision requiring Part B premiums to cover at least 25 percent of the program's cost, was part of the Senate's bill. The latter was dropped in conference at House insistence. The pattern of greater Senate severity noted for 1980 was thus repeated in 1981 with a different party majority and leadership.

Two provisions targeted hospitals. The larger came as a reduction in the nursing differential in caring for elderly patients; although the administration had recommended complete elimination of the nursing differential, it was only reduced under OBRA. Small savings were also achieved by reducing reimbursements for care considered inappropriate in an acute-care setting. Neither physicians nor employers/insurance companies were targeted for any OBRA cuts.

Finally, Congress reversed its 1981 decision to provide coverage for alcohol detoxification treatment, and also changed coverage for occupational therapy. Both changes meant financial losses for these particular providers. No increases in benefits were proposed, and none was enacted.

TAX EQUITY AND FISCAL RESPONSIBILITY ACT
(TEFRA), 1982

By 1982 the problem of Medicare costs and cuts was becoming more salient to Congress as a whole, for several reasons. First, of course, was the continued rise in costs, which led to discussion of basically revamping the health care system (*CQ Weekly Report*, February 20, 1982:331–33).

Second, however, liberals were beginning to complain that cuts on Medicare providers did not actually reduce costs, but simply shifted them to the elderly and poor. On the other hand, hospitals were contending that they were losing money and were increasingly unable to shift losses incurred by their traditional role of caring for the poor (*CQ Weekly Report*, July 17, 1982:1707–11). Though these disagreements were particularly prominent in the committees of jurisdiction, they also tended to spill over into the rest of Congress, particularly in an election year.

Finally, the determination of congressional leaders to raise revenues as a way of offsetting the deepening deficits led to development of a separate tax bill for FY83. This, of course, would involve Medicare in a very prominent way.

The House proved hard put to resolve these problems. In late May it defeated six separate versions of a budget resolution. Though it finally accepted a Republican version in June, the conference committee report on the resolution passed by only two votes.

The actual development of a tax bill proved even more painful. The Senate produced a package of fairly vigorous cuts; as Senate Finance chairman Robert Dole (R-Kan) noted: "We probably don't want to do any of this, but things are getting out of hand" (*CQ Weekly Report*, July 17, 1982:1711). But after prolonged fights both within Ways and Means and between that committee and Energy and Commerce, the House finally voted, on Ways and Means' recommendation, to go directly to conference with the Senate without passing *any* bill of its own. This meant, of course, that TEFRA would be largely a Senate product. But for the House, it had a major advantage: members would have to take only *one* vote on the whole unpleasant business—on the final conference report. And while that conference's proceedings were officially open to the public, actual decisions were made in private discussions (*CQ Weekly Report*, August 21, 1982:2038).

The lists of TEFRA cuts in Table 2.2 demonstrates how unique this piece of legislation was—all possible targets were hit but not evenly. It also demonstrates how much Congress had involved itself in the management of particular Medicare reimbursements. Savings are projected in millions for FY83–FY87.

As before, Congress solved part of its immediate budget problem by accounting maneuvers—here, suspending hospital payments in the last six weeks of FY83 and FY84 until the following fiscal years. This produced savings for those years of $750 million and $100 million, respectively, but at the cost of an $870 million addition for FY85.

The most striking aspect of TEFRA, however, was the sheer size of the cuts made—$22 billion over five years—and the fact that 70 percent fell on hospitals (see Table 2.2). Several reasons help account for why Part A, hospitals, was targeted early and heavily: (1) The costs of hospital rooms were up 17 percent (*CQ Weekly Report*, February 20, 1982:331–33); (2) Part A costs represented 72 percent of the Medicare totals over the decade (see Table 2.1); (3) Part A was financed under the HI trust fund from Social Security taxes and was rapidly approaching its upper limit (in comparison to Part B, which was financed from general tax revenues and premiums);

and (4) physicians' interest groups—and specifically the AMA—were considerably better organized, better financed, and more prestigious than hospital associations in this period, and thus better able to defend themselves.

Ironically, the hospital cuts were at least as stringent as Carter's old cost-cutting proposals. In addition to the payment delays mentioned above, $19 billion would be slashed through very strict annual caps on Medicare reimbursements through FY87. The nursing differential was now entirely eliminated. And the Department of Health and Human Services (HHS) was required to contract with independent claim reviewing organizations not owned or controlled by providers (*Congress and the Nation*, 1985:535).

TEFRA also targeted hospital-based physicians for a total of $2.4 billion (over five years), half of which came from cutting radiologist and pathologist reimbursements to the 80 percent of Medicare-approved charges allowed all other physicians. The other two provisions also tightened the strings on services supplied by hospital-based physicians or assistants. Community-based physicians were not touched by TEFRA. A 5 percent cap on physician fee increases was in the original Senate bill, and was vigorously pursued in House Energy and Commerce, which shares jurisdiction over Part B with Ways and Means. However, the provision somehow disappeared in the course of the conference. Although the community-based doctors won this battle, we shall see in DEFRA that Congress still considered them lively targets.

Some costs were also assigned to other providers and employers. A single payment rate for skilled nursing facilities and home health agencies was set, and duplicate outpatient payments were eliminated. Employers (and their insurance companies) were required to offer equal coverage for workers aged 65–69.

The elderly, however, were again hit, this time with an increase in Part B premiums. Originally intended to cover 50 percent of Part B costs, the premiums had been limited in 1972 to the percent increase of overall Social Security benefits. As these benefit increases never matched physician price increases, the proportion of Part B costs covered by premiums had fallen to about 24 percent by 1982. TEFRA reversed this trend by requiring that the premiums cover 25 percent of costs at least through 1984. Consequent savings to Medicare were estimated at $1.505 billion over five years. Moon (1988:324–25) contended that these changes had a large direct effect; for example, under the old (1972) system the 1987 premium would have been $13.70 monthly but would now be $17.90. (The administration and Senate had also proposed to have beneficiaries pay 5 percent of home health visit costs, and to index rises in Part B deductibles to the Consumer Price Index, but these were not enacted.)

The only significant addition was an expansion of Part A to include hospice services at least through FY86, for a cost of $320 million; hospice care being less intensive than traditional acute care hospitalization, this change was partly justified as contributing to long-range savings. The overall picture of TEFRA, then, is one of fairly unrelieved reductions.

SOCIAL SECURITY AMENDMENTS, 1983

As part of TEFRA, Congress had also instructed the Department of Health and Human Services to submit legislation revamping the entire system of hospital payments under Medicare. Instead of paying hospitals retrospectively for costs incurred, the new Prospective Payment System (PPS) would set a single price for each of 467 types of illnesses (Diagnosis Related Groups). This "revolutionary" legislation was submitted in draft by the end of November; hearings began in the new Congress in early February; and the legislation cleared for presidential signature in the third week of March.

In view of the furor that had greeted President Carter's hospital cost containment plan back in 1977, one might wonder how this plan succeeded so swiftly. *Congressional Quarterly* analyst Elizabeth Wehr summarized it nicely:

Hospitals believe the new plan would be better than the progressively harsher 1982 Medicare payment limits. The administration wants the greater control over Medicare spending promised by the bill, and *many members of Congress feel compelled to do something about inexorably rising medical costs without directly increasing medical costs of the people covered by the program.* (CQ Weekly Report, March 5, 1983:456; emphasis added)

Besides, a vehicle was at hand. The Old Age and Survivors' Insurance trust fund of Social Security was very rapidly approaching bankruptcy, and with the aid of a national commission's recommendations, a bipartisan compromise revamping the program financially had at last been reached. PPS (with some modifications easing the hospitals' TEFRA burdens) was simply attached to that "must" legislation as it moved along the congressional fast track. Even opponents of PPS, such as insurance lobbyists who feared that hospitals might shift unreimbursed Medicare costs to private insurers, felt it would be pointless to try to interfere. "This is not a train we want to get in the way of," one of them observed (ibid.). The success of this maneuver is indicated by the fact that only 17 senators even addressed the PPS portion of the bill during debate (Fuchs and Hoadley, 1984).

The Social Security bailout itself involved a number of tax increases and benefit cuts for Old Age and Survivors Insurance (OASI)—artfully disguised as "tax acceleration," "taxation of benefits," and "permanent COLA [cost-of-living adjustment] delays," and generally handled so as to reduce traceability (Light, 1985:236). These provisions did not apply to Medicare directly, but its revenues did benefit from the addition of new federal employees, top federal officials, and employees of nonprofit organizations, as well as an increase in the taxes for self-employed individuals. In addition, the program gained revenue from automatic increases in the total Social Security tax rates and wage bases scheduled back in the 1970s for future years. The 1983 legislation was by no means the only time that Medicare has, in one way or another, hitched a ride on the Social Security train.

DEFICIT REDUCTION ACT (DEFRA), 1984

With hospitals in transition to PPS, one major source of Medicare savings had been removed from the game. But further savings, and further revenue increases for a 1983 reconciliation bill, would still be necessary.

At this point, differences among the various players visibly widened. The Reagan administration, adopting the assumption that rising health costs stemmed from Americans' overuse of medical services, proposed a rise in Part B premiums to cover 35 percent of program costs, and more out-of-pocket costs for short hospital stays (though reductions for longer, "catastrophic" ones). It also proposed, however, to tax workers' health benefits, and to freeze physician payment levels for Medicare services.

Many in Congress had a quite different perspective, viewing physicians as the primary source of health cost increases. The budget resolution for FY84 therefore stipulated that Medicare savings must *not* be made at the expense of beneficiaries. However, the physician freeze—the obvious alternative—brought its own problems. A simple freeze would not stop doctors from raising their prices anyway, and passing on the difference to patients. But forcing the doctors to accept Medicare payments as reimbursement in full (mandatory "assignment") was anathema to the AMA. They argued that it not only would constitute a violation of promises made at the start of Medicare in 1965, but also would discourage doctors from accepting Medicare patients at all (*CQ Weekly Report*, October 10, 1983:2098).

Furthermore, there were other, separate claims on the health care budget that implicitly competed with Medicare. A large number of members wanted to provide continuing health insurance for the unemployed victims of the 1982 recession, but were opposed to taxing workers' health benefits to pay for it (or cutting Medicare, for that matter). Others, most notably Henry Waxman (D-Cal), chairman of the Energy and Commerce health subcommittee, had a particular interest in improving health programs for poor women and children; some competition between health care for the elderly and health care for the poor was therefore beginning to appear. All of these interests were represented on the committees with Medicare jurisdiction.

Again, the conflict proved too much for the House. Benefits for the jobless were passed, but with no money to pay for them. In mid-November, the House rejected the rule for the Ways and Means tax package, whereupon the Senate quit working on its own version; and amid extensive mutual recriminations, Congress adjourned without any reconciliation bill at all.

In 1984 the entire can of worms was reopened, now complicated by a new presidential budget submission and the need for a new budget resolution for FY85. Both chambers did manage to pass tax and reconciliation bills, and after a long conference, which frequently threatened to founder over the Senate's generally tougher provisions, a final package was cleared.

Even the most careful reader, however, would find it difficult to grasp the exact development of the 1984 action, not least because the tax and reconciliation package actually *preceded* the budget resolution. On top of that, Ways and Means marked up its part of the bill behind closed doors, and obtained a closed rule barring amendments on the floor. On the Senate side, debate stretched over three weeks; by the end, strategy was changing almost hourly, so that interest groups could hardly tell what was happening, much less alert their membership. Last-day conference sessions on June 22 lasted for almost 21 hours in order to get the package cleared before Congress recessed for the Democratic National Convention. It is most unlikely that ordinary voters could *ever* trace their own legislators' part in DEFRA. Indeed, the complexity even discouraged media coverage.

Table 2.2 shows total Medicare savings for DEFRA in millions of dollars for FY84–FY87. One difference in the DEFRA cuts is that for the first time, community-based physicians were seriously targeted (19.2 percent of total cuts, see Table 2.2). Between 1980 and 1983 Medicare costs for physician services increased an average of 12 percent per year (adjusted for inflation) versus only 6.5 percent for *all* physician costs (U.S. Senate, *Developments in Aging*, 1987:236). Not surprisingly, their reimbursement levels under Part B were frozen for 15 months beginning July 1, 1984. The Senate, but not the House, had supported mandatory assignment; the controversy was finally resolved by a compromise on voluntary assignment with financial penalties for nonparticipants. Those who did accept assignment for all their patients were offered expedited payment procedures and an advantage when postfreeze reimbursement rates were calculated. Doctors who accepted Medicare patients but increased their fees were subject to stiff fines (*Congress and the Nation*, 1985:545). Overall estimated savings were estimated at $1.025 billion through FY87.

Beneficiaries, however, were the largest target, representing 41 percent of the total cuts. The requirement that Part B premiums cover 25 percent of costs was extended for two more years, with a net savings against other premium provisions of $2.136 billion for FY85–87. These cuts, although contrary to the original budget resolution, were far less than the proposals initially approved by the Senate. It voted to index Part B deductibles against inflation and to delay Medicare eligibility dates by one month, a seemingly minor change that would have targeted beneficiaries for $630 million (*CQ Weekly Report*, June 2, 1984:1296). Both provisions were dropped in conference, indicating once again the comparative reluctance of the House to assign visible costs, especially to beneficiaries.

Other groups, such as employers and outpatient labs, were again targeted for $865 and $660 million, respectively. Hospitals, which had already felt significant cuts in TEFRA, now found themselves deprived of scheduled fee increases (for cuts of $615 million). Only minor new services were added by DEFRA. Their estimated cost was $15 million over two years.

CONSOLIDATED OMNIBUS BUDGET RECONCILIATION ACT (COBRA, 1985)

Throughout these accounts we have seen that the Republican-controlled Senate consistently pushed for heavier Medicare cuts than the House was willing to accept. This stance seems to have been based both on principle and political strategy. Less than a month before the 1984 elections, Finance Committee Chairman Dole and a number of other GOP senators called a press conference to defend the cuts as a way of saving the program with "across-the-board fiscal discipline" (*CQ Weekly Report*, October 13:2649).

By early 1985, however, their strategic position was weakening; the 1984 elections did not seem to have provided any particular reward to Senate Republicans for their "general benefit" stance. Furthermore, there were signs that previous cost-cutting attempts were not working out quite as planned. The move to DRGs had resulted in shorter hospital stays, leading not only to claims that elderly patients were being discharged "sicker and quicker," but also to a swift rise in the average cost per day. This in turn raised the first-day deductible paid by the patient. It appeared, too, that doctors were beginning to respond to the freeze on Medicare payment levels by increasing the volume of service (*CQ Weekly Report*, January 1, 1986:119); and of course, as not all doctors accepted assignment, additional charges would accrue to some patients. All this was apart from additional costs, such as rising premiums, actually intended under previous legislation. The House Select Committee on Aging reported that out-of-pocket expenses by older Americans represented 15 percent of mean income in 1984, about as high as before the whole Medicare program was enacted in 1965 (*CQ Weekly Report*, March 10, 1985:578).

In view of this evidence, it is perhaps not surprising that when the Senate came to consider the White House-GOP budget proposal for FY86, even a number of Republicans deserted the fold on amendments increasing cuts in various areas, including Medicare. Though a much-altered version did squeak through, agreement could not be reached with the House until August 1 on the basic budget resolution; and agreement on House and Senate reconciliation packages could not be reached at all. Again Congress adjourned without a reconciliation bill, though in a last-minute effort it did extend the physician freeze and the hospital freeze from DEFRA through March 1986.

Part of the problem was that most of the reconciliation conferees were also involved in a higher priority conference on the Gramm-Rudman-Hollings proposal to require automatic program cuts if preset deficit targets were not met. Here too Medicare was a bone of contention. If it was included in the "uncontrollable" category (programs whose costs increase automatically by indexing or COLAs), then cuts in defense would be larger because defense would be the main item under "controllables." The Senate had placed Medicare among the controllables, but the House wanted it in uncontrollables so that no cuts could be made in basic benefits. Ultimately the House won; the bill's final version limited Medicare cuts to 1 percent in FY86 and 2 percent thereafter—with no increase in costs to the elderly.

As 1986 began, it appeared that the deficit was going to be far worse than originally envisioned, with the prospect of unpleasantly deep automatic cuts under Gramm-Rudman. Efforts began to revive the old reconciliation act, despite the fact that with the passage of time its savings had dwindled substantially. Though it might more appropriately be called the "1986 Shuttlecock Bill," for it bounced back and forth between House and Senate nine times, it was finally sent to the president on April 1, 1986, as the Consolidated Omnibus Budget Reconciliation Act of 1985.

Table 2.2 demonstrates the estimated savings obtained by COBRA for FY86 and FY87 (in millions of dollars). *Hospitals* were again the largest target, taking 49 percent of total cuts (see Table 2.2). The largest monetary savings came from reducing supplemental payments for *in*direct training costs. Special payments for "return on equity" to for-profit, investor-owned hospitals were also scheduled to be eliminated, but only after FY89.

Second in importance was extension of the freeze in physician fee increases through December. However, "participating physicians," who accepted assignment for all Medicare patients, would be freed in May with an increase of 1 percent plus inflation—a sign of congressional determination to prevent cost-shifting. Congress was also intent on cutting costs through "micromanagement" of Medicare expenditures; for example, hospital-based physicians' assistants were denied reimbursements for routine cataract surgery and limits were set on reimbursements to beneficiaries for prosthetic lenses in cataract surgery.

The requirement that the elderly's Part B premiums cover 25 percent of program costs, originally enacted in 1982, was again extended, through 1988 (savings not shown above because not effective in FY87). However, a number of proposals relating to beneficiaries were dropped in the course of COBRA passage. Among them were the administration's repeat recommendations for increasing Part B premiums to 35 percent of costs, indexing the Part B deductible, and requiring copayments for home health visits. A Ways and Means subcommittee provision to link the size of Part

B premiums to annual income so as to charge wealthy beneficiaries more was dropped after strong protestations from the American Association of Retired Persons.

Hospital Insurance tax revenues were to increase as Medicare contributions were mandated for all new state and local government employees. But the Senate's plan to enroll *all* state and local government employees in Medicare was reduced in conference to only the newly hired.

COBRA also reversed the trend of little or no increases. Hospitals were allowed a .5 percent reimbursement increase beginning May 1. However, as the Gramm-Rudman cuts going into effect in March reduced payments to hospitals by 1 percent, the hospitals actually *lost* .5 percent in the conjunction of the two laws. (Previous laws would have allowed a raise of more than 5 percent for inflation). COBRA also made permanent a temporary provisions to pay for hospice care. It required that extra payments be made to hospitals heavily serving low-income patients and delayed the transition from regional DRG rates to one national rate. GAO estimated total benefit costs at about $280 million for FY86.

OMNIBUS BUDGET RECONCILIATION ACT (OBRA), 1986

Even before COBRA had passed, both chambers had begun work on the FY87 budget. The Senate Republicans, still obsessed with deficit reduction but nervous about election prospects, were by March in open revolt against President Reagan's insistence on domestic cuts, defense increases, and no new taxes. Joining with Democrats, they passed a budget resolution that, though rather less generous than the House resolution, imposed Medicare cuts almost entirely on providers. Despite a relatively easy budget conference, the reconciliation bills differed on an amazing number of points, and a bill passed only in mid-October. It marks a natural end to this study's sequence, for it actually *increased* Medicare costs.

The GAO report calculated only OBRA 86 savings for FY87; therefore, a listing comparing this act to the multiple-year savings noted above would be misleading. But cuts were clearly both minor and "picky" in nature: a 10 percent reduction in payments for cataract surgery; substitution of optometry for ophthamology services; reduction of payments to hospitals for capital-related costs; and elimination of certain advance payments to most hospitals. All the major administration proposals for cuts disappeared long before the budget resolutions were passed.

Thus most OBRA provisions actually increased costs to the program, though in a somewhat backhanded fashion. Physicians were finally released from the freeze and allowed to increase their Medicare charges 3.2 percent in 1987. But to raise the proportion of "participating physicians," Congress also made permanent their 4.15 percent higher levels of reimbursement.

Hospital payments were also increased, though only by 1.15 percent, for a cost of $230 million in FY87. Concerned about reports that hospitals were prematurely discharging patients under PPS, Congress required hospitals to develop procedures to safeguard patient rights and quality care, but simultaneously directed HHS to submit legislation revising the PPS payment structure to allow for severity of illness and case complexity.

The elderly benefited more directly. The steady increase in the Part A deductible had turned into a series of leaps; having increased 173 percent from 1980 to 1986 (from $180 to $492), it was scheduled to jump to $579 the next year. OBRA capped it at $520 for 1987 and stipulated that future rises would be tied to any increases in hospital reimbursement rates. In addition, several small types of expanded coverage were granted, some of which benefited providers as well as the elderly. *CQ Weekly Report* (September 27, 1986:2258) observed that the increases in spending in the reconciliation bill, though offset by revenue gains for FY87, would make the FY88 Gramm-Rudman targets almost impossible to meet.

LESSONS FROM MEDICARE IN THE 1980s

What, then, can we conclude from this account of the Medicare legislation passed in the 1980–86 period? We think there are a number of broader lessons about the nature of congressional action that can be drawn from the sequence; we have listed them informally below.

1. *When costs are intractably visible, Congress will target narrow interests.* Table 2.2, which summarizes the percentages and amounts of Medicare cuts overall and in each bill, makes that clear. Contrary to the conventional wisdom, but in accord with Arnold's argument, narrow provider health groups received the bulk of cuts in the six reconciliation laws—in fact, 76 percent of them. Hospitals were targeted in every act reviewed and were the primary targets in both TEFRA 1982 and COBRA 1985. In addition, the 1983 PPS legislation instituted a major reform of hospital reimbursements.

Physicians, either hospital- or community-based, were targeted in five of the acts. Though the 1980 ORA cuts really just shut accounting loopholes, the physician payment freeze that began under DEFRA was a significant blow to this powerful and well-organized group.

Other providers (skilled nursing facilities, home health agencies, outpatient facilities, clinical labs) were never major targets, but still received 7.7 percent of the cuts—greater than their approximately 6 percent of the Medicare budget. And another interesting target emerged from the analysis—employers and their insurance companies. Beginning with OBRA 1981, Congress progressively expanded the conditions under which they would retain primary insurance responsibility for the working aged and their dependents.

Even beneficiaries, whom one might presume enjoyed a favored status, received cuts in their benefits. Though members of Congress clearly were not very happy about this, they in effect preferred it to a clear, direct raise in taxes, or simply ignoring the tremendous rise in costs.

2. *But targeting such interests is far from easy.* Making programmatic cuts remains a perilous undertaking politically. In most of the cases we detailed there were severe struggles over Medicare within House and Senate, between the chambers, between them and the administration, or all three. Even though Congress seems to have adopted a "spread the pain" mechanism by targeting everyone in sight, it still encountered fierce resistance from the targets and their supporters. The AMA, in fact, went so far as to file in federal court against the DEFRA freeze (*CQ Weekly Report*, October 20, 1984:2714).

Considering this sort of resistance, the erosion of potential savings as reconciliation acts were delayed, and the occasional accounting tricks used to produce "savings," one might ask how effective the cuts were anyway. GAO (1988:19) estimated that "actual inflation-adjusted Medicare costs were about $17.3 billion less (measured in 1986 dollars) in the years after the laws became effective than they would have been had the prior cost growth trend continued." This translates into a decline in Medicare growth rates from 16.8 percent in 1970–80 to 13.8 percent in 1981–86 (see Table 2.3). But except for TEFRA, the cuts were not large in comparison with total Medicare expenditures; and furthermore, they hit largely at Part A, as Table 2.3 also shows. Part B expenditures, slowed down markedly by the DEFRA freeze, promptly rebounded. And as Congress neared the end of this sequence, it found itself engaged in the most marginal shaving of costs—the sort of legislative micromanagement that some scholars have deplored. The efforts required to cut Medicare were no doubt truly heroic; whether the results were is another question.

3. *The House is institutionally more resistant to domestic cuts than the Senate.* This merely confirms the observations of previous writers on the federal budget, but it is very clear indeed in the context of Medicare. Repeatedly the House offered smaller cuts in these programs than the Senate, and this was even true for the one year in our sequence when the Senate was under Democratic control. It was in fact a Democratic Senate that originated the attachment of reconciliation instructions to the first budget resolution.

This greater House reluctance seems to be a function of several things. Shorter House terms, exposing representatives to greater continual pressure, and narrower areas of specialization, which give members greater investments in particular programs, are two obvious possibilities. These factors are only partly offset by the Senate's greater individualism.

In fairness, however, we should point out that although much more willing to cut domestic programs and reduce the deficit generally, the Senate was also considerably less willing to restrain defense spending than the House,

Table 2.3
Medicare Growth, 1981–87

Year	Total Part A+B Expend (in mil)	Percent Change Prev. Yr Total	Percent Change Prev. Yr Part A	Percent Change Prev. Yr Part B	Part A as Percent Total
1981	$41,499	20.0	16.7	16.5	69.8
1982	$49,267	18.7	16.2	14.8	70.1
1983	$56,914	15.5	12.3	16.0	69.2
1984	$62,843	10.4	8.6	11.3	68.5
1985	$68,392	8.8	7.5	9.5	68.1
1986	$74,785	9.3	4.9	15.5	65.4
1987	$81,639	9.2	3.8	19.3	62.2
	$435,339 Sum	13.1 Avg	10.0 Avg	14.7 Avg	67.6 Avg

Source: GAO (1988).

especially in the early years. Although Peroff and Podolak-Warren (1979) did not find much evidence of a defense-health spending trade-off, we find it hard to escape the conclusion that such a trade-off did exist in the 1980s. And this leads us to another point:

4. *Philosophy has a lot to do with targeting.* Many of the Reagan administration's proposals for cuts in Medicare revolved around the belief that cost rises stemmed from unnecessary utilization of services. In contrast, many House liberals believed firmly that providers were either inefficient or taking advantage of the programs. These differing interpretations of the facts led inexorably to different targets for cost-cutting efforts.

5. *However, immediate pressures are even more important.* As we suggested early in the Medicare discussion, there were very good reasons why hospitals were targeted for cuts so early in comparison with community-based physicians. The primary ones were that hospitals drew so large a portion of the Medicare budget, and that Parts A and B drew on different financing sources. With Part A's hospital services financed by the rapidly diminishing HI trust fund, Congress really had to take its first major actions against the hospitals. Physician services, smaller and largely financed out of general revenues, could wait a while.

6. *It's easier to target narrow groups when you have White House cover.* Though some members had advocated a freeze on physician fees early in the 1980s, the freeze made no real headway until Reagan included it in his FY83 budget request. Then it was enacted in DEFRA, the next reconciliation bill. The AMA was outraged, but had no good place to take its appeals. Conversely, the administration did *not* request an extension of the physician freeze for FY86, and it was dropped in OBRA.

7. *It also helps a great deal if the action itself can be partially hidden.* The Ways and Means Committee had clearly learned this lesson by 1981, when it began holding all its tax markups in closed session (*CQ Weekly Report*, May 3, 1986:963). But action can be effectively hidden in other ways: closed rules, hitching a ride on more prominent legislation, omnibus packages handled in one overall vote, and sheer confusion. All of these devices were employed in the bills we studied—some of them repeatedly.

8. *And a "good cop/bad cop" routine can be useful.* A heavy cut seems to incline groups toward more cooperation in the future. After the imposition of TEFRA, hospital groups were eager indeed to participate in the PPS restructuring. And the AMA, though angered by the physician pay freeze, found it convenient thereafter to emphasize the number of physicians who had voluntarily accepted assignment.

9. *But congressional willingness to target may well exceed its ability.* This is one of the most important lessons to emerge from our investigation. Throughout the period, Congress found that its attempts to target provider groups were plagued by the problems of cost-shifting. The installation of the PPS system immediately resulted in a *rise* of costs to the elderly in the form of increased deductibles, as the hospitals shortened patient stays and thus increased the average cost per day. The desire to limit physician fees constantly ran afoul of physicians' ability simply to charge patients for any additional fees not allowed by Medicare; while some members wanted to require mandatory assignment to eliminate such cost-shifting, others feared it would scare doctors away from even accepting Medicare patients. A partial (and probably temporary) solution was found in the differential incentives allowed "participating physicians."

Cost shifting was by no means the only sort of problem Congress experienced in hitting its target. The ability of physicians to offset the fee freeze by raising the volume of services was, according to GAO (1988:25) probably a major reason for the lesser effects of the Part B cuts.

10. *Finally, no policy is an island.* It is not just winners and losers that are entangled together; policies themselves are. The passage of at least two sets of Medicare provisions was hampered by entanglement with other, irrelevant provisions—everything from Superfund financing to industrial development bonds. On the other hand, the Medicare provisions themselves sometimes constituted major stumbling blocks to other legislation.

Beyond that, no policy can be presumed free of the provisions in other legislation. The fight over categorizing Medicare for Gramm-Rudman purposes illustrates the way in which priorities and policies interlock.

Budget issues for Medicare were far from over in 1986. In 1990 Congress reconstructed the physician payment system to institute a Resource Based Relative Value Scale giving more money to primary-care doctors and less to surgeons. However, the mandatory Expenditure Targets, which would have limited future fees according to Part B expenditures per year, were changed to an advisory system under ardent AMA lobbying. The tension and competition among targets will continue as long as the costs of these programs—and the political costs of cutting them—are so high. That, we think, will be for a very long time.

REFERENCES

Arnold, R. Douglas. 1990. *The Logic of Congressional Action*. New Haven, CT: Yale University Press.

Birnbaum, Jeffrey H. and Alan S. Murray. 1987. *Showdown at Gucci Gulch: Lawmakers, Lobbyists, and the Unlikely Triumph of Tax Reform*. New York: Random House.

Congress and the Nation. 1985. Washington, DC: Congressional Quarterly Inc.

Congressional Quarterly Weekly Reports. 1980–86.

Copeland, Gary W. 1984. "Changes in the House of Representatives after the Passage of the Budget Act of 1974." In *Congressional Budgeting: Politics, Process and Power*, W. Thomas Wander, F. Ted Hebert, and Copeland, eds. Baltimore: Johns Hopkins University Press, 51–77.

Derthick, Martha and Paul J. Quirk. 1985. *The Politics of Deregulation*. Washington, DC: The Brookings Institution.

Fuchs, Beth C. and John F. Hoadley. 1984. "The Remaking of Medicare: Congressional Policy-making on the Fast Track." Paper presented at the annual meeting of the Southern Political Science Association, Savannah, Georgia.

General Accounting Office. 1988. *Medicare and Medicaid: Updated Effects of Recent Legislation on Program and Beneficiary Costs*. GAO/HRD-88-85. Washington, DC: GAO.

Health Care Financing Administration. 1983. *Medicare and Medicaid Data Book, 1983*. Baltimore: Department of Health and Human Services.

Light, Paul. 1985. *Artful Work: The Politics of Social Security Reform*. New York: Random House.

Lowi, Theodore J. 1963. "American Business, Public Policy, Case-Studies and Political Theory." *World Politics* 16:766–815.

Marmor, Theodore R., Donald A. Wittman, and Thomas C. Heagy. 1983. "The Politics of Medical Inflation." In *Political Analysis and American Medical Care: Essays*, Theodore R. Marmor, ed. Cambridge: Cambridge University Press.

Mayhew, David R. 1974. *Congress: The Electoral Connection*. New Haven, CT: Yale University Press.

Moon, M. 1988. "Increases in Beneficiary Burdens: Direct and Indirect Effects." In

Lessons from the First Twenty Years of Medicare, M. Pauly and W. Kissick, eds. Philadelphia: University of Pennsylvania Press.

Peroff, Kathleen and Margaret Podolak-Warren. 1979. "Does Spending on Defense Cut Spending on Health? A Time-Series Analysis of the U.S. Economy 1929– 1974." *British Journal of Political Science* 9:21–39.

Public Policy and Aging Report. 1988. Vol. 2, no. 2.

U.S. Senate Special Committee on Aging. *Developments in Aging: 1987*, Vol. 1. (January 28, 1987). Washington, DC: Government Printing Office.

Wilson, James Q. 1973. *Political Organizations*. New York: Basic Books.

3

Evaluating the Social Impacts of Health Insurance Policy

Anona F. Armstrong

INTRODUCTION

Evaluation of public policy at a macro level is particularly difficult because the chain between the allocation of resources and the final outcome is a long one, the links are not always clear, to determine causality is almost impossible, and there are many contingencies and variations in the planning, implementation, and delivery stages of a program. Even if successfully concluded, no evaluation produces results unless it is used. Among the reasons for lack of utilization of results are inappropriate personnel to conduct the evaluation, the lack of evaluation expertise (Scriven, 1984), the perceived threats of evaluation, the political constraints (Weiss, 1986), the daily clashes of those involved (Patton, 1978), lack of involvement with decision-makers or users (Stake, 1983), the overinvolvement of the commissioners of evaluation (Scriven, 1984), the lack of appropriate communication between evaluators and those who could use the information, and the lack of evaluation implementation skills (Armstrong, 1986).

Despite the difficulties, evaluation of government programs is essential to provide knowledge of how a community values a program, what is the impact of a program, some comparisons of the impact of a program on the state of the community with and without a program, the desirability of alternatives to a program, and the costs and benefits of a program and its alternatives. The evaluation intervention can occur at different stages in the design, implementation, and delivery of a program, and at different levels of decision-making (Armstrong, 1990). In each case, the information obtained serves different decisions and decision-makers.

At a policy level, an evaluation can indicate whether a program is better or worse than alternatives. The evaluation question is whether a program should be terminated or continued. At an administrative level, the information required is usually formative—that is, it answers questions about how the program is being delivered and how the delivery can be improved. Consumers make decisions about the use of services. Consumer evaluation examines the impacts of a program and addresses the evaluation question: to what extent is the program meeting the needs it was designed to serve.

The purpose of this chapter is to present a systemic framework for examining the interaction between political, administrative, and consumer decisions. The utility of the model is illustrated by its application to determining the effectiveness of health insurance policies. Before describing the model, it may be useful to describe the goals of health insurance policies and some of the major evaluation questions.

EVALUATION OF HEALTH INSURANCE POLICIES

The goals of a national health insurance policy are to improve the health of the population by enabling access to services and operate efficiently in terms of costs and management. This means that among the major tasks of evaluation are to: monitor the health status of the public; evaluate different methods of providing health care; analyze the interaction between consumers and providers of health services to determine what leads to effectiveness of program delivery, consumer satisfaction, awareness of available services, and efficient programmatic management; and determine the effectiveness of current and proposed health insurance procedures.

The sources of this information may be all those involved in the process—the stakeholders—or only those directly concerned in the decision-making process. The stakeholders in a health insurance program include politicians, administrators of public and private health insurance funds, those involved in service delivery, and the clients or the community at large. Each group of stakeholders—the legislators in government, public service or health fund administrators, the providers of services (physicians, nurses, psychologists, dentists, etc.), and the consumers of services (individual and community)—can be described by a variety of roles, attitudes, values, and so on, described in more detail in the section entitled "System Inputs." Because of these differences they make different decisions affecting the health insurance system.

If information is gathered from all the stakeholders, some of the disadvantages are the size and cost of the operation, the time constraints imposed on decisions, and the interruptions to the decision processes of attempting to accommodate various points of view. The advantages are the breadth of knowledge gained, slower implementation of programs is less threatening, and people are more committed to decisions in which they have shared.

Figure 3.1
A Social Policy Analysis Model

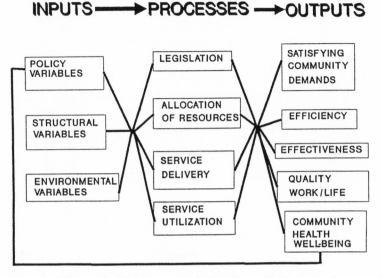

The most significant decisions are made by the politicians at the top of the hierarchy. Those most removed from the political decisions are the clients. Nevertheless, the more politically important a program, the more significant are clients' decisions. This is particularly true of health insurance programs.

All stakeholders are consumers of health services and health insurance, but as members of each category of stakeholders they have different characteristics and perceptions, and play different roles in the health insurance system. Politicians are concerned about policy issues. Should a health insurance program be compulsory or voluntary? Should it be privately or publicly funded? Administrators will be concerned with issues affecting program costs, and program managers with modification that may make the program better. Clients make decisions about utilization—that is, about their kind of health insurance cover, whether to use a health service, and how often to use it.

The following policy analysis model provides a systemic framework that guides the selection of useful information to examine issues linking these political, administrative, and consumer decisions.

A SOCIAL POLICY ANALYSIS MODEL

The four basic requirements for a system model are system inputs, processes, outcomes, and a set of structural relationships between the sets of variables. Figure 3.1 shows the components of a social policy analysis model. Each component in the whole system can be decomposed into various subsystems, and each system or subsystem's inputs, processes, or outcomes can be evaluated or judged against some criteria such as normative standards, needs, or performance standards.

System Inputs

System inputs include policy manipulable variables, structural variables, and environmental variables. Examples of policy variables are the government's stated policy on health insurance, and the resources devoted to health insurance industry funds, staff, building facilities, etc.

Structural variables include the characteristics of the participants: the legislators (the government), the administrators of services (the public service), the providers of the services (physicians, nurses, psychologists, dentists, etc.), and the consumers of services (individual and community). Each subgroup of participants can be described by their roles, demography, habits, attitudes, values, motives, dispositions, and abilities.

Habits are defined as activities that through prolonged practice have become relatively automatic. They may be consistent patterns of thought or attitudes or an acquired drive, such as drug addiction.

Attitudes are a function of beliefs about the object, the evaluation of the importance (the value or worth of an object) to the individual (Fishbein and Coombs, 1974). Attitudes are tendencies to respond to people, institutions, or events either positively or negatively. This implies classification or categorization of related events so that a conservative voter with a favorable attitude toward a conservative political party is likely to react favorably to all of that party's policies on health insurance, irrespective of their individual merits or differences. Should an evaluation study find that a government was out of step with its party members, it could expect some repercussions at the next elections.

Values are the evaluation of the excellence of anything or the social goals or ends that are considered desirable of attainment. Goals are the ends toward which an individual strives. Values affect community attitudes toward equity issues that determine policy options such as whether premiums should be the same for everyone, or whether higher insurance costs should be paid by higher income groups or higher risk groups. When there is a generally held belief that people who are ill should have access to medical care, values determine whether insurance should cover the cost of abortion, plastic surgery, or unlimited access to high-cost technology.

Administrative decisions are influenced by consumer attitudes toward, for example, the public or private ownership of health insurance funds, whether health insurance should be voluntary or compulsory, and utilization of services. The selection and utilization of a fund are determined by the reasons people have for choosing a fund, how satisfied they are with a service, the type of cover that they prefer, and the options available for paying different types of premiums.

Data information systems contain records of patients and service deliveries, types of services, and frequency of use. One of the administrative maintenance functions is checking for fraud and overservicing by service delivery agents. The success of the operation will be influenced by community attitudes toward the protection of the medical profession and perceived responsibility for the cost of health care. Habits, attitudes toward accountability and responsibility, and preferences for alternative packages of premiums and services directly affect the cost of health care.

The environment, the third of the system input variables, refers to a multidimensional organizational domain composed of physical, social, economic, and political factors (Armstrong and Wearing, 1977). It is the context within which people live. An individual's experience of his or her environment can be described through one's perceptions of life concerns such as family structure, access to health services, and opportunities for participation in all areas of life (Andrews and Withey, 1976).

Processes

Processes in the policy analysis model describe how the decisions and activities of participants lead to outcomes. The relationships between the characteristics of stakeholders (inputs in the model) and their decisions and activities (processes) determine the social impacts of the program.

Changes in activities occur because of the decisions or transactions of stakeholders. Decisions are influenced by the characteristics of participants, habits, attitudes, beliefs about an issue, the importance of the issue to an individual, and their goals and expectations.

Administrators allocate resources. Drawing on their specific expertise, providers of services decide on the factors affecting the costs of health care. They include the quality of care and the allocation of care such as frequency of services and when to hospitalize a patient. Individual consumers make decisions affecting the utilization of services, such as their choice of health insurance, consulting a general practitioner, or attending a community health clinic.

Outcomes

Outcome variables describe the results of a program. The stated goals of a national health insurance policy are to improve the health of the population by enabling access to services and to operate efficiently in terms of costs and management.

Multiple outcomes reflect how the goals of the policy programs differ for each subgroup of stakeholders. Outcomes for government and legislators are the extent to which programs meet community needs and acceptable levels of efficiency and effectiveness in the provision of services. For providers of services, outcomes include variables such as income generated and the quality of life. An assumption underlying the implementation of social policy by the provision of health and welfare services is that the well-being of the community can be improved. Hence, individual and community goals are represented by the state of health and well-being in the community.

Measures of health outcomes could include objective measures of health status, morbidity, mortality, life expectancy (OECD, 1973), aggregates of the frequency of illness and the duration of illness (Jazairi, 1976), various dimensions of health function/dysfunction (Fanshell and Bush, 1970), and subjective measures such as those developed by Bradburn (1969), Goldberg (1972), Hall (1976), Andrews and Withey (1976) and Armstrong (1983).

Secondary intended and unintended impacts may occur. For example, one of the goals of introducing a policy of compulsory health insurance was to make health care accessible to all members of the Australian community (the introduction of Medicare extended public medical benefits to the whole population [Deeble, 1987]). Among the unintended results were a rise in the use of high-cost, high-technology services (an annual increase between 1983 and 1987 of 20 percent [Deeble, 1987]) and the demand for health services (a 34 percent increase in the number of services from 85 to 90 percent [Deeble, 1991]).

The structural relationships between variables in this system are extremely complex. Relationships occur among variables within each subsystem of the whole system and between each component or set of input, process, and output variables. Changes in any of the system components may initiate feedback loops that may alter the relationships within other components of the system. When additional services—for example, psychological services— were made accessible through health insurance, this new health care option could change the pattern of health care access for consumers who may choose to visit a psychologist instead of their local practitioner.

CONCLUSION

The assumptions underlying this approach to evaluation are that programs are not only cycles of events but more importantly chains of decisions and that the decisions are not just the result of social pressures, but that people make decisions based on their knowledge, information, and experience and that their decisions have consequences at each step of the design, implementation, and delivery of a program. The social policy analysis model suffers from many of the limitations common to macroanalyses of social issues. The model provides an overview of the relationships between the components, but collecting all the data required to fully explore the model is an expensive and difficult task. The model was used to explore the issues

(Armstrong, 1980) but the measures were taken at only one point in time. Although the relational properties of the components of the system were observed, it is difficult to make inferences about the probability or magnitude of how a change in one component would affect or be affected by a change in other components.

An advantage of using a systemic framework that links political, administrative, and consumer decisions is that it increases the utilization of the results by providing information that is relevant to and can be used to improve decisions that determine the effectiveness of the program.

REFERENCES

Andrews, F. M. and S. B. Withey. 1976. *Social Indicators of Well-Being: American Perceptions of Life Quality*. New York: Plenum Press.

Armstrong, A. F. 1980. "Health Policy and Subjective Social Indicators." Unpublished Ph.D. thesis.

———. 1983. "Health Indicators for Victoria." Paper presented to *Social Factors and Mental Illness, 12th Meeting of Australian Social Psychologists*, Institute of Administration, Prince Henry Hospital, May 12–15.

———. 1986. "The Skills of Evaluation." In *The Skills of Evaluation*, Vol. 1, A. Armstrong, ed. Proceedings of the Second National Evaluation Conference, 1984. Melbourne: Department of Psychology, University of Melbourne.

———. 1990. "Evaluating Health Education Programs." *Network* 6(3).

Armstrong, A. F. and A. J. Wearing. 1977. *The Social Impact Assessment of Some Current and Expected Changes in the Social Environment of the Mornington Peninsula*. Melbourne Psychology Reports 33, University of Melbourne.

Bradburn, N. 1969. *The Structure of Psychological Well-Being*. Chicago: Aldine.

Deeble, J. 1987. "Health Care Under Universal Insurance: The First Three Years of Medicare." Paper presented to the 1987 conference of the Australian Medical Writers Association, Canberra, September 18.

———. 1991. *Medical Services through Medicare*. National Health Strategy Background Paper No. 2. Canberra: National Health Strategy Unit (Australia), Department of Community Services and Health.

Fanshell, F. and J. W. Bush. 1970. "A Health Status Index and Its Application to Health Service Outcomes." *Operations Research* 18(6):1021–66.

Fishbein, M. and F. S. Coombes. 1974. "Basis for Decision: An Attitudinal Analysis of Voting Behavior." *Journal of Applied Social Psychology* 42:95–124.

Goldberg, D. P. 1972. *The Detection of Psychiatric Illness by Questionnaire*. Oxford: Oxford University Press.

Hall, J. 1976. "Subjective Measures of Quality of Life in Britain: 1971 to 1975. Some Developments and Trends." *Social Trends* 47–60 (HMSO).

Jazairi, N. T. 1976. *Approaches to the Development of Health Indicators*. Special Studies No. 2. Paris: OECD.

OECD (Organization for Economic Co-operation and Development). 1973. *List of Social Indicators Common to Most OECD Countries*. Paris: OECD.

Patton, M. 1978. *Utilization-focused Evaluation*. Beverly Hills, CA: Sage.

Scriven, M. 1984. "Checklist Evaluation." Paper presented to Evaluation Workshop, Canberra.

Stake, R. E. 1983. "Stakeholder Influence in the Evaluation of Cities-in-Schools." In *Stakeholder Based Evaluation*, A. S. Bryk, ed. San Francisco: Jossey-Bass.

Weiss, C. H. 1986. "Increasing the Likelihood That Evaluation Research Influences Decisions." In *The Skills of Evaluation*, A. Armstrong, ed. Melbourne: Department of Psychology, University of Melbourne.

PART II

PROVISION OF CARE
FOR THOSE IN NEED

Part II of this volume focuses on equity in health care insurance. How is one to provide for those most in need? The chapter authors examine care given to those largely abandoned by the system.

In Chapter 4 Vaughan and Buss examine the plight of workers displaced in plant closings who need health insurance. Two out of three workers laid off carry no insurance and could be pushed into poverty if they required expensive health care. The authors suggest that during periods of unemployment, displaced workers be given loans to purchase private health insurance for a period up to two years. The loans would be repaid through the existing unemployment payroll tax system when they find replacement jobs.

The proposed health insurance loan would be self-financing and managed by the state or privately by a health care providers consortium. Federal and state governments are currently willing to offer health care to elderly displaced or impoverished individuals. The health insurance loan program suggested here would be a voluntary option, permitting displaced workers to purchase peace of mind. The trauma of unemployment, coupled with unfinanced health programs, could lead to significant cost to the economy through discouraged and displaced workers. Layoffs create temporary financial problems, including the loss of health coverage. More critically, workers would then have to satisfy new waiting periods if they allowed their insurance to lapse.

Rice and Jones in Chapter 5 examine public and/or charity hospital use, which has increased due to changes in Medicaid eligibility requirements,

Medicare reimbursement, increasing numbers of uninsured, and transfers of uninsured and underinsured from private to public hospitals. Increasing numbers of transfer patients require emergency care upon arriving at public hospitals. The transferring hospital may claim that the transfer is for medical reasons, when, in fact, the major ground is the patient's poverty.

Most dumping is done within the emergency room. Hospitals can exclude the poorer patient by requiring advance payment, refusing care to those whose physicians do not have admitting privileges, or by a blanket refusal to accept Medicaid patients. In those states where for-profit hospitals have expanded, dumping has become more prevalent. Given the fact that there is no universal health insurance, many patients will be considered financially unattractive. Furthermore, by totally refusing treatment, the hospital escapes liability. The only hope for uninsured or underinsured patients is the dubious protection of antidumping legislation.

Sanders examines charity care and community benefit in Chapter 6. Hospitals have generally been considered nonprofit, but there is a question as to the justification for treating nonprofit hospitals differently than the for-profit hospitals. Nonprofit hospitals have been assailed for unfair competitive advantage. Do the revenues lost to the locality from tax exemption exceed the benefits that nonprofit hospitals contribute to the public?

The government has established organizational and operational tests to determine tax-exemption status. The first test requires that the proceeds cannot be distributed and the second test is that hospitals must provide services at free or reduced costs for charity cases and that they must provide community benefits. But there are certain practical difficulties in determining these measures. It is sometimes hard to distinguish bad debts from charity care. If a substantial portion of the bad debt is actually charity care improperly designated, then the charity care contribution is overestimated. By the same token, if significant portions of bad debts reflect fees that might have been collected but were not, then the size of hospital charity care contribution could be overstated. Sanders notes that community benefits are exceedingly difficult to quantify monetarily. The whole definition of community has broadened because of transportation and communication differences. Nonprofit hospitals are generally faithful to the dual obligations of charity care and community benefit. The continuation of these dimensions of care is, however, questionable within the current environment.

4

Financing Health Care Coverage for Displaced Workers

Roger S. Vaughan and Terry F. Buss

INTRODUCTION

Paying for health care is a growing burden, but only a small fraction of the population must carry the weight unaided. The elderly and those on welfare are assisted by publicly financed programs. Three-quarters of the American work force are covered through health insurance plans at work and pay premiums through payroll deductions that are shared with their employers—and, because coverage is not a taxable benefit, with taxpayers (Podgursky and Swaim, 1987). For the self-employed, plans are available for those who can afford them.

But the unemployed can draw on none of these benefits. Cut off from health plans, too rich for Medicaid, and unable to pay for the premiums out of benefits that replace, on average, less than half of their income, the majority survive without coverage. A sick child, a personal accident, or a spouse's serious illness can render them medically indigent. Most of the working poor also lack coverage and the means to pay for it. For many, their problems are chronic and must be addressed through a different program than that described in this chapter.

Federal and state governments have tried various ways to extend health services to the medically indigent (King, 1986). Congress requires employers to allow those laid off to remain enrolled in the plant's health plan at their own expense while at least one employee remains on the local payroll. Massachusetts and Connecticut mandate extension of health coverage for several months after a closing. Yet these measures do not help displaced workers pay for the coverage, particularly when the previous employer is bankrupt or closed—the case for 40 percent of displaced workers in Youngs-town, Ohio, for example (Buss and Redburn, 1987). State regulators, health care providers, and the health-insurance industry have developed many different ways of paying the medical bills for those who have no money. These programs deal with emergencies, but they do not prevent people from becoming indigent.

This chapter explores the feasibility of providing loans to the unemployed to pay all, or part, of the cost of health insurance premiums, which would then be repaid when the borrower returned to work. The program would be self-financing. It is not intended to supplant other initiatives to aid the medically indigent or as a way to help the working poor, but as a way to help people who are experiencing a temporary spell of unemployment to maintain access to quality medical care.

The Health Insurance Loan (HIL) option offers two benefits. It would improve access to health care for displaced workers and their families and thus allow them to live healthier lives. It would also reduce the number of people who fall back on welfare and on special plans for the indigent when they do suffer serious health problems.

The first section describes the extent of the problem—the number of displaced workers without health insurance coverage and the number that suffer medical expenses beyond their means. It also discusses the different approaches that states have adopted to deal with the problems of the med-ically indigent.

The second section discusses the elements of health coverage that affect the cost of purchasing insurance, including age and family characteristics of the displaced worker; deductibility—the expenses that the individual must bear before insurance takes over; and copayment—the share of medical expenses the patient must bear. Each of these factors will influence the cost of coverage and therefore the amount of the loan for the unemployed.

The third section examines the design of a loan program, including how eligibility would be established, how the loan would be made available, how interstate relocation would be handled, how it would be repaid, and how defaults would be accommodated. The program must extend financial assistance to those most in need but should not continue to advance loans to those displaced workers who seem to have little prospects of or ambition for reemployment.

UNEMPLOYMENT, HEALTH INSURANCE, AND THE
MEDICALLY INDIGENT

In 1986 Americans spent $462 billion on health care—11 percent of GNP and nearly $2,000 per capita. But 75 percent of expenses were incurred by 20 percent of the population. Some 25 percent of households in 1977 in-curred health care expenses in excess of $500 and 10 percent in excess of

$1,000 (Robert Wood Johnson Foundation, 1983). Three million families in that year suffered out-of-pocket medical expenses exceeding 20 percent of family income.

Against large, unexpected expenses, seven out of eight people carry private health care insurance or are covered by one of the major public programs for the poor, the elderly, or veterans. But one out of eight people (208,000 families) and two out of three unemployed Americans are not covered by health insurance (Regula, 1987). The number has grown by 33 percent since 1976.

The Bureau of Labor Statistics estimates that, of the 5 million workers displaced between 1981 and 1985, 1.2 million were without health insurance coverage in January 1986 (Horvath, 1987). Of these, half had found other jobs but without health insurance coverage—these "uncovered workers" represented 22 percent of the reemployed. Almost 400,000 of those without coverage were unemployed, and represented 60 percent of the unemployed. Some 265,000 had dropped out of the labor force, and those without coverage represented about half of the discouraged workers. In Youngstown, Ohio, lack of health insurance was one of the most important concerns of displaced workers (Buss and Redburn, 1983).

Lack of health insurance leads to health and financial problems. Families without health care coverage may suffer serious health problems because they are unwilling to seek treatment at an earlier stage or because the provider refuses care to the uninsured. People under the age of 65 with health insurance receive 54 percent more physician ambulatory care than those without insurance (Davis and Rowland, 1983). They also receive twice as much hospital care, and they suffer much higher mortality rates (Hadley, 1982). When the medically indigent use health services, the costs have to be met by others. Hospitals reported over $7 billion in uncompensated costs in 1986, driving up costs for other patients and often raising the cost of health insurance. For example, in Arizona businesses pay an estimated $100 per worker annually in additional premiums toward the cost of uncompensated health care (Hadley, 1982).

In response to the problems of the medically indigent, state and local governments and the health care industry have enrolled uncovered people in existing public and private health plans or have created funding pools to pay for their health care directly.

Enrolling in Existing Health Plans

State and local governments have found ways to offer health insurance at subsidized rates to those with low incomes (King, 1986). The additional groups covered include the children of two-parent families living below the AFDC (Aid to Families with Dependent Children) cash assistance level and families with unemployed parent(s) below the AFDC cash assistance level.

Some 56 percent of the costs of coverage for these groups would be met through federal Title XIX funds. Medicaid coverage for acute care services can be extended to those whose net income falls within 133.3 percent of the AFDC income standard when their medical expenses are deducted.

State Funding Mechanisms for Uncompensated Health Care

Most states have created funding mechanisms to pay for health care for the indigent. These mechanisms include (King, 1986):

Assessments on Hospitals and other health care providers. Care providers pay an assessment based on their gross receipts to a state agency that then reimburses hospitals for care delivered to indigent people. Legislation has been passed in Florida, New York, South Carolina, West Virginia, and Wisconsin.

Assessments on Insurance Premiums. Legislation has been enacted in Iowa.

Minimum Care Requirements. Care providers are required to deliver a minimum level of charity care—equivalent to the tax (above) but paid in kind. Legislation has been enacted in Arkansas and California. Nonlegislative programs are operating in Georgia and Kentucky.

Rate Setting Add-on Mechanisms. In those states with a rate-regulating agency, providers are allowed to charge higher rates to allow for the amount of uncompensated care they have provided. Legislation has been enacted in Connecticut, Maine, Maryland, Massachusetts, New Jersey, and New York. Massachusetts covers an estimated $200 million annually in this way.

Employer Contributions. Hawaii requires employers to make health care available to all employees, which has increased the number of low-wage employees covered by health insurance.

Earmarked Revenues. Pennsylvania earmarks about $100 million of lottery proceeds, New Jersey uses about $70 million from gambling revenues, and Montana sets aside the proceeds from money seized for violating gambling laws for indigent health care. Oklahoma sponsors a check-off against the state income tax for people to donate a portion of their tax refund for the indigent.

In addition to these formal, mandated programs, an unknown—but presumably large—amount of health care is paid through charitable contributions and local tax levies.

Conclusion

The inability of people to pay for either health insurance or health care is a major problem that cannot be met through existing public- or private-sector initiatives. The unemployed comprise a large share of the population that needs coverage but is unable to afford it.

THE COST OF HEALTH INSURANCE

The cost of health insurance depends on the insurer's estimate of the policyholder's future demands for health services. This depends on the health characteristics of those to be covered by the policy that may predict need for health care—such as age, overall health, and occupation. It also depends on the nature of the coverage requested. If the policyholder bears part of the cost of the health services or undertakes or agrees to a deductible, they are likely to make less use of health services than people who carry full coverage for all expenses ("How Many Americans Are Adequately Protected?" 1988).

This section reviews three factors that determine the cost of health insurance: the health services covered, the obligations of the policyholder, and the characteristics of the policyholder.

Services Covered

Health insurance can cover a wide array of medical expenses—from outpatient care and major medical expenses to dentists and psychiatrists. Insurance covers nearly 90 percent of inpatient hospital care, about 40 percent of ambulatory physician care, and only about 20 percent of dental and prescription medicine (Kasper et al., 1980).

The more extensive the coverage the more expensive the coverage. Monthly coverage for major medical expenses only—including all expenses beyond the first $1,000—costs an average of $72 per capita. The lowest rates are for policies that cover catastrophic health problems. The policyholder is expected to cover the first $1,000 in household medical expenses each year.

Policy Characteristics

The most important determinants of the cost of insurance coverage are the size of the deductible—how much the policyholder must pay before the carrier contributes toward the expenses—and the copayment—the share of each expense that the policyholder must pay. The higher the deductible and the larger the copayment, the lower the premium.

From the perspective of displaced workers, the two most important characteristics of the policy are the deductibility and copayment provisions. Several studies have found that copayment discourages physician use more strongly among those with low incomes than among higher income patients (Beck, 1974). However, there is little evidence that this leads to poorer health.

Some displaced workers may have acquired considerable assets and may receive severance payments. Others may be poor. The former may be interested in low-cost health insurance because they can afford deductibles and copayments. The latter may wish to protect their small incomes and assets by investing in more complete health insurance coverage.

Companies—and some public agencies seeking coverage for low-income people—have achieved considerable savings through group rates. However, in many states, the formation of groups, simply for the purpose of purchasing health insurance, is illegal.

Policyholders' Characteristics

The characteristics of the individuals seeking insurance do affect premiums, but the difference between the group that pays the highest rates—older people with preexisting medical conditions—and those paying the lowest rates is not as great as the range between the lowest cost and the highest cost policies above.

Conclusion

The purchase of health insurance is complicated. Most people are used to selecting among a few relatively simple options through an employer's health plan. If the unemployed are to use their insurance loans effectively—to meet their own particular situation and resources—they will need access to advice and information that, at present, is not available. For example, the Ohio Department of Insurance cannot provide a list of insurance providers, options, and costs to consumers.

THE DESIGN OF A HEALTH INSURANCE LOAN PROGRAM

A program to help people pay for health care should achieve three ends. First, it must reach those least able to afford health care from their own resources without imposing a financial penalty on participants who successfully improve their financial position. Second, it must aid those whose employers do not provide coverage without encouraging all employers to reduce coverage. And third, the way in which assistance is offered should neither deny valuable health services to participants nor encourage them to overuse the services.

Political, economic, and financial considerations make the achievement of these ends difficult. For example, means-tested health care programs such as Medicaid make it financially difficult for welfare recipients to return to the labor force unless they can find well-paid work that offers generous benefits (Hopkins, 1987). Yet they may not be qualified for such employment. Mandating companies to provide health insurance to all their employees (as Hawaii does) dramatically increases the cost of low-skilled labor, which will reduce the number of such jobs. Providing either public health insurance coverage to low-income households or directly paying for the medically indigent may discourage companies from providing their own health plans for individuals otherwise insuring themselves.

When targeting on the unemployed, these problems loom very large because so many people experience spells of unemployment during their working lives. In Youngstown, Ohio, for example, steelworkers laid off in 1977 experienced on average two additional spells of unemployment through 1985 (Buss and Redburn, 1983). If a program for which all unemployed people were eligible reduced the incentives to return to work, it would be very expensive.

The Health Insurance Loan Program would extend loans to unemployed people to pay for the purchase of private health insurance. Loans are suitable to bridge temporary spells of low income caused by the loss of a job, because most of the unemployed will return to work and therefore would be able to repay. The amount of time one is unemployed does vary during recessions (Horrigan, 1987). In 1981–82, for example, mean unemployment duration was 21 weeks. In 1986 it had dropped to 15 weeks. Loans would not be suitable for the long-term poor because their needs would be much greater relative to their ability to repay and their chances of soon finding a well-paid job are much less. To simplify the administration of the program and to reduce the chances of misuse of the funds, the proceeds of the loan would go directly to health insurance providers—acting as a "voucher" for premium payment. The loan would be repaid through a direct payroll deduction when the borrower returned to work—collected from the employer as an add-on to the Unemployment Insurance (UI) tax.

The three considerations—eligibility, incentives for private provision, and incentives for the efficient use of health services—are valuable yardsticks to apply when determining the details of the program. Each is discussed in turn below.

Who Should Be Eligible?

The goal of the program is to help the unemployed pay for health care insurance during the financially painful transition from one job and another. But not all the unemployed have an equal probability of returning to work and thus of repaying the loan (Horvath, 1987; Horrigan, 1987; Hopkins, 1987). As the number of such risky borrowers increases, then the repayment rates of those that do return to work will have to increase to cover the delinquent debts of others.

Those least likely to find regular employment within a decade of being laid off are workers over the age of 55—who are likely to choose early retirement—and unskilled female household heads with preschool children. To lend to the former, future Social Security or union pension benefits may have to be tapped to repay loans. Unskilled women, and other chronically poor people, may be best served by enrolling in Medicaid rather than loaned money. They need more than "bridge financing" in order to escape from poverty.

It may be possible to extend the program to some of the working poor who are not eligible for Medicaid by linking the program to activities that will raise their potential long-term income. For example, those without a high school graduation certificate who enrolled in an education or training program might be extended a loan for the duration of their enrollment (provided they maintained progress toward their education goals). It might also be possible to extend loans for a limited period to people undergoing on-the-job-training in a company if they are moving from jobs that offer no health care coverage to jobs that do. People moving out of state would no longer be eligible for additional loans and would repay through the same type of reciprocal mechanisms established by the Unemployment Insurance system.

How Much Could People Borrow?

Over time, the size and duration of the loan would have to be determined by experimentation. The system could increase the size if the overall fiscal viability could support either raising the maximum amount or extending the period during which people may borrow. As a starting point, the monthly insurance premium for a family of three ranges from about $100 to $150, depending on the level of coverage. Loans of $100 a month for two years would enable displaced workers to ensure that their families enjoyed continued access to basic health care. Those that wished could supplement the loan to purchase more coverage.

For How Long Could Participants Continue to Borrow?

Loans should probably be available for up to two years after the worker is laid off. In Youngstown, two years after the closing of Youngstown Sheet and Tube in 1977, nearly 50 percent of the workers had found other jobs and 30 percent had retired. It may be worth extending the eligibility period when overall economic conditions deteriorate—much as the duration of UI benefits lengthens during recessions. In 1983, just after a deep recession, the average duration of unemployment was 21.2 weeks. By 1986 this had fallen to 15.2 weeks (Horrigan, 1987).

At a minimum, workers should be eligible for loans while they are receiving UI benefits. In most areas, this coverage lasts for only 26 weeks (longer in high-unemployment areas where people are eligible for supplementary benefits for several more weeks). Eligibility could be extended for this period.

However, in Youngstown nearly one-third of displaced steelworkers remained unemployed after they were no longer receiving UI checks. A major part of the "at-risk" population would be omitted if HIL loans expired with benefits. A two-year period would broaden coverage, and only experience will be able to determine if this is too broad.

The period of eligibility need not terminate when the worker has found another job. A transitional period of three or four months (providing it fell within the overall eligibility period) could be allowed in which either loans were still available or repayments did not begin. This would reduce some of the costs of returning to work.

Will the Program Discourage Employers from Covering Workers?

The HIL program would provide loans to the unemployed to pay the premiums of private health insurance programs. There are no disincentives for carriers or the providers of health care to treat participants any differently from the majority of the population covered by health insurance. Because the loans or vouchers cover only basic coverage, most people would be adding their money to purchase whatever additional coverage they wanted. They would therefore be "price sensitive." Because the program is no more than the transfer of a voucher, it will not produce disincentives for employers.

Will Participants Use Health Care Services Efficiently?

Access to free health care leads people to use more health services. People who must share a part of the cost of visits to a doctor or hospital make fewer visits. Does this lead to better health? If so, should the loan program be used to encourage people to purchase comprehensive health insurance with neither a deductible level of expenditures nor copayments?

The most extensive experiment with health insurance coverage, conducted by the Rand Corporation, found that adults who had to share the costs of care make about one-third fewer ambulatory visits and were hospitalized one-third less often than those whose expenses were wholly covered by their insurer (Newhouse et al., 1981). This translated into reduction in medical expenses incurred. Annual per capita expenses were $750 for families in which the insurer covered all expenses, $617 where people had to pay 25 percent of the expenses, and $540 where 95 percent of expenses were paid by the policyholder (for the first $1,000 of expenses, zero thereafter) (Manning et al., 1987).

But these significant differences in use and expenses have little impact on the health of the insured person. The Rand researchers (Brook et al., 1983) summarize:

First of all, free health care had no effect on the major health habits that are associated with cardiovascular disease and some types of cancer. Enrollment in a more generous insurance plan, resulting in an average of one or two more encounters with a physician each year for several years, had no impact on smoking, weight, or cholesterol levels.

Second, we detected no effects of free care for the average enrollee on any of the five general self-assessed measures of health.

Third, people with specific conditions that physicians have been trained to diagnose and treat (myopia, hypertension) benefit from free care. At the end of the experiment, persons receiving free care had better visual acuity, and some of them had lower blood pressure....

These mortality reductions, in and of themselves, are not sufficient to justify free care for all adults; investing in more targeted programs such as hypertension detection and screening would be a more cost-effective way of saving lives.

How Would Loans Be Repaid?

As soon as the borrower returned to work they would begin repaying the loan into the HIL Trust Fund at a rate intended to cover the full cost of the loan plus whatever allowance for bad debts is needed to maintain the solvency of the system. The average repayment period could be five years, with prepayment allowed, and, perhaps, even encouraged. For a dislocated worker who had borrowed $2,400 over two years, the monthly payments would vary with the interest rate and the repayment period:

Interest Rate	Repayment Period	
	4 Years	5 Years
8.0	55.92	47.27
10.0	60.89	51.48
12.0	63.22	53.40

Loans might also be repaid by providing labor in exchange for premium payments. For example, a displaced worker might agree to work 20 hours a month in a local hospital in exchange for all or part (depending on the prevailing wage for the work) of the monthly voucher of $100—with the hospital paying the HIL program on behalf of the worker. This would help hospitals with their growing shortage of help as well as providing the unemployed with meaningful work while they search for more permanent employment.

If the system is to be self-financing, the cost of defaults must be borne by charging those who do not repay higher interest rates. If default rates become too high, the program will no longer be attractive to borrowers. Several state student loan programs have experienced very high default rates, a reduction in federal guarantee payments, and a necessity for large subsidies from state revenues to maintain the system.

The experience with the Guaranteed Student Loan (GSL) Program suggest several ways in which defaults could be minimized. First, the loan should be backed by strong collateral by the borrower. These need not include the limited assets that the borrower needs for her- or himself and her or his family. They could include future income payments—even if the worker relocates out of state—and retirement benefits if the worker never returns to the work force. States already operate interstate agreements for managing the UI system. These could be extended to allow the imposition of the UI surcharge to repay debts owed to out-of-state agencies.

Second, the job of collecting delinquent payments should be contracted with a private financial institution. Public agencies rarely have the resources and the flexibility to collect effectively. Under the GSL program, when public agencies turned over bad loans they had failed to collect to private financial institutions, nearly half the money owed was returned.

In several states the entire student loan program is operated by private financial institutions. These tend to enjoy lower default rates and costs. This approach would be possible for HIL loans providing that the employment service would cooperate in certifying workers eligible for the loans—a process that could coincide with the determination of UI benefit eligibility.

Ultimately, if default rates prove uncomfortably high despite these measures, it may be necessary to limit the term of eligibility or the maximum amount that can be borrowed. If the fiscal integrity of the program is maintained, it will be possible, over time, to evolve an effective loan program that does not require massive public subsidies yet meets a clearly identified need.

CONCLUSION

The unemployed need temporary help to maintain coverage for themselves and their families. Layoffs create temporary financial problems that, despite some well-intentioned but ineffective federal and state policies, result in most displaced workers losing health insurance coverage. For those who suffer illness, the financial consequences may be grave.

The Health Insurance Loan Program would offer the unemployed the chance to purchase health insurance from private vendors and to repay the loan when they returned to work. Purchasers would also be given information describing the health insurance options they can adopt and a comparison of the prices of premiums from companies offering individual coverage within the state.

The program should be entirely self-supporting, with repayments covering the amortization and interest costs of the loans. Delinquent loans would require a surcharge or repayments.

REFERENCES

Beck, R. G. 1974. "The Effects of Copayment on the Poor." *Journal of Human Resources* 20:1–20.

Brook, Robert H. et al. 1983. "Does Free Care Improve Adults' Health?" *New England Journal of Medicine* 309:1432ff.

Buss, Terry F. and F. Stevens Redburn. 1983. *Shutdown in Youngstown: Public Policy for Mass Unemployment.* New York: State University of New York Press.

———. 1987. "Plant Closings: Impacts and Responses." *Economic Development Quarterly* 1:170–77.

Davis, Karen and D. Rowland. 1983. "Uninsured and Undeserved: Inequities in Health Care in the United States." *Milbank Memorial Fund Quarterly* 61:149–76.

Hadley, J. 1982. *More Medical Care, Better Health.* Washington, DC: The Urban Institute.

Hopkins, Kevin R. 1987. *Welfare Dependency.* Washington, DC: U.S. Department of Health and Human Services, September.

Horrigan, Michael W. 1987. "Time Spent Unemployed." *Monthly Labor Review,* July: 3–15.

Horvath, Francis. 1987. "The Pulse of Economic Change: Displaced Workers of 1981–85." *Monthly Labor Review,* June: 4–11.

"How Many Americans are Adequately Protected?" 1988. *Perspective,* Spring: 1–9.

Kasper, J. et al. 1980. "Expenditures for Personal Health Services." Paper presented at the Annual Meeting of the American Public Health Association, November.

King, Martha P. 1986. "Alternative Funding Sources for the Case of the Medically Indigent." Washington DC: National Conference of State Legislatures, July.

Manning, Willard G. et al. 1987. *Health Insurance and the Demand for Medical Care,* R–3476–HHS. Santa Monica, CA: The Rand Corporation.

Newhouse, J. P. et al. 1981. "Some Interim Results from a Controlled Trial of Cost Sharing in Health Insurance." *New England Journal of Medicine* 305:1501–7.

Podgursky, Michael and Paul Swaim. 1987. "Health Insurance Loss: The Case of the Displaced Worker." *Monthly Labor Review,* April: 30–33.

Regula, Ralph. 1987. "National Policy and the Medically Uninsured." *Inquiry* 24 (Spring): 48–56.

Robert Wood Johnson Foundation. 1983. *Report on Access to Health Care for the American People,* Special Report No. 1. Princeton, NJ: Author.

5

The Uninsured and Hospital Care in the Inner City: Patient Dumping, Emergency Care, and Public Policy

Mitchell F. Rice and Woodrow Jones

INTRODUCTION

According to the 1988 U.S. Bureau of Census Current Population Survey (CPS), 31 million Americans or some 15 percent of the population do not have some form of medical insurance or are not covered by Medicare or Medicaid. This figure, while an increase of 2 million since 1980, is less than the widely held figure of some 37 million (U.S. Congress, 1988). The considerably fewer number of uninsured individuals is due to two major reasons: (1) the health insurance questions on the CPS were asked of more adults and include more health insurance programs, and (2) additional questions were asked about coverage of children by Medicaid and private health insurance (Moyer, 1989). About 25 million of these individuals are workers and their dependents (Moyer, 1989). The firms that employ these individuals provide no health insurance or the employed has opted not to pay for health coverage. Further, one-fifth of the uninsured are children under the age of 15 (U.S. Congress, 1988).

The vast numbers of uninsured have generated much policy debate about the responsibilities of hospitals and medical centers in being responsive to the hospital and medical needs of uninsured patients. Many of the uninsured delay seeking medical care until their illnesses have become most severe. As a result, the cost of providing care increases because the severity of medical conditions being treated increases. Many hospitals are forced to stabilize these patients and attempt to transfer them to facilities that are willing to accept high-risk and high-cost patients who have limited insurance coverage or lack the ability to pay. This transfer practice is referred to as *patient dumping, inappropriate transfers, case shifting, or economically motivated transfers* (Duncan and Vogel, 1988). Ansell and Schiff (1987:1500) define "patient dumping as the denial of or limitation in the provision of medical services to a patient for economic reasons and the referral of that patient elsewhere." While dumping can be divided into two categories—inpatient and outpatient—it most commonly occurs in the emergency room (outpatient) (Schiff et al., 1986). In the emergency room a hospital may exercise judgment regarding who it will and will not treat.

A growing body of literature suggests that dumping has become a serious problem and public policy has sought to address the problem. A study of 26 urban hospitals in 12 states and the District of Columbia involving 1,066 patients indicates that dumping has become a widespread phenomenon. The study points out that at least 15 percent of emergency transfers to public hospitals qualify as dumping (*Hospitals*, 1986). In Washington, D.C., transfers from private hospitals to public hospitals increased from 169 to about 1,000 annually between the years 1981 and 1984 (Greensberg, 1984). The number of transfers to Cook County Hospital in Chicago increased by more than five times between 1980 and 1983 (Schiff et al., 1986). During a 99-day period from June 1 to September 1, 1986, at the Memphis Medical Center, some 91 percent of requested patient transfers were for economic reasons (Kellerman and Hackman, 1988).

While hospital dumping has been more pronounced in urban areas, it has been occurring repeatedly in smaller cities and rural areas. In Texas, hospitals that were undergoing severe financial strain were frequently perpetuators of patient dumping (more than 40 such hospitals were recently documented as sites of dumping [Rice, 1989]). Most dumping is profit motivated, which leaves the uninsured in a vulnerable position: pay or not receive care. This kind of health system responsiveness has been referred to as "Kentucky Fried Medicine" or "wallet biopsy": the assurance that one can pay for health services before they are provided (Berlinger, 1988).

The focus of this chapter is on the relationship between the growing numbers of uninsured Americans and patient dumping. The growing numbers of both phenomena in the American health care system provide an impetus for the installation of a national health insurance system. Although present reform efforts are incremental, they have not adequately addressed the issues of the uninsured nor the escalating cost of delivering health services to these individuals. This chapter also explores the federal and state policy responses to patient dumping and indigent care given the present cost-oriented health care system.

Table 5.1
Characteristics of the Uninsured Unemployed Population, 1987

	# of uninsured (in millions)	% of uninsured	Probability of being uninsured
Annual Work Experience			
Total	31.1	100%	12.9%
None	7.7	24.8%	11.1%
Full-time, all year	7.7	24.7%	10.0%
Part-time, all year*	1.4	4.4%	16.5%
Full-time, part year	5.4	17.4%	23.3%
Part-time, part year*	2.1	6.9%	20.3%
Under age 15	6.8	21.8%	12.9%
Employed subtotal	16.6	53.3%	13.9%
Poverty Status of Family			
In poverty	9.4	30.1%	28.7%
100-124 percent	2.9	9.3%	26.3
125-149 percent	2.7	8.8%	25.0%
150-184 percent	3.3	10.7%	20.9%
185 percent	12.8	41.1%	7.5%
Family Type			
Single with children	5.1	16.4%	19.2%
Huband, wife w/children	11.2	36.1%	11.0%
Single, no children	8.9	28.6%	18.9%
Two or more adults, no children	5.9	18.9%	9.0%
Census Region			
Northeast	4.4	14.1%	8.8%
Midwest	5.5	17.7%	9.3%
South	13.4	43.1%	16.3%
West	7.8	25.1%	15.7%

*Part-time employees work 18 plus hours per week.
Source: Preliminary data, March 1988 Current Population Survey.

THE UNINSURED AS DUMPING VICTIMS

Profile of the Uninsured

Of the 31 million Americans who are without health insurance, some 13 million (40 percent) have incomes 185 percent or more below the federal poverty level and 43 percent live in the South. About 7.7 million (nearly 25 percent) of the uninsured work full time and 36 percent are families with children. Table 5.1 points out the number and characteristics of the uninsured as of 1987. The ability to finance medical care depends on employment and the extent of insurance coverage. As income increases, there

Table 5.2
Characteristics of the Employed Uninsured, 1987

	# Employed Uninsured (in millions)	Percent	Probability of Being Uninsured
Work Experience			
Full-time, all year	7.7	46.2%	10.0%
Part-time, all year	1.4	8.2%	16.5%
Full-time, part year	5.4	32.7%	23.3%
Part-time, part year	2.1	12.9%	20.3%
Total	16.6	100.0%	13.9
Self-Employed	1.8	10.8%	20.4%
Age			
Under 18	0.4	2.3%	15.6%
18-24	4.5	26.9%	23.4%
25-54	10.6	63.7%	12.9%
55-64	1.1	6.8%	9.3%
65+	0.1	0.4%	1.9%
Sex			
Male	10.1	60.9%	15.3%
Female	6.5	39.1%	12.3%
Race			
White	10.5	63.1%	11.1%
Black	2.6	15.8%	21.7%
Hispanic	3.5	21.0%	28.8%

Source: Preliminary data, March 1988 Current Population Survey.

is an expansion of the amount of coverage that an individual can afford. However, without employment those who are poor are more likely to be uninsured or underinsured. These individuals are most likely to be Hispanics and black Americans (Gold, 1989). For the poorest segment of the population there is the Medicaid program, but only half of the poor population qualify for this assistance and this figure is steadily decreasing (Treiger, 1986).

The working poor represent the largest percentage of persons without health insurance (see Table 5.1). Their income and employment prevent them from receiving Medicaid but do not allow them to self-insure. Table 5.2 shows the characteristics of the employed uninsured. Some 45 percent of this group are employed either part time or full time for part of the year. Many of these workers are intermittent, persons who frequently change jobs, employees of small firms, and workers in labor-intensive industries that rely on transient labor. Some 46 percent of the uninsured are employed full time all year (see Table 5.2). Teenagers and young adults (18–24 years of age) represent nearly 27 percent of the employed uninsured. Employed blacks and Hispanics have the highest probability of being uninsured (see Table 5.2).

The distribution of the uninsured is important in understanding the development of the practice of patient dumping. The uninsured includes the homeless and socially dislocated, recent labor force entrants or persons otherwise considered the working poor, and a small group of uninsurables. More of the uninsured are in urban areas than rural settings. This is a reversal of the trend that existed in 1980. At that time 37 percent of poor rural residents and 34 percent of poor urban residents were uninsured (U.S. Congress, 1988). Many of the urban uninsured are not poor but can be classified as the working poor. Their numbers are indicative of the need and demands experienced by hospitals to provide indigent care.

Race and Economics of Dumping

In some states where profit-oriented hospital chains have proliferated and acquired a large share of the market, dumping has been an extremely serious problem (Relman, 1985). In most cases the likely victim of patient dumping is an uninsured minority patient. Schiff et al. (1986) found that 89 percent of the transfers involved blacks and Hispanics. They also estimated the cost of care provided to these patients to be $3.35 million. In addition, 77 percent had no third-party insurance. Himmelstein et al. (1984) found that of the 458 patient hospital transfers in Oakland, California, 63 percent had no insurance, 21 percent had Medicaid, and only 3 percent had private insurance. They also concluded that a high percentage of the patients transferred were minorities. Kellerman and Hackman (1988) found that 68.3 percent of patient transfers in their study were blacks. Ansell and Schiff (1987) estimated that 250,000 patients in need of emergency care annually are transferred for economic reasons and represent a cost of $1.04 billion to public hospitals.

Economic reasons dominate the justifications for most transfers (Reinhardt, 1985). By transferring patients to public hospitals, many private hospitals are able to avoid not only the cost of treatment but also the cost of collection efforts. These costs are compounded by the fact that patients who are uninsured are usually without assets to cover costs. This situation leaves hospitals with few avenues in which to recover costs.

Community hospitals provided a total of $6.2 billion of uncompensated care in 1982, with approximately $1.7 billion representing charity care (Bookheimer, 1989). Uncompensated care grew from $4.2 billion in 1978 to $6.2 billion in 1982, an increase of nearly 50 percent in four years. By 1985 total uncompensated care had risen to $9.5 billion (Brider, 1987). Much of this increase has been attributed to a growing competitive economic environment for hospitals (Treiger, 1986) and the shifting ownership matrix with many not-for-profit hospitals being purchased by large for-profit hospital chains (Rice, 1987). Thus, there are a limited number of public hospitals that take on the burden of delivering care without fair compensation.

The data on economically induced dumping of the uninsured are not as available given different accounting procedures. More than 72 percent of 1,066 patients transferred to 26 public hospitals in 1985 needed emergency care or inpatient admissions according to the National Association of Public Hospitals (*Hospitals*, 1986). In a 1986 General Accounting Office report, 80 percent of 868 transfers to Washington, D.C. General Hospital were for economic reasons. The justification by hospitals for dumping the uninsured is linked directly to hospital competition. The competition between hospitals in urban areas has generated some use of dumping to hamper competitive opponents.

FEDERAL AND STATE POLICY RESPONSES

Federal Policy Response

The enactment of Medicare and Medicaid was merely a partial solution to the problems of the uninsured. While Medicare addresses the needs of those who are 65 years of age and older by providing access to hospital care and physician services, Medicaid attends to the problems of the poor and near poor. However, these two broad policies were not designed to address the problems of the uninsured directly but to protect the interest of the providers from uncompensated care. Although these two programs have done much to alleviate the level of uninsurance, they are subject to political and administrative changes that lessen their effectiveness.

The changing eligibility and reimbursement policies of Medicare and Medicaid have had a reverse effect on the number of uninsured individuals. Instead of reimbursing hospitals for the actual cost of treating Medicare patients, the federal government has instituted a system of payments based on Diagnosis Related Groups. The incentive for hospitals within this system of prospective payment is to spend less than the fixed reimbursement rate of the federal government. The Medicaid program during the Reagan administration underwent changes in eligibility requirements that led to a significant decline in the number of individuals covered. In 1984 Medicaid covered some 38 percent of the poor, compared with some 65 percent in 1976 (Brider, 1987).

Furthermore, the ability to pass on costs for treating the uninsured has become much more difficult. Hospitals had relied on the practice of cost-shifting to cover unreimbursed costs. Private health insurance carriers, charitable foundations and private donations, and private pay patients have been hospitals' major sources in absorbing unreimbursed costs. However, charitable and philanthropic donations have declined dramatically and cost containment strategies have reduced many hospitals' ability to shift costs to the privately insured (Milligan, 1986).

In addition, the changing Medicaid eligibility requirements only exacerbate the number of uninsured—many of whom fail to fall into eligibility categories for non-income-related reasons, having incomes over a state's mean test level and having failed to apply for benefits (Wilson, 1988). As the health care system becomes more efficient in the allocation of medical services, there is less room for free riders. The response to the free rider problems has been the use of patient transfers as a tool by which private facilities can pass on the excess cost to public institutions who are already overburdened. Consequently, the uninsured become the victims of a health care system that attempts to rationalize methods of payment and organization.

The initial Consolidated Omnibus Reconciliation Act (COBRA) legislation (P.L. 99–272) enacted by Congress in 1985 prohibits patient dumping. The law requires hospitals to stabilize and provide a medical examination and necessary treatment before transferring a patient. The original penalty for patient dumping was $25,000 per case. If found in violation, the hospital would not only be subject to civil penalty as prescribed by law but would also be denied Medicare/Medicaid reimbursements. The legislation requires that in an emergency a hospital must stabilize before transfer unless another facility can offer better treatment. By late 1987 the U.S. Department of Health and Human Services (HHS), which has enforcement responsibilities for the antidumping law, had received 33 complaints of patient dumping. More than 50 percent of the complaints came from the State of Texas and only five actions were taken against hospitals (Burda, 1987).

From the enactment of the law through mid-1988, the agency had received 188 complaints regarding patient dumping (Holthaus, 1989). Of these, 177 were investigated and 53 hospitals were found not to have been in compliance with the law (Tolchin, 1988). Two hospitals failed to change their procedures within 30 days and were disqualified from participating in the Medicare program. Two small community hospitals in Texas—Charter Community Hospital (Cleveland, Texas) and Brookside Hospital (San Pablo, Texas)—were faced with Medicare termination. Termination was later rescinded for Brookside Hospital (Committee on Government Operations, 1987). The most prominent hospital charged with dumping was the University of Chicago Hospital, where an allegedly illegal transfer of a gunshot victim took place in July 1987. HHS issued termination of Medicare participation against the hospital; however, after adding a trauma team and assuring that such an incident would not occur again, Medicare termination proceedings were discontinued (*Hospitals*, 1987). By late 1988, 61 hospitals were found by HHS to have violated the antidumping law (Ansberry, 1988).

Federal revised regulations adopted in 1988 to implement the COBRA Act require hospitals with emergency rooms to examine all patients who seek treatment, and to treat all those suffering medical emergencies and all women in labor regardless of their ability to pay. Penalties were raised from $25,000 to $50,000. Further, all transfer decisions require the appraisal of a qualified staff member and the receiving hospital is required to be informed of the pending transfer and to agree to receive the patient. The regulations formalized the process used by HHS to protect Medicare patients from early discharge from hospitals. All hospitals treating Medicare patients are required to give formal notice to patients concerning rights about discharge. This was a congressional concern given reports of early discharge when patients were not medically ready (*Hospitals*, 1987). A significant provision in the legislation was the definition of the term "stabilize" as "providing medical treatment of the condition necessary to assure, within reasonable medical probability, that no material deterioration of the condition is likely to result from the transfer" (*Hospitals* 1987:35–36).

Texas and Illinois Policy Responses

The variation of state policy response can be explained by state political culture and severity of the dumping problem. The degree of indigent care provided by a state is an outcome of the social values reflected in state policymaking. Public hospitals are the recipients of most hospital dumpings. The degree of funding for a public hospital system and the degree of support for indigent care are important determinants of a state's response to the problem of indigent patient dumping.

Texas and Illinois are the two states that have surfaced as major sites of patient dumping. Texas, because of an oil bust and a resulting downturn in the economy, has had a particularly difficult time funding indigent care. Its indigent care system is one of a last resort. By law all other remedies for care must be exhausted before hospitals can make claims for reimbursement for the treatment of indigent patients. However, hospitals and physicians are liable for felony prosecutions if they deny medical care to individuals because of socioeconomic status.

Texas became the first state to effect comprehensive regulations that specifically deal with the dumping problem (*Texas Medicine*, 1986). The regulations that are mandated by Texas law and were promulgated by the Texas State Board of Health became effective April 1986 (Ellis, 1985). The law prohibits dumping of emergency patients and insures that patients are transferred only with their informed consent (when possible) and for valid medical reasons (Relman, 1986). The regulations also require hospitals to submit a transfer policy to the Texas Department of Health. Hospitals not submitting an acceptable policy by a specified time risk losing their license to operate and fines of not more than $1,000 for each act of violation (*Texas Medicine*, 1986). The legislation was provided impetus by Parkland Hospital in Dallas, which effectuated a policy and study of patient transfers in 1983 (Reed, Cawley, and Anderson, 1986).

Texas state law governing the transfer of patients deals specifically with the responsibilities of hospitals in the emergency room. No medical officer can deny emergency services to a person who is diagnosed by a physician as requiring medical services. In addition under the Patient Transfer Act, the Texas Board of Health is required to set the minimum guidelines for transfer (Ellis, 1985). However, the law applies only to a transfer from one hospital to another and does not apply to nursing homes. This loophole may lead to nursing homes becoming dumping grounds for elderly and disabled individuals who have limited insurance or are unable to pay for prolonged hospital care (Jones, 1989). Upon initiating a transfer, the sending hospital must notify the receiving hospital and the records of the patient must follow the patient to the receiving hospital. The receiving hospital has only 30 minutes to respond to a request for a transfer or face a fine of $1,000 a day per violation (*Texas Medicine*, 1986).

Illinois uses a statewide selective contraction program to reduce state medical assistance costs for inpatient hospital care. The Illinois Competitive Access and Reimbursement Equity (ICARE) program was implemented in 1985 with a goal of shifting patient care from higher cost teaching hospitals to lower cost community hospitals. In the first year of implementation, there were fewer hospital transfers. However, from a critical view many patients were lost from the system (Christoffel and Snelling, 1988). The utilization decline within the ICARE system resulted from patients being denied access to care at the hospitals they had been accustomed to using, and not being effectively provided with alternative access to hospital care (Smith, 1987). Understandably, public-aid patients and the uninsured tend to be limited in transportation, education, language, and finances, and thus are easily deterred when rebuffed at their usual source of health care.

The disappearance of these patients is symbolic of the experiences of all patient dumpings. Rather than dumping for institutional protection, patients were being dumped in Illinois as a part of an effort toward institutional reform. The system was creating a concentration of poor patients in a few hospitals and disrupting the continuity of patients' care as they are dumped from one hospital to another (Goodman, 1986). The pressures of ICARE have created a two-track medical system with public-aid and indigent patients in poorer community hospitals and academic and teaching hospitals providing specialized services not available elsewhere.

Texas and Illinois are examples of the problem faced by state governments in trying to reform problems in both patient dumping and indigent health care. In the case of Texas, a simple reform measure using the legal powers of the state was enacted simultaneously with a poorly coordinated indigent care system. In Illinois, a more comprehensive effort involving rate setting, discharge planning, and institutionalized dumping has creased a dual health care system with many for-profit hospitals not assuming their share of the indigent health care population. Thus, in these two state policy examples, there is a matrix of reform efforts short of national health insurance.

Nationwide Policy Responses

Overall, some 25 states have enacted legislation requiring hospitals to provide emergency care regardless of ability to pay and requiring that patients be stabilized before transfer (Ansell and Schiff, 1987). In 1983 New York State passed a statute that makes economic emergency refusals a misdemeanor punishable by a fine of $1,000 and a year in jail for the hospital personnel involved. New York may also revoke a hospital's operating license for denying emergency care after a judicial hearing. In June 1985 South Carolina enacted an antidumping law that included a civil penalty of up to $10,000 if violated by a hospital (Rice, 1989).

Despite the widespread passage of state antidumping legislation, many of the statutes are ineffective and are rarely enforced. Treiger (1986) points out that the central weakness of most state statutes is that they do not contain a clear definition of "emergency services" and those states that have remedies have weak ones.

CONCLUSION

The need for reform of the American health care system is quite obvious and necessary. A strategy is needed that will make the health care system less inflationary, less wasteful, and accessible to all. Present government policies have emphasized cost control and cost consciousness. As hospitals become more competitive there is a corresponding need for the provision of care to the uninsured. Competition produces hospital behavior that has already exacerbated the uninsured and indigent care problem. Effective policy solutions are required that will not continue to grossly neglect these types of patients (Rose, 1989). The present alternatives to the patient dumping problem are at best an incremental solution. Federal and state policy responses are merely a "patchwork quilt" that needs total reform. An impending reform is the movement for a national health insurance similar to the Canadian health care system (Relman, 1989). Universal coverage will solve the gravest problem in health care by eliminating financial barriers to care for the uninsured and underinsured. A single comprehensive health coverage program is necessary not only to insure equal access but also to reduce the complexity of government health administration and accounting.

The United States spends some $500 billion annually on health services, which is 120 percent of the amount spent in the Canadian health care system (Moloney and Paul, 1989). Canada's universal system is more efficient and less inflationary than that of the United States. In 1987 health care costs in

Canada had stabilized at 8.6 percent of national income as compared to 11.5 in the United States (Moloney and Paul, 1989). Stated another way, Canadian health expenditures per person are 40 percent less than in the United States. Canada's system of universal coverage has eliminated the problem of uncompensated care and there are no competitive pressures from the market to discrimination against the uninsured to bring about patient dumpings. Needless to say, there are many arguments that will be made against the establishment of such a program. These arguments, however, wane in response to the denial of the basic human right for health care. However, in the United States the need for fiscal restraint in the period of deficit-driven policy decisions is unlikely to change in the near future. Any change in the health care system requiring increased funding through taxation is unlikely to garner much political support. Furthermore, the growing trend toward the privatization of health care services has resulted in less opportunity for a public response to the patient dumping and uninsured problems.

REFERENCES

Ansberry, C. 1988. "Dumping the Poor: Despite Federal Law, Hospitals Still Reject Sick Who Can't Pay." *Wall Street Journal*, November 29:A1, A10.

Ansell, D. A. and R. L. Schiff. 1987. "Patient Dumping: Status, Implications and Policy Recommendations." *Journal of the American Medical Association* 257:1500–2.

Berlinger, H. S. 1988. "Patient Dumping: No One Wins and We All Lose." *American Journal of Public Health* 78:1279–80.

Bookheimer, S. 1989. "Uncompensated Care and the Hospital: A Political-Economic Perspective." *Journal of Health and Human Resources Administration* 11:328–40.

Brider, P. 1987. "Too Poor to Pay: The Scandal of Patient Dumping." *American Journal of Nursing* 187:1447–49.

Burda, D. 1987. "Dumping Law Spurs Look at E D Risk Management." *Hospitals*, July 20:34–38.

Christoffel, T. and P. Snelling. 1988. "How the Poor Fared in a Competitive Model: Assessing the Illinois Selecting Contracting Approach." *Public Health Policy* 7:519–36.

Committee on Government Operations. 1987. *Equal Access to Health Care: Patient Dumping*. Hearing before Subcommittee on Government Operations, House of Representatives, 100th Congress, 1st session. Washington, DC: Government Printing Office, July 22.

Duncan, R. P. and W. B. Vogel. 1988. "Uncompensated Care and the Inpatient Transfer." Paper presented at the Annual Meeting of the American Public Health Association, Boston.

Ellis, V. 1985. "Compromise Paves Way for Outlining 'Patient Dumping.' " *Dallas Times Herald*, December 13:1, 6.

Gold, A. R. 1989. "The Struggle to Make Do Without Health Insurance." *New York Times*, July 30:1, 11.

Goodman, J. 1986. "Medicaid Fund Crash Stuns Area Hospitals." *Crain's Chicago Business*, March:1, 12.

Greensberg, D. S. 1984. "Health Care Thrift Spurs Patient Dumping." *Los Angeles Times*, November 12:1, 8.

Himmelstein, D. V., S. Woolhander, and M. Harnley. 1984. "Patient Transfers: Medical Practice as Social Triage." *American Journal of Public Health* 74:494–97.

Holthaus, D. 1989. "Patient Dumping: A Gray Area of Enforcement." *Hospitals* 63:58, 60.

Hospitals. 1986. "15% of Transfers Seen as 'Dumping.' " October 5:146.

———. 1987. "Patient Dumping Regulations Offer Little Guidance." September 5:35–36.

Jones, D. B. 1989. "The Devil or the Sea: Transfer Regs Create A Dilemma." *Texas Medicine* 85:70–75.

Kellerman, A. L. and B. B. Hackman. 1988. "Emergency Department 'Patient Dumping': An Analysis of Interhospital Transfers to the Regional Medical Center at Memphis, Tennessee." *American Journal of Public Health* 78:1287–92.

Milligan, C. J. 1986. "Provisions of Uncompensated Care in American Hospitals: The Role of Tax Code, the Federal Courts, Catholic Health Care Facilities and Local Governments in Defining the Problem of Access for the Poor." *Catholic Lawyer* 31:7–34.

Moloney, T. W. and B. Paul. 1989. "A New Financial Framework: Lessons From Canada." *Health Affairs* 8:149–59.

Moyer, M. E. 1989. "A Revised Look at the Number of Uninsured Americans." *Health Affairs* 8:102–10.

Reed, W. G., K. A. Cawley, and R. J. Anderson. 1986. "Special Report: The Effect of a Public Hospital's Transfer Policy on Patient Care." *New England Journal of Medicine* November 27:1428–32.

Reinhardt, E. 1985. "Health and Hot Potatoes." *Washington Post*, March 16:2.

Relman, A. S. 1985. "Economic Considerations in 'Emergency Care': What Are Hospitals For?" *New England Journal of Medicine* February 7:372–73.

———. 1986. "Texas Eliminates Dumping: A Start Toward Equity in Hospital Care." *New England Journal of Medicine* February 2:278–579.

———. 1989. "American Medicine at the Crossroads: Signs from Canada." *New England Journal of Medicine* 320:590–91.

Rice, M. F. 1987. "Inner-City Hospital Closures/Relocations: Race, Income Status and Legal Issues." *Social Science and Medicine* 24:889–96.

———. 1989. "Medical Indigency and Inner-City Hospital Care: Patient Dumping, Emergency Care and Public Policy." *Journal of Health and Social Policy* 1:1–29.

Rose, C. 1989. "Patient Dumping: The Physician Dilemma." *Chest* 95:490–91.

Schiff, R. L., D. A. Ansell, J. E. Schlosser, A. H. Idris, A. Morrison, and S. Whitman. 1986. "Transfers to a Public Hospital: A Prospective Study of 467 Patients." *New England Journal of Medicine*, February 27:552–57.

Smith, W. 1987. "Hospitals Shut Doors to Indigent." *Chicago Tribune*, May 7:1, 9.

Texas Medicine. 1986. "TDH Rules on Hospital Transfers Take Effect April 1," 82:59–62.

Tolchin, M. 1988. "U.S. Seeks to Require Treatment of All Hospital Cases." *New York Times* June 18:1, 8.

Treiger, K. I. 1986. "Preventing Patient Dumping: Sharpening the COBRA's Fangs." *New York University Law Review* 61:1186–1223.

U.S. Congress. 1988. *Unpublished Statistics from the Current Population Surveys for 1980 and 1987.* Washington, DC: Congressional Budget Office.

U.S. General Accounting Office. 1986. *Medicare: PPS Impact on Post Hospital Long-Term Care Services.* Washington, DC: GAO/PEMO 85–8, February 21.

Wilson, T. M. 1988. "Health Care Insurance in Alabama: Some First Approximations of Coverage and Problems of Access to Care." *Journal of Health and Human Resources Administration* 11:328–40.

6

Does Mission Really Matter? Measuring and Examining Charity Care and Community Benefit in Nonprofit Hospitals

Susan M. Sanders

Since the adoption of the federal corporate income tax in 1909, the majority of hospitals have generally been accorded tax-exempt status as part of their nonprofit incorporation (see Section 501(c)(3) of the Internal Revenue Code [IRC]). However, nonprofit hospitals have been exempt not only from the federal corporate income tax, but also from state sales taxes, from local property taxes and federal unemployment taxes, and from the communications excise tax. In addition, nonprofit hospitals are eligible to receive discounts on postal rates and may apply for tax-exempt revenue bonds to finance capital projects. Moreover, individual contributions made to nonprofit hospitals are tax deductible for the donor under Section 170(c)(2) of the IRC.

At the legal and policy levels, these circumstances suggest questions about the justification for treating nonprofit hospitals differently from their for-profit counterparts. At philosophical and organizational levels, the treatment and behavior of nonprofit hospitals relative to their for-profit counterparts raise questions about the mission of nonprofit hospitals.

LEGAL AND POLICY QUESTIONS

From legal and policy perspectives, nonprofit hospitals have been criticized for the unfair competitive advantage they have over their for-profit competitors. For example, local businesspeople have argued that they have a competitive disadvantage because nonprofit hospitals operate tax-exempt businesses such as gift shops, restaurants, laundries, food services, and medical equipment stores. This position has found some sympathy with the U.S. Congress and with the state legislature in Pennsylvania, where a special legislative committee has been formed to study competition between for-profit and nonprofit enterprises.

In addition to objections about nonprofits having an unfair competitive advantage, for-profit hospitals have argued that there are few, if any, substantial differences between for-profit hospitals and nonprofit hospitals. Specifically, using empirical data that are generally inconclusive, for-profit hospitals have argued that they provide ostensibly the same services as nonprofit hospitals—and at a comparable cost and quality.

Private entrepreneurs and Pennsylvania legislators are not the only ones troubled by current U.S. tax-exemption policy, however. Legislators in many states and municipalities that are feeling the effects of the antitax movement and chronic budgetary shortfalls have also begun to question whether the foregone revenues from tax exemption substantially exceed the benefits that nonprofit hospitals contribute to the public.

ORGANIZATIONAL AND PHILOSOPHICAL QUESTIONS

From an organizational perspective, research into the activities of health care organizations that exist in both the for-profit and nonprofit forms raises questions about the relationship between organizational form and economic activity. Are some types of economic activity appropriate only to the public or private sectors? If appropriate to the private sector, is the nonprofit or for-profit form better-suited to producing equitable or efficient outputs? What can be said of public-private partnerships?

Moreover, a consideration of the nature, mission, and behavior of non-profit organizations raises questions about the roles and responsibilities of large institutional actors to the communities in which they are situated. What can the local community legitimately expect of institutional actors such as hospitals? What responsibility do institutional actors share for the well-being of the community in which they are situated?

From a philosophical perspective, these questions become even more difficult to answer. For example, those who sponsor nonprofit hospitals often voice concerns about how the nonprofit health care mission is being communicated to and realized in society. Some sponsors, typically those with religious affiliations, wonder aloud whether they should discontinue their sponsorship of nonprofit health care organizations because market considerations now seem to make it impossible for them to fulfill the traditional nonprofit mission. Why, they query, should they continue to commit resources to health care when their service to the poor or socially dispossessed—the traditional target groups of the nonprofit hospital—may be little better than that of their for-profit competitors?

THE RESEARCH SAMPLE

Using a sample of Catholic nonprofit hospitals,[1] the research discussed in this chapter (see Sanders, 1991) addresses some of these questions in terms of the operational criteria that the Internal Revenue Service (IRS) has proposed for tax-exemption eligibility. In particular, this research reports on how well the hospitals in the sample "measure up" in terms of their contributions of charity care and community benefit.

Toward this end, this chapter first discusses the challenges of defining and measuring charity care and community benefit. Subsequently, the results of the charity care and community benefit analyses are reported. Having identified and characterized the charity care and community benefit contributions in the sample, the chapter concludes with a discussion of the implications of the research findings for current tax-exemption policy and for the mission of nonprofit hospitals. However, before reporting the results of this analysis, the section that immediately follows provides some background on the policy of tax exemption.

THE FEDERAL REQUIREMENTS FOR TAX EXEMPTION

At the federal level, the U.S. Congress has established two tests—one organizational and one operational—to determine whether a nonprofit organization should be granted tax-exempt status. Broadly defined in Section 501(c)(3) of the IRC, these two tests require that "no part of the net earnings of [the nonprofit corporation] inures to the benefit of any private shareholder or individual" (the organizational test); and that the nonprofit organization be "operated exclusively for religious, charitable, scientific, testing for public safety, literary, or educational purposes" (the operational test).

The Organizational Test

Passing the organizational test is usually a matter of corporately structuring an organization so that it complies with the incorporating state's rules for nonprofit organizations. That is, a hospital incorporates as a nonprofit organization, but in so doing the nonprofit hospital is not prohibited from making a "profit"—that is, from having more revenues than expenses. However, the hospital is forbidden from distributing these proceeds to anyone who has a stake in the organization. Thus, unlike for-profit hospitals, nonprofit hospitals do not have stockholders who profit from their activities.

Concerned more with form than substance, the organizational test is the easier of the two tests to clear because it has not suffered from the legal ambiguity that complicates the application of the operational test (Hopkins, 1979). Thus, matters of "greater substance" center around the operational test of how an organization engages in "exclusively . . . charitable . . . purposes."

The Operational Test

The meaning of "exclusively . . . charitable . . . purposes" has evolved throughout the development of English and American case law. Currently, judicial and administrative precedents have established two criteria against which the charitable purposes of nonprofit organizations, and nonprofit hospitals in particular, may be evaluated: (1) that nonprofit hospitals engage in charitable works such as providing services at free or reduced cost (charity care); and (2) that hospitals engage in activities that benefit the local community (community benefit).

Despite recent judicial and administrative efforts to clarify these terms, the meanings of charity care and community benefit are still ambiguous. Moreover, little has been said by either the legal or the evaluation research communities about how to measure these two operational criteria.

To address these problems, the sections that follow discuss the difficulties of defining and operationalizing measures of charity care and community benefit. Then, having developed measures of charity care and community benefit, the extent of these contributions was measured across the research sample.

CHARITY CARE

Social scientific researchers have been relatively inconsistent in their definitions and applications of the term "charity care." For the research described in this chapter, charity care has been defined as the financially quantifiable costs of activities, services, or programs that a hospital provides for an individual, but for which the hospital is not fully or partially compensated. Thus, the hospital alone bears the costs of charity care. No other source of payment is forthcoming to the hospital that provides the services for free or below cost. That is, a hospital cannot look to the government, to private insurers, or to the patient as a source of revenues to offset the costs of the services the hospital provides. While this definition of charity care is relatively unambiguous, it is nevertheless replete with measurement issues. Three issues are of particular importance.

First, given current hospital accounting practices, it is virtually impossible to separate the costs of providing service from the charges for providing service. To promote efficiency within a hospital, a charity care measure that is based on costs, not on charges, is desirable. Otherwise, adopting a measure that incorporates charges rather than costs, especially when the charges are substantially higher, provides an incentive for hospitals to mark up their services. The extent to which a markup can occur, however, is subject to what the market will bear. Moreover, if charity care contributions are based on foregone charges rather than on foregone costs, a hospital with a higher markup might appear to be contributing a higher level of charity care than a hospital with lower markups.

Second, current hospital accounting and admitting practices also make it difficult to separate bad debts from charity care. Why? Because research (see Center for Health Policy Research, 1986, as cited in Lewin, Eckels, and Roenigk, 1988) suggests that a large part of that which a hospital itemizes as bad debt may actually be charity care that inadvertently had not been so identified.

That many hospitals have been relatively unsuccessful in separating charity care from bad debt has two opposing consequences for evaluating how well hospitals measure up in terms of their charity care contributions. On the one hand, if a substantial part of bad debt is actually charity care that has been improperly categorized, then charity care contributions could be underestimated. If, on the other hand, the more substantial part of bad debts is debts that should have been collected from patients but were not, then the size of a hospital's charity care contribution could be overestimated. Moreover, to "reward" a hospital based on charity care measures that reflect a hospital's inability to collect its outstanding debts would not provide an incentive to organizational efficiency—the type of organizational efficiency that encourages hospitals to engage in a rigorous and consistent classification and separation of charity care and bad debts.

Third, as the preceding difficulties suggest, how well hospitals "measure up" in terms of their charity care contributions very much depends on the way that charity care is measured. For example, should a measure of charity care include the costs of Medicaid shortfalls or Medicare contractual allowances? That is, should the measures include the costs of being reimbursed by the government for Medicare and Medicaid programs at substantially lower rates than what the hospitals argue it costs to provide the service?

Responding in the negative, there are those, typically governmental representatives, who argue that a hospital freely enters into a contract with the state or federal government to provide services at the contract rate. Presumably, if the service could not be provided at that rate, a hospital would not enter into the agreement, especially if it jeopardized its financial integrity or survival.

Responding in the affirmative, there are those who argue that hospitals are being shorted by the government if the costs of contracted allowances or shortfalls are not included. These shortfalls, they argue, must be made up from other revenue sources. Those who argue this position— typically hospital administrators—maintain that governmental reimbursement rates severely understate the true costs—the real value—of the contributions that a hospital makes to society for the care of its poor. Further, hospital administrators argue that their hospitals have entered into what amounts to a forced agreement with the government—that they have no other choice if they want to serve any significant number of poor people and still survive.

Neither health care practitioners nor academicians currently agree on the answer to the question of whether to include Medicare and Medicaid contractual allowances/shortfalls in the calculus of charity care. Recognizing this debate, as well as the debates about costs, charges, and bad debts, this researcher adopted a "something for everyone" approach. Specifically, four measures of charity care were developed, each having different financial components:

1. *Pure Charity Care*, which includes the write-off "up-front"—that is, prior to services being rendered, of all or part of the costs to patients that a hospital has classified as being unable to pay.

2. *Uncompensated Care*, which includes the costs of pure charity care and bad debts, where bad debts include the costs of care that a hospital has been unable to collect from patients who were identified as being able to pay their bills, but who do not do so.

3. *Unreimbursed Care*, which includes the costs of pure charity care and shortfalls from Medicaid and Medicare contractual allowances.

4. *Total Charity Care*, which, as the name implies, includes the costs of pure charity care, bad debts, and shortfalls from Medicaid and Medicare contractual allowances.

Besides taking a "something-for-everyone" approach, the research described in this chapter incorporated the fact that cost figures are not generally available for individual services or procedures. Thus, the four measures used in this research incorporate a method for estimating the *costs* of charity care (see Lewin, Eckels, and Roenigk, 1988). Finally, in addition to adjusting gross revenue figures to reflect costs rather than charges, the four measures of charity-care dollars were normalized to take into account the different sizes of the hospitals in the sample.

COMMUNITY BENEFIT

Evidence of charity care is only one criterion prescribed in the IRC as part of its operational test for tax-exempt status. The IRC also requires that tax-exempt organizations engage in activities that benefit the community. Unlike the extensive discussion about how to measure charity care, however, there has been little written about how to define and measure the beneficial contributions that a nonprofit hospital makes to the local community.

For this research, a community benefit occurs when a hospital bears or donates all or part of the relatively unquantifiable costs of promoting, sponsoring, or engaging in religious, educational, scientific, or health-related activities or programs that have been designed to link with the community to improve its health levels. As such, neither the individual nor society bears the true costs of the hospital's efforts to improve individual and societal health care levels.

In addition to being private goods that are "consumed" exclusively by an individual, community benefits are also economic public goods. That is, they are goods that are nonexcludable and indivisible and cannot be easily circumscribed by legal or geographic boundaries. For example, when a hospital inoculates a child against measles, the individual child benefits directly. However, the inoculation efforts benefit not only those who participate in such health programs, but also the members of society at large. For example, society at large does not have to bear the costs of the inoculation in the form of a tax expenditure for measles vaccinations. Moreover, society benefits because the inoculation itself reduces the probability of a measles outbreak among those not yet vaccinated.

Unlike charity care, the costs associated with most community benefits are relatively difficult, if not impossible, to quantify monetarily. One reason for this relates to the public goods dimension of community benefits. The other relates to current hospital accounting practices.

In terms of the public goods dimension, changes in transportation and communications have made it virtually impossible to define geographically the specific community that benefits from a hospital's activity. Rather, the salutary effects of community benefit policies, activities, and programs transcend spatial limitations and accrue both directly to individuals and indirectly to society at large.

In terms of current hospital accounting practices, hospitals are not required to establish a cost center for each community benefit activity. Consequently, it is impossible for most hospitals to measure accurately the costs of non-revenue-producing services or in-kind gifts. Conceivably, this problem could be addressed if new technologies were available to make it easier and cheaper to identify the costs of these activities and the number of people that these activities benefit.

Since relatively little research has focused on the meaning of community benefit, it follows that attempts to measure community benefit activities are only beginning. This being the case, the challenge becomes one of identifying the various dimensions of community benefit activity, and then of delineating indicators within each dimension that measure whether and to what extent the activities of a nonprofit hospital benefit the local community.

Religious, Educational and Scientific Activities. There are two sources of information or research that suggest indicators of community benefit activity. First, the IRC itself gives a description, albeit very limited, of the activities that it deems charitable, namely those that are religious, educational, and scientific. Although the IRC does not give examples of the types of activities that would be included within these categories, they do constitute one dimension of community benefit activity.

Second, the work of Sigmond, Seay, and Vladek (see Seay and Sigmond, 1989; Seay and Vladek, 1988; Sigmond, 1985 and 1988) and the contributions of the American Hospital Association (1988) and the Catholic Health Association (1989) suggest five more dimensions of community benefit activity.

Mission and Policy Statements: This dimension includes the extent to which a nonprofit hospital's mission and policy statements make an explicit commitment to the improvement of the health status of the local community and to the promotion of cost-effective services. While indicating intent more than performance, mission and policy statements reflect a conscious and tangible commitment to improving the health and welfare of the local community.

Linkages to the Local Community: This dimension includes a hospital's efforts to connect and interact with community members, the poor, and community-based agencies that affect health status. Thus, this dimension not only includes outreach programs and activities sponsored by a hospital, but also formal and informal efforts to meet with the public and with representatives of the local civic and political communities to explore health-related concerns.

Public Advocacy: This dimension derives from a nonprofit hospital's becoming involved in public advocacy efforts to secure resources related to the health and welfare of the local community. As distinct from engaging in political campaigns, these efforts can legally take place at various levels of government.

Special Efforts for the Poor: This dimension is expressed in hospital activities that are specifically designed to benefit the poor. These endeavors include outreach to the poor, including the involvement of the poor in assessing community needs and in shaping health care programs. Moreover, it includes emphasis on family care, primary care, and continuity of care. Further, it addresses the special problems of the poor, such as transportation, cultural and language barriers, and hours of operation that often hamper the access of the poor to hospital services (Sigmond, 1985).

Non-Revenue-Producing or In-Kind Services: This dimension may be expressed in terms of the in-kind contributions that a hospital makes. While not generally means tested, the hospital makes these contributions at no or reduced cost. For example, when a hospital nurse staffs a satellite clinic in an economically deprived area, the clients at the clinic do not receive a bill for the services they receive. Nevertheless, the hospital incurs the costs of staffing the clinic.

From these six dimensions, an index of community benefit activity was developed (see Sanders, 1991). Subsequently, the index was used to measure the type and the extent of a hospital's community benefit activity.

RESULTS OF THE ANALYSIS

In general, two results of the analysis stand out. The first concerns the distribution of charity care across the sample, irrespective of measure. The second concerns the extent and diversity of the contributions that the non-profit hospitals in the sample made to their communities. In the sections that follow, these and other results of the charity care and community benefit analyses are discussed.

Charity Care Analysis

Research using the four charity care measures proposed earlier indicates that, irrespective of measure, there were substantial differences in charity care contributions among the sample hospitals. Specifically, and depending on the measure, approximately 25 percent of the hospitals in the sample were responsible for 60 percent of all the charity care contributions being made by the hospitals in the sample. Conversely, 75 percent of all the nonprofit hospitals in the sample accounted for 40 percent of all the charity care contributed at the time of the study.

Estimates using multiple regression techniques and based on a model developed by Aday, Andersen, and Newman (Aday and Andersen, 1974; Andersen and Aday, 1978; Andersen et al., 1983; and Andersen and Newman, 1973) indicated that while several factors were correlated both positively and negatively with the charity care levels, charity care per bed contributions seem to be caused by factors that characterize the local population. For example, depending on the charity care measure, the factors that influence levels of charity care included the percentages of children, senior citizens, and Afro-Americans in the community; the generosity of state public aid payments; the percentages of Medicare and Medicaid inpatients; and the percentage of people living in poverty. In addition, the number of emergency room visits and the mortality rate of the hospitals, the number of a hospital's community-based programs, and a hospital's being a teaching hospital also appeared to be causally related to levels of charity care, variously defined.

Thus, in general, this research suggests causal relationships between levels of charity care and factors such as the age of the people in the community, local Medicare and Medicaid reimbursement practices, and public policies that affect the amount of a state's welfare payments. Further, this research suggests that a hospital's location plays a key role in determining the extent of its charity care contributions.

Community Benefit Analysis

In contrast to the charity care measures, where the distribution was very unequal, the distribution of community benefit activities was much more equal. That is, on average, the majority of the hospitals in the sample tended to respond positively to most of the indicators of community benefit activity. However, the hospitals in the sample scored higher on the advocacy, the linkages, and the mission and policy dimensions than they did on the education/religious/scientific, the special initiatives for the poor, or the non-revenue-producing services dimensions.

In particular, the data showed that almost all the hospitals engaged in a variety of activities that have an educational or training dimension. However, very few hospitals in the sample were formally affiliated with educational or training institutions such as medical schools. Moreover, very few hospitals in the sample engaged in scientific or research-oriented activity.

POLICY IMPLICATIONS

The research described in this chapter has shown that most of the non-profit hospitals in the sample engage in a wide range of activities and programs that benefit the local community. Moreover, these hospitals seem well-linked to their local communities insofar as most of their patients, their employees, and their board members live in that community. In addition, they are linked with their local communities through outreach services to the community, and through off-campus meetings with community groups. However, most hospitals appear to be very careful to control how and when formal encounters with community members are arranged.

The result is that while the needs of the local community are represented indirectly through intermediaries—typically community or business elites whose health care needs may have little in common with those of the majority of the community—the "folks" seldom have the opportunity to express their needs directly to hospital administrators and policymakers—for example, at a hospital-sponsored forum. This finding suggests that nonprofit hospitals may not be as directly accountable to the people in their local communities as they could be. Such being the case, the tax-exempt status of some of these hospitals could be called into question insofar as it is the local community, acting through its elected officials, that authorizes and pays for the variety of tax exemptions that a nonprofit hospital receives.

The findings about community benefit activities are not the only data that have policy implications for tax exemption. The research described in this chapter has also shown that many of the nonprofit hospitals in the sample serve society by making extensive contributions of charity care. However, some hospitals are making relatively smaller contributions. Factors more associated with location and less with hospital policy, resources, and/or organizational structures seem to be causally related to changes in levels of charity care.

How charity care contributions are distributed, the differences among the four charity care measures, and the importance of location in affecting changes in levels of charity care also have three important implications for public policy.

First, the finding of a great inequality in the distribution of charity care across the sample implies that some of the hospitals may not be doing enough charity care to meet this one criterion for tax exemption. However, the data also show that many hospitals are making extraordinarily large contributions of charity care. Consequently, policymakers would be overreacting if they were to legislate a blanket revocation of tax exemption on the assumption that very few hospitals are making substantial contributions of charity care.

Second, it is not at all clear that making accurate distinctions between high and low charity care contributors is a simple process. Rather, it is easier to argue that a hospital should be evaluated on its charity care contributions than it is to design a measure of charity care that not only is accurate but also promotes organizational efficiency.

The research summarized in this chapter described the difficulties of designing such a measure of charity care and illustrated that the choice of a charity care measure is not inconsequential. For example, the pure charity care measure, which consists of those costs written off by the hospital before the patient receives services, "behaved" quite differently from the uncompensated, unreimbursed, and total charity care per bed measures. The most conservative measure in terms of the types of costs it incorporates,[2] the pure charity care measure showed a substantially greater inequality in the distribution of charity care across the sample. Moreover, if the pure charity care measure were to be adopted by policymakers as a measure for assessing the charity care contributions of nonprofit hospitals, then the charity care contributions would look significantly smaller—perhaps unjustifiably—than would be the case if any of the other three less "conservative" measures had been used.

Third, along with or before the adoption of new tax policies that require an evaluation of a hospital's level of charity care contributions, hospitals will need to redesign current accounting practices in order to differentiate between the *costs* of charity care and the *charges* that have been written off from charity care activities. In addition, hospitals will need to be given some time to monitor admitting procedures so that bad debts and pure charity care can be better distinguished.

THE NONPROFIT HOSPITAL MISSION AND CURRENT TAX-EXEMPTION POLICY

Accepting the political and economic roles that nonprofit hospitals play, how might those responsible for developing public policy best promote the socially beneficial contributions that nonprofit hospitals make? Clearly, one form of promoting the contributions of nonprofit hospitals has been to grant them a variety of tax exemptions—exemptions that, at the federal level, are estimated to cost the government approximately $12 billion in foregone tax revenues (Office of Management and Budget, 1987). These are substantial revenues to forego if the policy of tax exemption is not the best way to promote charitable activities that benefit the local community.

Would tax-exemption policy as a vehicle for supporting the nonprofit health care mission of providing charity care and community benefits be necessary if a policy of comprehensive national health insurance were adopted? For that matter, would there still be a role for the nonprofit health care sector?

While there would be no need for charity care contributions because everyone would presumably have access to all the health services they need, there would still be a demand for community benefit activity. As such, this type of activity could be promoted through some form of tax-exemption subsidy.

However, if national health insurance means that nonprofit hospitals would come to rely even more on the sale of services and on third-party and governmental reimbursements and even less on charitable contributions than they do today, then nonprofit hospitals could risk losing their sectoral and behavioral distinctiveness (Ferris and Graddy, 1988). So suggest Hollingsworth and Hollingsworth (1986).

According to these researchers, the loss of the distinctiveness of the non-profit health care sector may already be occurring *absent* a national health insurance policy. That is, Hollingsworth and Hollingsworth, in studying the changes in the nonprofit hospital's funding patterns, have documented what they consider to be the growing commercialization of nonprofit hospitals and the subsequent erosion of their legitimacy and mission. Specifically, they argue that changes in a nonprofit hospital's external funding sources have begotten changes in organizational goals and behavior—changes that divert nonprofit hospitals away from their service mission and, subsequently, divest them of the public trust. While acknowledging the influence of increased dependence on medical technology and the demands of accreditation, Hollingsworth and Hollingsworth cite the influence of the public and private third-party payers, who have made it possible for any of the three economic sectors—the public, the private, or the nonprofit—to compete for fee-paying patients. As evidence, their research, which compares hospital operation and performance by sector, suggests a growing similarity across the different economic sectors. This similarity is most obvious when measured in terms of length of stay, cost, and occupancy rates.

Ironically, direct health care financing methods that preclude the need to provide charity care but that promote community benefit contributions may actually dilute the differences among nonprofit, public, and for-profit hospitals. Were the result the provision of more "undersupplied" public or quasipublic goods, the results of these types of changes would not be altogether bad. However, to the extent that the trustworthiness of nonprofit hospitals erodes because of becoming too businesslike, the raison d'être for nonprofit hospitals will become less legitimate. As a consequence, the distinctive economic role of the nonprofit hospital as a means of signaling information about the quality of its products will also diminish.

The traditional mission of the nonprofit hospital is historically linked to its service of the poor and the disenfranchised (Sanders, 1991). The research reported in this chapter shows that nonprofit hospitals are still faithful to this traditional dimension of the nonprofit health care mission because they engage in extensive charity care and community benefit activities. However, whether nonprofit hospitals can continue—with or without a tax exemption—to fund these activities, survive in a highly competitive environment, and avoid the loss of the public's perception of trustworthiness and legitimacy is a matter still open to speculation.

NOTES

1. The data for this research were drawn from a number of sources. Foremost among them were the 1986 Catholic Health Association Care of the Poor Survey; the 1988 Catholic Health Association Annual Survey; the 1987 Annual Survey of the American Hospital Association; a survey of Catholic hospitals constructed by the researcher; and the CACI 1986 Sourcebook of Demographics and Buying Power. The sample consisted of 595 acute care Catholic hospitals, which compose approximately 10 percent of all nonfederal hospitals and which control approximately 15 percent of all nonfederal hospital beds in the United States (Unger, 1990).

2. The pure charity care measure, however, is probably the least statistically reliable measure. This conclusion was reached after discovering the fact that 40 of the hospitals in the sample recorded $0 of charity care on the pure charity care line item of the hospital's income and expense statement. In all probability, these hospitals, like most hospitals, had a difficult time actually separating pure charity care from bad debts. If this were the case, the pure charity care measure could be greatly underestimated. For a more detailed discussion and statistical illustration, see Sanders, 1991.

REFERENCES

Aday, L. A. and R. M. Andersen. 1974. "Framework for the Study of Access to Medical Care." *Health Services Research* 9:208–20.

American Hospital Association. 1987. *Annual Survey.* Chicago: American Hospital Association.

———. 1988. *Community Benefit and Tax-Exempt Status: A Self-Assessment Guide for Hospitals.* Chicago: American Hospital Association.

Andersen, R. and L. A. Aday. 1978. "Access to Medical Care in the U.S.: Realized and Potential." *Medical Care* 16:533–48.

Andersen, R. M., A. McCutcheon, L. A. Aday, G. Y. Chiu, and R. Bell. 1983. "Exploring Dimensions of Access to Medical Care." *Health Services Research* 18(1):49–74.

Andersen, R. and J. Newman. 1973. "Societal and Individual Determinants of Medical Care Utilization." *Millbank Memorial Fund Quarterly* 51:95–124.

CACI. 1986. *The 1986 Sourcebook of Demographics and Buying Power.* Fairfax, VA: CACI Marketing Systems.

Catholic Health Association of the United States. 1988. *Annual Survey 1988.* St. Louis: Catholic Health Association.

———. 1989. *Social Accountability Budget.* St. Louis: Catholic Health Association.

Center for Health Policy Research. 1986. *State University Study of Indigent Care.* Unpublished data runs by Center for Health Policy Research, University of Florida Health Center, Gainesville.

Federal Corporate Income Tax Act of August 5, 1909, Ch. 6, Sec. 38, 36 Stat. 112 (1909).

Ferris, J. J. and E. Graddy. 1988. "Fading Distinctions Among the Three Public Sectors: Implications for Public Policy." Unpublished paper prepared for 1988 Spring Research Forum, San Francisco, March 17–18.

Hollingsworth, J. R. and E. Hollingsworth. 1986. "A Comparison of Non-Profit and For-Profit Hospitals in the United States: 1935 to the Present." Program on Non-Profit Organizations. Institution for Social and Policy Studies, Yale University. (PONPO Working Paper No. 113, June.)

Hopkins, B. 1979. *The Law of Tax-Exempt Organizations.* New York: John Wiley.

Internal Revenue Code. 1987. Section 170 (c) (2), 99th Cong., 2d Sess. St. Paul: West Publishing.

———. 1987. IRC Sec. 501 (c) (3), 99th Cong., 2d Sess. St. Paul: West Publishing.

Lewin, L. S., T. J. Eckels, and D. Roenigk. 1988. "Setting the Record Straight: The Provision of Uncompensated Care by Not-for-Profit Hospitals." Paper presented for the Volunteer Trustees of Not-for-Profit Hospitals, Washington, DC, April.

Office of Management and Budget (OMB). 1987. *Special Analysis G-Tax Expenditures.* Washington, DC: U.S. Government Printing Office.

Sanders, S. M. 1991. "The Measurement of Charity Care and Community Benefit in Catholic Nonprofit Hospitals: Implications for Tax-Exemption Policy." Unpublished dissertation, University of Chicago.

Seay, J. D. and R. M. Sigmond. 1989. "Community Benefits Standards for Hospitals: Perceptions and Performance." *Frontiers* 5(3)–39.

Seay, J. D. and B. C. Vladek (eds.). 1988. *In Sickness and Health: The Mission of Voluntary Health Care Institutions.* New York: McGraw-Hill.

Sigmond, R. 1985. "Reexamining the Role of the Community Hospital in a Competitive Environment." Pamphlet published by the University of Chicago Graduate School of Business, Center for Health Administration Studies.

———. 1988. "Hospital's Tax-Exempt Statute and Paying for Municipal Services." Draft paper prepared for presentation in session at the Graduate School of Public Health, University of Pittsburgh, November 16.

Unger, M. 1990. "Personal Communication." Catholic Health Association of the United States of America, St. Louis.

PART III

HEALTH INSURANCE
IMPLEMENTATION

Part III considers better implementation of health care to promote responsive collaboration. Structural and procedural approaches have very human impacts on care and well-being.

Retired middle-class individuals face the dire prospect of divesting themselves of most assets and income in order to qualify for Medicaid, the major public program to pay for long-term care. Brandon in Chapter 7 suggests that it is improper to force those to whom financial security has been promised as a right through Social Security and Medicare into a welfare program that defines poverty. Although costly and debilitating, in actuality the need for long-term care is relatively rare for the elderly population. Only 24 percent of those turning 65 in 1990 will have a cumulative lifetime use of one or more years.

Social insurance is suggested as an appropriate mechanism for long-term institutional care. Brandon's proposal for a Medicare Part C long-term care insurance proposal would draw its revenue from current Medicaid and Medicare payments for institutionalized long-term care, old age survivors and disability trust funds, and copayments from Social Security checks or publicly administered pensions. The chief protection against overuse of even the best institutional long-term care derives from the widespread reluctance to enter a nursing home. Having insurance for that purpose would not exacerbate elderly people's use of such services, but it would help cushion the blow for those who have no choice but to use long-term care when medically necessary.

In Chapter 8 Jacobson reviews the Arizona Medicaid program, which selects providers through competitive bidding. This decision suggests that requiring the development of a unique information system serves as a barrier to new entrants. States considering similar programs should provide a standardized information system so that providers can focus on efficiently providing medical care. This is a particularly serious problem for state governments that operate Medicaid programs of health care delivery to the poor.

The Health Care Financing Administration agreed to waive certain traditional requirements for Medicaid participation so that states could develop innovative delivery systems. Prior to 1981, Arizona was the only state that did not have a Medicaid program and, partially for this reason, was empowered by HCFA to establish a demonstration project. Information systems are necessary for three reasons: first, so that utilization of services can be tracked; second, reliable data are needed to determine accurate bidding prices; and third, data are required to monitor the performance of subcontracting physicians and hospitals. The demonstration project in Arizona can serve as a model for other states striving to contain Medicaid costs. Jacobson suggests that more competitors can be invited by establishing standard information systems permitting easier comparison. Arizona has developed its own version of managed care Medicaid known as the Arizona Health Care Cost Containment System linking the public and private sectors.

Many large employers are limiting coverage by providing less complete hospital coverage and higher deductibles. In Chapter 9 Larson calls for a balance between the government's responsibility and that of private insurance companies vis-a-vis extraordinary risk. Larson strives to achieve balance between equity and risk in insuring people with AIDS. The government proposes mechanisms to limit the growth of Part B. One approach is to narrow the gap made to specialists as contrasted to physicians.

In considering another high-risk area, the best way of mainstreaming the severely disabled could be achieved through health insurance rather than through special targeting. Another way would be to regulate insurance companies' broader coverage. While private insurance is helpful in protecting the working disabled, there are still considerable burdens placed by insurance companies on the working well, with higher deductibles and coinsurance. The private insurance industry assumes risk but strives to maintain profits by cautiously accepting only certain calculable risks. On the other hand, Larson notes that the public sector concerns itself with the issue of equity in terms of providing health care to the citizenry. As U.S. health care costs increase steadily relative to other countries with national health insurance, the likelihood of a national health insurance program becomes steadily more feasible despite many objections.

Mills examines the impact of Diagnosis Related Groups, a prospective reimbursement formula, on hospital finance in Chapter 10. While the initial impetus for such a program was to contain runaway prices within health care, there have been unexpected dislocations within health care operations. Measures of successful performance have now changed to emphasize cost containment over traditional outcome evaluation of patient well-being. Economy, efficiency, and equity have become the watchwords of hospitals under regulation.

This chapter examines the impact of the prospective reimbursement formula on the hospital structure, including unintended consequences such as the trade-off in technology and innovation and the development of what may be termed the codification of compassion. Mills considers that the nature of physicians drawn to Medicare in the future may differ. The greater the emphasis on cost containment and routine care, so much less will be the growth of innovation and productive risk taking. Careful monitoring may also tend to overemphasize the easily quantifiable. DRGs may ultimately represent a critical initial step in nationalizing American health care.

7

Fulfilling the Promise of Medicare

William Brandon

The media and personal knowledge have made increasing numbers of ordinary Americans aware of the plight of retired middle-class individuals or
couples faced with a Hobson's choice of either allowing the expenses of
long-term care (LTC) to make them destitute or divesting themselves of
assets and income in order to become sufficiently poor to qualify for Medicaid, the principal public program that pays for long-term care in institutions. For the policy analyst, this dilemma becomes an anomaly in social
policy: significant numbers of the only major group that is covered by social
insurance—Social Security and Medicare—are forced to rely on means-
tested welfare for extended medical care.

The anomaly is clearly malign, for it results in particularly egregious
institutionalized two-class medical care. Long-term care institutions are no-
torious for separating into those that will accept new patients on Medicaid
and those that select private payers and sometimes only those patients who
are thought likely to remain self-paying.[1] Moreover, it is cruel to perpetuate
a system that forces many of those to whom minimal financial security in
old age has been promised as a *right* through Social Security and Medicare
into the welfare programs that publicly define poverty in America.

The remarkable repudiation by the elderly of the Catastrophic Coverage
Act of 1988 resulted in part from their belief that the act failed to give them
new protection of much value. The act, which provided protection against
financially catastrophic acute health care, failed to address the more common catastrophic costs associated with the need for nursing home care. A
host of government studies at both the federal and state level, such as the

Pepper Commission Report (1990), have endorsed the reality of the need for coverage for long-term care. However, none has yet managed to craft a feasible proposal that shows a way out of this vexed policy impasse.

The situation is remediable. Because the need for long-term care is *relatively* rare in the elderly population, but financially catastrophic when it occurs, it is precisely the sort of contingency against which insurance can be effective. Only an estimated 43 percent of those turning 65 in 1990 will be admitted to a nursing home some time prior to death; 24 percent will have a cumulative lifetime use of one year or more. At an average cost of about $25,000 for a year in a nursing home in the early 1990s, a lengthy stay in a long-term care institution is a genuine financial catastrophe (Kemper and Murtaugh, 1991).

This chapter argues for broadening Medicare to cover long-term care in institutions. It focuses on *institutional care*—skilled nursing and intermediate care facilities—instead of home care, because lengthy institutional care constitutes the greatest remaining financial catastrophe typically encountered by the elderly. This objective is also suggested by the fact that potential increases in the costs of institutional care are easier to control than those of home care, and services in institutions are currently more uniform and universally available. The funding proposal and most of the analysis can easily be expanded to include home and community care by anyone who judges that the political system can cope with an even more sweeping proposal.

The approach is *national* because increasing differences in the proportion of the population 65 and over among the states as well as economic disparities among the states will make state-based financing of nursing home care increasingly difficult and unjust (Kovar and Feinleib, 1991; Thompson, 1987). Fortunately, the Social Security Act—which includes Medicare, Supplementary Security Income, and disability legislation—and the Employee Retirement Income Security Act of 1974—which regulates private pensions—have effectively made retiree income maintenance and health a federal responsibility.

The argument begins by exploring the principles of social insurance and means-tested welfare. The analysis reveals that social insurance is manifestly more appropriate to the realities of long-term institutional care. The second section focuses on the problem of financing a public program for long-term care. The last section proposes a specific plan for new revenue streams to cover extended care with a minimum of disruption in either individuals' lives or in current political and administrative arrangements.

SOCIAL INSURANCE OR MEANS-TESTED WELFARE FOR LTC COVERAGE?

Social Insurance Versus Welfare

Social insurance is characterized by its nonvoluntary nature and its universality: it covers all persons in a broad and therefore heterogeneous group

Table 7.1
Comparison of Social Insurance and Means-Tested Welfare

Social Insurance	Means-Tested Welfare
1. Eliminates Stigma	Social Control
2. Improves Quality/Quantity	Inferior Services; Concentrates Public Funds on Greatest Need
3. Simplicity	Complexity
4. Equality	Deserts
5. High Public Costs (due to large population and potential overutilization)	Low Public Costs (but possible high societal inefficiency)

by virtue of their group membership.[2] Many examples of social insurance such as the Social Security program encourage the illusion that each person pays for what he or she may receive. Because both the ability to pay and the likelihood of benefiting are unequally distributed in a society, such programs are in fact invariably redistributive (see Table 7.1).

Requiring means-tests (or some other narrow criteria like moral character or single-parenthood) for the receipt of communally provided benefits distinguishes the recipient in some respect beyond the material need or condition that occasions the benefit. Such programs, which are also usually redistributive, seldom try to hide the fact that beneficiaries should be grateful. However, it is sometimes far from obvious from which private pockets the benefits ultimately stem.

Social insurance has three chief advantages:

• No stigma is involved in receiving benefits, for the universality of the scheme implies an ideal equality in the chances of benefiting and its claim to be insurance permits benefits to be regarded as deserved payments or services for which one has already paid.

• The universality of coverage is likely to produce a constituency with sufficient power and self-interest to insure that benefits are maintained at a decent level of quantity and/or quality.

• Universal entitlement avoids or reduces technical complications, such as the need for elaborate certification or information-gathering, to insure that beneficiaries actually qualify for benefits. Social insurance can also generally be designed so that it avoids the "notch effect," in which the potential loss of a benefit creates an incentive to maintain the characteristic used as a test for program qualification.[3]

A disadvantage of social insurance is that the public costs of covering a population—even one limited to retired workers and their elderly dependents—may appear high. Moral hazard—the tendency for events covered by insurance to occur with greater frequency than similar events in the absence of insurance—is also a problem. For long-term care one must decide whether, in the absence of other measures to discourage utilization, a significant increase in the use of publicly financed extended care would result from easing the burden of private payment. The important questions of cost will occupy the next section.

Means-testing has other benefits:

- It can discourage unwanted behaviors and encourage those that are considered desirable.
- Concentrating limited public funds on a small population can increase their impact.
- Selecting a characteristic that accompanies some instances of a need may be the most effective way that bureaucracies, which are always imprecise instruments, can calibrate just deserts. For example, the conjunction of medical need and a history of military service is judged to merit government health care through the Veterans Administration (VA), while the general public that is ineligible for Medicare does not deserve publicly provided health care. The principle that individuals must be rewarded according to just deserts is important to thinkers who fear that individuals will be demoralized or debased if individual responsibility should be eroded.

Two disadvantages of means-testing mirror the advantages of social insurance. Means-tested programs often have low levels of indemnification or inefficient and underfunded service benefits. Notch effects and technical complexities in administration are also greatly increased (Davidson and Marmor, 1980, Ch. 4).

Implications for LTC

The application of these general observations to the case of long-term care is obvious. No question of stigma nor just deserts ought to be attached to the actual need for long-term care. On the contrary, we want patients to feel as good as possible under the circumstances about using the benefit— at least so long as that feeling does not encourage unnecessary use. In addition, social insurance promises to reduce bureaucratic complexity and improve the overall quality of services.

The only question of influencing behavior by the application of stigma might arise long before the actual need, when individual self-reliance and financial prudence in preparation for self-payment might seem to be possible.[4] This concern has not got much to do with the realities of long-term care, however valid it may be in other contexts. Very few healthy individuals or couples can reliably (1) predict whether they will incur long-term care expenses in the future, (2) estimate the cost of those expenses in current dollars, (3) and then follow a prudent investment strategy that not only protects against general inflation but also permits sufficient capital growth to offset future increases in long-term care costs in excess of inflation. To insist that individuals should take these three steps to protect themselves against the risk of requiring long-term care is to push the admirable principle of individual prudence too far. Indeed, a conservative can probably most effectively foster self-reliance by providing individual decision-making with a background of security in regard to such unmanageable risks.

If only a few wealthy Americans can adequately protect themselves as individuals against the potential but unlikely event of incurring catastrophic long-term care expenses, what other alternatives exist? The problems of maintaining the current system in which patients must exhaust personal resources before receiving public assistance through Medicaid are widely recognized, as suggested at the beginning of this chapter. In the U.S. political culture, the only other politically possible long-term care options are private insurance and social insurance.

Private insurance would not cover the entire population at greatest risk for long-term care (Rivlin and Wiener, 1988:59–82; Brandon, 1989:447–49). Moreover, most of the elderly no longer receive the economic and actuarial advantages of purchasing insurance through employment groups, which effectively spreads risk across a healthy population of various ages, while reducing administrative costs. These difficulties have inhibited private carriers and the "Blues" (Blue Cross and Blue Shield) from marketing adequate catastrophic coverage.

In the contemporary U.S. health care system, social insurance is the only reasonable way to provide for the cost of an individual's potential long-term care, which is unpredictable in duration and intensity on a personal but not on a collective basis. Unlike either the conservative's "rational" couple striving for self-reliance or private insurance, social insurance need not maintain current resources adequate to fund future obligations. The obligations created by social insurance differ from those involved in market contracts and the fluctuations to which they are subject. Despite the recent financial difficulties encountered by Social Security and Medicare, the government's promises of basic security in old age, which are backed up by the taxing power, are entirely worthy of trust (Bernstein and Bernstein, 1988). The reliability of federal guarantees, for example, has recently been demonstrated by the government's dependability in making good the losses of insured savings and loan depositors.

COSTS AND FINANCING

So far I have tried to make the case that the *ideal* way to pay for long-term care in institutions is through some form of social insurance. Maintaining that long-term care coverage is *practical* requires one to address the difficult problem of raising sufficient public revenue to cover the costs. The question has two parts: (1) Can the public budget sometime in the 1990s bear the burden of current long-term care costs? (2) How can such an expansion of Medicare be financed?

Public Versus Private Financing

We can begin with an observation made by many proponents of comprehensive National Health Insurance when that subject was debated during the Carter administration. The proponents pointed out that because current services are paid out of current dollars, the public assumption of responsibility for health care costs need not lead to an increase in overall health care costs. By emphasizing total expenditures by the entire society, NHI advocates hoped to focus the debate on whether those dollars ought to flow through the public purse and the consequences of such a change. Unfortunately for the NHI case, conservatives campaigning against government spending succeeded in making a national statistical fetish out of the percentage produced by dividing public budgets by the gross national product. Subsequently, the Reagan administration's principal success in health policy was to formulate and implement the Prospective Payment System to reduce the rate of increase in government Medicare payments to hospitals (Brandon, 1991). The attempt to reduce the government proportion of health expenditures did little to restrain the increase in costs billed to nongovernment payers. Some now argue that to control the increase in health costs the United States should follow Canada in making government a monoposonistic buyer of health services (Himmelstein et al., 1989; Evans 1987; Evans et al., 1989; New York State Department of Health, 1989).

Unlike full-fledged universal compulsory national health insurance, an expansion of Medicare to cover catastrophic institutional long-term care expenses can claim to bow before the conservatives' fear of increasing the government share of health care costs: *about half of the dollars currently used to finance long-term care in institutions are already public dollars.* Medicaid pays for about 45 percent of nursing home care; federal funds alone constitute more than 28 percent of all long-term care expenditures (Office of National Cost Estimates, 1990:34). Therefore, any federal system for financing long-term care must be designed to capture the state dollars that are currently used for this purpose. It should not be difficult for the federal government to reduce its Medicaid contribution to each state by the amount of the state's long-term care expenditures that it takes over.

It is also revealing that roughly 40 percent of direct payments from patients for nursing home care stem from Social Security checks rather from their assets, savings, or private pensions. Private long-term care insurance constituted only a negligible 1.1 percent of all nursing home expenditures (Office of National Cost Estimates, 1990:15, 34). The unimportance of private long-term insurance and the role of private funds derived from Social Security are both significant for the social insurance approach to funding long-term care that is developed in the next subsection.

An expansion of Medicare to cover long-term care does not involve large amounts of additional money, either in absolute dollars or relative to what the federal government is already paying. Nursing home care constitutes only 8 percent of total U.S. expenditures for health or 9 percent of what is spent on personal health services. (Actually, these figures overestimate the costs of normal nursing home care for the elderly, because they include almost $4 billion for intermediate-level care of the mentally retarded.) In the 1988 national health accounts, the category of nursing home care amounted to $43.1 billion out of total health expenditures of more than $539.9 billion. Since the federal government paid $12.5 billion for nursing home care, the incremental federal costs for paying the entire tab would have amounted to a little over $30 billion. State and local payments were $8.4 billion. Thus, public coverage of *all* nursing home costs in 1988 would have required taxes or borrowing of no more than an additional $22.2 billion or less than half a percent of GNP (Office of National Cost Estimates, 1990).

Paying for LTC

Of course there is no free lunch. Liberal proponents of social insurance for health care can satisfy their consciences in setting humane goals for programs, but it is necessary to be as hard-headed as any fiscal conservative in thinking about the financing. The harsh reality is that no government in the United States has uncommitted revenues that it can dedicate to a long-term care entitlement. Therefore, in addition to capturing current federal and state expenditures, any plan for public financing of long-term care must collect private dollars to cover the additional $20–25 billion (in 1988 dollars). The policy choices range along a spectrum between attempts to capture the private dollars that would be spent for long-term care in the absence of any new federal program and reliance on general sources of new tax funding.

Obviously the patients' dollars that now pay for long-term care should not be the major source of funding: the whole point of expanding social insurance is to spare individuals and families from extreme financial hardship caused by the costs of long-term care. Nonetheless, carefully designed patient participation through a deductible and copayments is needed to aid in financing the program and to discourage unnecessary utilization.[5] Other than out-of-pocket payments by patients, private funds for long-term care are currently insignificant. Private insurance has not yet developed into a major payment source for long-term care.[6] (In contrast, NHI proponents can point to widespread insurance among the under-65 population that can be "federalized" as part of a social insurance scheme for acute health care.)

The chances of securing financing from sources at the other end of the funding spectrum—by increasing tax revenue—appear equally dismal. Further increases in payroll taxes (such as revenue from the recent rise in the salary base on which payroll taxes are due) need to be devoted to insuring the integrity of the basic pension and Medicare Part A trust funds. In the current political climate, the general tax revenues must also be rejected as a source of funds for an expansion of Medicare.[7] Moreover, it is probably not prudent to increase the differences—and, consequently, potential antagonism—between those who pay payroll and income taxes and the elderly who stand to benefit in the short term from reduction in the risks that they face (Longman, 1987; Hayward et al., 1988; Hess, 1990).

If the two extremes on the continuum between actual patients and faceless, ageless taxpayers or workers are eliminated, a plan is needed to raise the $20 billion from identified taxpayers who are closer to the actual risk, but who are not yet likely to be long-term care patients.

Two important principles that future health legislation must embody are implicit in the traumatic politics that led to the repeal of the Catastrophic Coverage Act of 1988. All potential beneficiaries must bear the same financial burden. The second lesson is that reformers should develop a financing system that does not remind those who pay of the annual income tax, which is the focal point of citizens' antagonism toward government. A plan to cover institutional long-term care should also aim at simplicity in administration and try to make any tax or premium as invisible and therefore painless as possible.

A PROPOSAL FOR MEDICARE PART C LONG-TERM CARE INSURANCE

One way to meet all these requirements is to create a new Medicare Part C Long-Term Care Trust Fund. Table 7.2 outlines the chief features of the plan. The heart of the proposal is its three revenue sources:

- Current federal and state Medicaid and Medicare payments for institutionalized long-term care tended to increase over the years with the medical care cost index.

- Premium payments from the Old Age, Survivors and Disability (OASDI) Trust Funds (or other government-administered pension funds) are to be deducted from the initial cost-of-living allowance(s) after a beneficiary enrolls. This premium, like the Social Security benefit, would increase as the Consumer Price Index (CPI) pushes up Social Security benefits.[8]

- Copayments are made from the monthly Social Security check (or from other publicly administered pensions for patients lacking Social Security) after the patient in a nursing home or intermediate care facility has met the required deductible. The copayment (unlike the deductible) represents living costs such as food, utilities, and shelter that are avoided because of institutionalization.

Table 7.2

A National Program to Cover Long-Term Care in Institutions: Plan Highlights

Administration and Coverage:

* Automatic enrollment of all beneficiaries of Social Security and federally administered pensions

* Reimbursement for qualifying care in skilled nursing and intermediate care facilities

* Revenues raised by DHHS through electronic transfers among federal trust funds

* Providers paid by DHHS through administrative mechanisms similar to those of Medicare Parts A and B

* Current Medicaid continued for ineligible patients or for care of low-income patients during deductible and waiting period

Financing:

* Current public funds (indexed to the cost of medical care)

* Premiums from a one-time diversion of federal beneficiaries' COLA (indexed to the CPI)

* Copayments of 80 percent of a patient's Social Security benefit after 90 days (informally indexed to the CPI)

* 90-day deductible to qualify as long-term care receiving Medicare Part C reimbursement

* 2-year waiting period after initial enrollment before a beneficiary becomes eligible for coverage (while premiums are paid)

The last two of these funding streams are novel and therefore require explanation and justification. Space constraints prohibit a full discussion of the administrative and coverage issues involved in the plan.

Premiums

The transfer from the OASDI Trust Funds to Medicare Part C is a premium paid by all beneficiaries from money that they have not yet begun receiving. The same amount should be deposited for each beneficiary without regard to when retirement occurs. Increases in nursing home costs above inflation in the CPI may, however, force Congress to increase the premium periodically. Because the premium reduces the Social Security COLA for the duration of an individual's benefit, inter-Fund transfers have no effect on the surplus that is building up in the Social Security Trust Funds to pay for the retirement of the baby-boom generation. (In other words, a liability is created by Trust Fund transfers to the Medicare Part C Long-Term Care

Trust Fund, but payments of Social Security benefits to individuals are reduced by exactly the same amount.)

Because the premium comes from the first COLA increase(s) of new beneficiaries, it will not reduce the amount of money that beneficiaries have been promised by Social Security when deciding to retire. Recent retirees tend to have higher incomes than those who have been retired for some years (Rivlin and Wiener, 1988:11–12). Financial problems are more likely to arise in the second and third decades of retirement. Thus, reduction of the initial increases in the Social Security benefit come when most can best afford to forgo an increase in monthly income. Well-informed workers in an era when retirement is increasingly an individual option may choose to compensate for the lost COLA increase(s) in the first year(s) of retirement by working a few quarters longer to raise average Social Security earnings. This outcome would be consonant with the need in the early years of the twenty-first century to encourage aging workers to remain in the labor force. Such a policy is necessary to help cope with expected labor shortages and the need to postpone receipt of Social Security benefits.

Copayment

The stream of income from the copayment into the Part C Trust Fund is somewhat easier to explain. A chief difference from the Part B copayment is that the federal government instead of the health care provider collects the copayment. The Part B copayment is in large measure intended to reduce utilization (which is conceived to be at least partly under the control of the patient). In contrast, the Part C copayment is mainly designed to increase Long-Term Care Trust Fund revenues by capturing "savings" that patients who are institutionalized may realize. Because copayments constitute diversions to the Medicare Part C Trust Fund from Social Security (or other pension) benefits paid to individual patients after they qualify for long-term care reimbursement, the government is again in the relatively simple bureaucratic position of paying itself.

This form of copayment is suggested by the health care reformers at Harvard (John F. Kennedy School of Government, 1986:26, 29–30):

To meet the objection that Medicare should not pay for the elderly's living expenses, we propose that Medicare beneficiaries in nursing homes pay a "residential copayment" that will partially cover the non-medical costs of nursing home care. This copayment recognizes the responsibility of elders and their families to plan for the "usual" costs of living—namely room and board.

    ... Their liability for these costs, however, should not exceed their ability to pay. To this end, we propose that this copayment equal 80 percent of their Social Security income (or, if there is a spouse, 80 percent of the difference in payments for individuals and couples). Setting copayments in this way establishes a reasonable charge that may rise over time with inflation but will not exceed a beneficiary's financial resources.

This copayment may be regarded as forcing all Medicare beneficiaries to experience some of the burden now borne by the large numbers of elderly who pay their own nursing home bills. A patient copayment of four-fifths of a major income stream like Social Security may seem unduly large, but it should be remembered that an extended nursing home stay is often a black hole that entirely wipes out such financial resources as investments, private pensions, and other income streams or assets. Because it formalizes current patterns of spending, this copayment can also be justified as adhering to the principle of capturing dollars that at present are spent on long-term care. The latest available health care expenditure data show that about 40 percent of the $20.8 billion of private out-of-pocket payments for nursing home care already come from patients' Social Security income (Office of National Cost Estimates, 1990:15, 34).

Integrating copayment revenues into a Medicare Part C Trust Fund recognizes the importance for cost control of the single-payment source. This principle, which stems from observations of the Canadian health care system (Evans, 1987; Evans et al., 1989), is incorporated widely in proposals for reform of the U.S. health care system (Himmelstein et al., 1989; New York State Department of Health, 1989). The Health Care Financing Administration will gain greater regulatory control by consolidating payments for all eligible nursing home patients. Implementation—the simple diversion of part of a government payment to the new Medicare Part C Trust Fund—is also simple.

Deductible and Waiting Period

The constant need to insure that any social insurance of long-term care should be fiscally prudent requires that the proposal include provisions for a sizable deductible and for a waiting period before new beneficiaries can use long-term care benefits. The calculations in this proposal use a deductible constituted by the first 90 days of nursing home care; Rivlin and Wiener (1988) use 100 days in many of their simulation models. Unlike the copayment, each nursing home should be responsible for collecting the cost of the first three months of care from individual patients and their third-party payers. Although only about half of nursing home patients stay as long as three months, the average length of stay for those who remain longer is more than two years (Technical Work Group on Private Financing n.d.:i). Thus, most patients who are discharged from hospitals to a nursing home for rehabilitation or additional recuperation in response to such incentives for early hospital discharge as PPS will not be affected by the new long-term care program.

Any proposal for social insurance must address the problem of unnecessary utilization. The chief protection against overuse of institutional long-term care comes from the widespread aversion to entering a nursing home on a long-term basis. Yet the deductible provides an added financial disincentive for unnecessary institutionalization. In passing, it ought to be pointed out that because patients and families find home care much more desirable, it would be more difficult to control utilization if the new long-term care program subsidized care in the home.

To further strengthen the proposed financing plan, it is also advisable to institute a two-year waiting period before nursing home benefits can be used. The COLA diversion would, of course, be paid into the Part C Trust Fund during the two years. Since few elderly require nursing home care immediately upon retirement, a waiting period as long as two years would cause little hardship. Deductions from the second-year COLA will normally complete the full funding of the Part C premium. If advocates for the elderly object to payment of premiums before the beneficiary is eligible for service, the plan could be modified to pay a nursing home benefit during a waiting period that is proportional to the percent of the patient's premium that had been paid into the Trust Fund at the time a patient meets the Part C deductible.

The choice of a two-year waiting period is somewhat analogous to the two years that disabled persons must wait for federal disability payments. Several considerations might suggest modifying the proposed waiting period for the population eligible through the Disability Insurance Trust Fund. This relatively small population (11 percent of OASDI recipients in 1988), which waited two years to qualify for disability payments, is more likely to need nursing home care than the typical healthy, "young" 65-year-old new Social Security beneficiary. As the AIDS epidemic expands, the increasing need to provide nonacute care for AIDS patients dictates lowering rather than raising bureaucratic barriers to care.

Cost and Revenue Estimates

To be credible, an innovative financing proposal must be accompanied by estimates of the amount as well as the sources of revenues to be raised. A crucial issue for the acceptability of this proposal is the size of the premium diverted from the COLAs of Social Security and other government-administered pensions. The inauguration of Medicare Part C would leave a portion of the $22.1 billion (for 1988) paid by nongovernmental sources to the private sector, because about half of all patients are discharged before the expiration of the 90-day deductible and because patients who do not qualify for Social Security or other government pensions will have to depend on private resources until they can qualify for Supplementary Security Income and Medicaid. To insure that estimates err toward overfunding the

Table 7.3
Total Funding for Institutional LTC Under Medicare Part C (in 1988 dollars)

Funding Source	Estimated Revenue (in billions)
Federal Funds under Current Programs*	$12.5
State Funds under Current Programs*	8.4
Premium ($375 per OASDI Beneficiary)	14.4
Copayment (80% of Mean OAS & DI Benefit)	6.1
Private Share of Deductible (51.4% of First 90 Days)	1.6
TOTAL ESTIMATED FUNDING	$43.0

Notes: Estimates are rough calculations developed from published data. The author has consistently adopted conservative assumptions regarding costs and revenues that should result
  in over-funding the proposed Long-Term Care Trust Fund.
*Current programs would require some of these funds to support care for patients ineligible
  for Medicare Part C or care delivered to eligibles who have not yet met the waiting period
  or deductible requirements for reimbursement. Figures include $3.7 billion in Medicaid
  expenditures for care of the mentally retarded in intermediate care facilities. Most of these
  patients would not be eligible for Medicare Part C.
Sources: Calvin Green, Office of Public Inquiry, Social Security Administration; *1989 and
  1990 Annual Reports* of the Federal Old-Age and Survivors Insurance and Disability
  Insurance Trust Funds (Washington, DC: GPO, 1989 and 1990); Task Force on Long-
  Term Health Care Policies, *Report to Congress and the Secretary* (Washington, DC, 1987),
  pp. 84–91; Office of National Cost Estimates, "National Health Expenditures, 1988,"
  Health Care Financing Review 11 (Summer 1990): 1–41.

proposed public long-term care program, only the 90-day deductible will
remain as private long-term care expenditures under the rough calculations
reported here.

   In 1988 the private share of the deductible would amount to about $1.6
billion; current government programs can be assumed to pay a similar
amount of the cost of the first three months (see Table 7.3). An 80 percent
copayment on Social Security income of eligible nursing home patients after
the 90-day waiting period would have generated about $6.1 billion in 1988
if all of these long-stay nursing home days were covered. To produce a
premium on the COLA that will raise the remaining $14.4 billion would
require about $375 per year. The monthly premium of $31.25 amounts to
one and a half times the value of the COLA awarded on the mean OAS or
DI benefit in 1988, but a much smaller proportion of subsequent COLAs.
(Table 7.4 shows that COLA increases have risen from 4 percent of the
benefit in 1988 to 5.4 percent in 1990.) Thus, assuming no major reduction
in recent COLA levels, by the end of a two-year waiting period the full
contribution would have been transferred from Social Security to Medicare
Part C. It should be emphasized that these estimates are based on *revenues*
from only part—the OASDI beneficiaries—of the entire population that will
contribute, but on long-term care *costs* incurred after the deductible by the

Table 7.4
Mean OAS and DI Benefits and COLA Increases, 1988–90

Year Benefit & COLA	Old-Age and Survivors Insurance	Disability Insurance
1988		
Mean Monthly Benefit	$516	$509
COLA Percent Increase	4.0%	4.0%
COLA Value for Mean Benefit	$ 20.64	$ 20.36
1989		
Mean Monthly Benefit	$537	$529
COLA Percent Increase	4.7%	4.7%
COLA Value for Mean Benefit	$ 25.24	$ 24.86
1990		
Mean Monthly Benefit	$571	$557
COLA Percent Increase	5.4%	5.4%
COLA Value for Mean Benefit	$ 30.83	$ 30.08

Note: Cost of Living Allowance (COLA) increases are announced in October of each year
and first appear in beneficiaries' December checks.

Sources: Calvin Green, Office of Public Inquiry, Social Security Administration; *1989* and
1990 Annual Reports of the Federal Old-Age and Survivors Insurance and Disability
Insurance Trust Funds (Washington, DC: GPO, 1989 and 1990).

entire patient population that currently depends on private resources. The
unfortunate fact that some patients will not be covered by the long-term
care program provides added financial integrity to the plan.

CONCLUSION

This chapter has offered fresh thinking in response to the paralysis in
public policy caused by the conflicting pressure of government deficits and
public demand for more humane and widespread financial support for long-
term care than that currently provided by Medicaid. The chapter initially
returned to general principles to make the case for social insurance of long-
term care. Then it outlined a feasible plan to raise the necessary resources
for a comprehensive public long-term care program. It advocated bypassing
the fiscal impasse by finding nontraditional resources that come from the
age cohort that uses most long-term care.

Because the chapter has focused on raising the revenue as painlessly and
efficiently as possible, it has remained silent on a number of important issues
of administration, coverage, and implementation. Many of these central
questions can be answered in a number of ways once new thinking has
shown how to raise the necessary revenue.

For example, an unexamined aspect of the plan that may be controversial
is its exclusion of coverage for community- and home-based services. Most

experts emphasize the importance of care outside of institutions. The proposed plan could be expanded to cover such services without much difficulty; therefore, critics should not dismiss the proposal on this account alone. The author does believe that the optimal way to inaugurate social insurance for long-term care is to restrict Medicare Part C reimbursement to care provided in skilled nursing and intermediate care facilities. Adequate explanation for this choice, however, would require another study.

NOTES

The study of this subject was begun by the author in a symposium published in *Policy Studies Review* (Brandon, 1989), which reviewed the three approaches to comprehensive reform in financing long-term care. That article's overview of the issue leads to this chapter, which argues for social insurance of long-term care and proposes a specific plan to finance it. The author wishes to thank Seton Hall University for the sabbatical-year support that allowed him to work on this chapter.

1. Outside of the long-term care field, the ideal of rich and poor, black and white receiving health care from the same sources has long been espoused even if the practice sometimes falls short. Support for the claim that nursing homes discriminate, if any is needed, can be found in Smith (1990), Feder and Scanlon (1980:58, 75), and Rango (1982). White admissions to nursing homes significantly exceeded those of blacks among those dying in 1986, even when longevity and sex were controlled (Kemper and Murtaugh, 1991:596).

2. Although traditional use restricts the term "social insurance" to public programs that are financed by premium-like payments that make one eligible to become a beneficiary, this chapter accepts the common extension of "social insurance" to include universal programs financed by general tax revenues. As Stephen Long and John Palmer (1982) point out, sometimes what they call "universal" programs may be designed with means-tested cost sharing. Because Medicaid pays Medicare co-payments and deductibles for the elderly poor, Medicare is a "universal program with income-tested cost-sharing."

3. For example, the loss of Medicaid coverage at a specific level of income discourages the economically rational welfare recipient from work. Some aspects of social insurance may also have notch effects. A cap limits earnings by Social Security beneficiaries who wish to receive full benefits.

4. It is also a mistake to think that individual action on the basis of our increasing understanding of health risks offers protection. Healthy living, which may postpone both death and the need for nursing home care, is unlikely to reduce greatly one's chances of institutionalization over a lifetime. Indeed, it may increase the probability that an individual will be confined to a nursing home by prolonging survival to advanced ages when the incidence of institutionalization is highest (Kemper and Murtaugh, 1991). The issue, which is complex and controversial, cannot be addressed in these few pages.

5. Even the liberal Medicare reformers responsible for the Harvard Medicare Project advocated a deductible equal to the cost of the first month in a nursing home for nonrehabilitative care and a "residential copayment" calculated as a proportion of the beneficiary's Social Security income to partially cover the nonmedical costs

of nursing home care (John F. Kennedy School of Government, 1986:28–31). Kane and Kane (1991) suggest going beyond recognizing the distinction in financing to radically restructure personal care vis-à-vis housing and hotel aspects of nursing homes.

6. In 1988 private insurance paid for only about $500 million worth of nursing home care; private philanthropy, for another $800 million (Office of National Cost Estimates, 1990).

7. General revenues finance much patient care under current arrangements. In addition to sizable health expenditures for the military and veterans, they provided 73.1 percent of the funds spent by Medicare Part B in 1988 (up from about 50 percent of a much lower total in 1972) (Office of National Cost Estimates, 1990:19–22).

8. In addition to Social Security, the federal government is responsible for railroad, military, and civil service pensions. If OASDI Trust Fund balances decline drastically, the COLA may be indexed to wages. If intermediate and worst-case scenarios are realized, this "stabilizer" could be used when the Trust Funds near exhaustion in the twenty-first century (Board of Trustees, 1990:39n).

REFERENCES

Bernstein, M. C. and J. B. Bernstein. 1988. *Social Security: The System That Works*. New York: Basic Books.

Board of Trustees, Social Security Administration. 1989. "The Federal Old-Age and Survivors Insurance and Disability Insurance Trust Funds." *1989 Annual Report*. 101st Cong. 1st Sess., April 1989.

———. 1990. "The Federal Old-Age and Survivors Insurance and Disability Insurance Trust Funds." *1990 Annual Report*. 101st Cong. 2d Sess., April 1990.

Brandon, W. P. 1989. "Cut Off at the Impasse Without Real Catastrophic Health Insurance: Three Approaches to Financing Long-Term Care." *Policy Studies Review* 8(2):441–54.

———. 1991. "Two Kinds of Conservatism in U.S. Health Policy: The Reagan Record." In *From Rhetoric to Reality: Comparative Health Policy and the New Right*, C. Altenstetter and S. C. Haywood, eds., pp. 165–206. London: Macmillan.

Davidson, S. M. and T. R. Marmor. 1990. *The Cost of Living Longer: National Health Insurance and the Elderly*. Lexington, MA: Lexington Books.

Evans, R. G. 1987. "Finding the Levers, Finding the Courage: Lessons from Cost Containment in North America." In *Health Policy in Transition: A Decade of Health Politics, Policy and Law*, L. D. Brown, ed., pp. 17–47. Durham, NC: Duke University Press.

Evans, R. G. et al. 1989. "Controlling Health Expenditures—The Canadian Reality." *New England Journal of Medicine* 320:571–77.

Feder, J. and W. Scanlon. 1980. "Regulating the Bed Supply in Nursing Homes." *Millbank Memorial Fund Quarterly* 58 (Winter).

Hayward, R. A. et al. 1988. "Inequalities in Health Services Among Insured Americans: Do Working Age Adults Have Less Access to Medical Care Than the Elderly?" *New England Journal of Medicine* 318:1507–12.

Hess, J. L. 1990. "Greedy Geezers II: The Catastrophic Health Fiasco." *The Nation*, 698–702.

Himmelstein, D. U. et al. 1989. "A National Health Program for the United States: A Physician's Proposal." *New England Journal of Medicine* 320:102–8.

John F. Kennedy School of Government, Center for Health Policy and Management. 1986. *Medicare: Coming of Age—A Proposal for Reform*. Cambridge, MA: Harvard University.

Kane, R. L. and R. A. Kane. 1991. "A Nursing Home in Your Future?" *New England Journal of Medicine* 324:627–29.

Kemper, P. and C. M. Murtaugh. 1991. "Lifetime Use of Nursing Home Care." *New England Journal of Medicine* 324:595–600.

Kovar, M. G. and M. Feinleib. 1991. "Older Americans Present a Double Challenge: Preventing Disability and Providing Care." *American Journal of Public Health* 81:287–88.

Long, S. and J. Palmer. 1982. "Financing Health Care." In *Income-Tested Transfer Programs: The Case For and Against*, I. Garfinkel, ed. New York: Academic Press.

Longman, P. 1987. *Born to Pay: The New Politics of Aging in America*. Boston: Houghton Mifflin.

New York State Department of Health. 1989. *Universal New York Health Care: Day-Care*. New York State Department of Health, September 1.

Office of National Cost Estimates, U.S. Department of Health and Human Services. 1990. *Health Care Financing Review* 11(4):1–41.

The Pepper Commission, Bipartisan Commission on Comprehensive Health Care. 1990. *Recommendations to the Congress: Access to Health Care and Long-Term Care for All Americans*. Washington, DC: Government Printing Office.

Rango, N. 1982. "Nursing-Home Care in the United States: Prevailing Conditions and Policy Implications." *New England Journal of Medicine* 307:883–89.

Rivlin, M. R. and J. M. Wiener. 1988. *Caring for the Disabled Elderly: Who Will Pay?* Washington, DC: The Brookings Institution.

Smith, D. B. 1990. "Population Ecology and the Racial Interpretation of Hospitals and Nursing Homes in the United States." *Millbank Quarterly* 69:561–96.

Task Force on Long-Term Health Care Policies, U.S. Department of Health and Human Services. 1987. *Report to Congress and the Secretary*. NCPA Pub. No. 87–02170. Washington, DC: Government Printing Office, September 21

Technical Work Group on Private Financing of Long-Term Care for the Elderly (U.S. Department of Health and Human Services). N.D. "Report to the Secretary. Draft manuscript by a work group in 1986 chaired by Steven A. Grossman.

Thompson, F. J. 1987. "New Federalism and Health Care Policy: States and the Old Question." In *Health Policy in Transition: A Decade of Health Politics, Policy and Law*, L. D. Brown, ed., pp. 79–101. Durham, NC: Duke University Press.

8

Health Policy Goals and Firm Performance: A Transaction Cost Analysis of the Arizona Medicaid Experiment

Carol K. Jacobson

INTRODUCTION

Access to health insurance and medical care services is restricted for the estimated 33 million Americans who do not have health insurance. As a partial solution to the problem of the uninsured, some proposals recommend expanding public Medicaid programs to the private sector.[1] Arizona is one state that has recently expanded its innovative Medicaid program and allowed plans delivering indigent medical care to offer coverage to small employers in the private sector. This chapter discusses the implications of Arizona's unique program for improving access to affordable health insurance.

Within the group of 33 million uninsured, only 15 percent are hard-core unemployed. The remainder are sometimes employed (27 percent), steady part-time workers (8 percent), or employed in full-time jobs (50 percent).[2] Many of the employed but uninsured have jobs in the secondary labor market, characterized by low wages, poor working conditions, and limited job security (Doeringer and Piore, 1971; Levitan et al., 1981). Such jobs do not offer health insurance or other fringe benefits.

Employer efforts to contain the costs of health care benefits are creating tense employer-employee relations (Luthans and Davis, 1990). The problems of small firms wanting to offer health benefits are particularly acute. Insurance companies either charge individuals and small groups a higher premium than they charge large groups or refuse to extend coverage to them. In addition, a small group may risk cancellation of coverage if only one employee incurs a large medical claim as a result of an illness such as cancer. Whether employees of a small firm are without coverage because the insurer cancels the policy or because the employer drops health insurance benefits when premiums rise or economic conditions force layoffs, the effect is an increase in the number of uninsured.

The problem investigated in this chapter is the evolution of the Arizona Medicaid demonstration project, which is considered a model for other states interested in implementing similar programs to deliver health care to the poor as well as other uninsured. In an effort to control the rapid growth in Medicaid expenditures,[3] the Health Care Financing Administration, as administrator of the Medicaid program, agreed to waive certain requirements of the traditional Medicaid program in order to allow states to start demonstration projects to test innovative delivery systems. Arizona received a waiver to introduce a unique competitive bidding system to select providers for Medicaid clients and proposed a future expansion of the program to allow winning bidders to offer insurance coverage to small firms and individuals in the secondary labor market.

This chapter uses transaction cost economics as the theoretical framework for understanding health policy actions and the strategic responses of firms (Williamson, 1975; Jones and Hill, 1988). Past research has produced comprehensive case studies that describe the evolution of the Arizona project and model the behavior of bidders (e.g., Kirkman-Liff, Christianson, and Hillman, 1985; Christianson, Kirkman-Liff, Guffey, and Beeler, 1987; Kirkman-Liff, Christianson and Kirkman-Liff, 1987). Two key aspects of the program depart from the outcome anticipated by the program's planners: the small number of firms involved in the annual competitive bidding process and the market share dominance of vertically integrated firms. The argument here is that many health plans were reluctant to enter the bidding because it was necessary to invest in specialized information systems. From the viewpoint of the bidding firm, the features of the Arizona project were not sufficient to encourage a large number of competitors to enter the market. In order to safeguard specialized as well as general-purpose assets from contracting problems, participating firms chose vertical integration as the dominant mode for organizing transactions between providers and the Arizona Medicaid program. The next sections discuss the theory of transaction cost economics, a brief history of the Arizona demonstration project, a transaction cost explanation of the key features of the Arizona project, and the implications for policymakers and small employers.

TRANSACTION COST ECONOMICS

Given the goal of improving efficiency in Medicaid programs, an efficiency-based framework such as transaction cost economics provides a theoretical basis for analyzing and understanding program outcomes. The main argument of transaction cost economics is that boundedly rational and potentially opportunistic economic actors will choose to organize trans-actions by structural arrangements that will increase the overall economic efficiency of the transaction (Williamson, 1975). Efficiency is achieved by reducing the transaction costs of negotiating, monitoring, and enforcing the agreement between the contracting parties. A firm will continue to inter-nalize transactions as long as the economic benefits of vertical integration exceed the bureaucratic costs of monitoring and managing the exchange internally (Jones and Hill, 1988).

The key attribute of transactions giving rise to transaction costs is *asset specificity* or the nontrivial investment in transaction-specific assets (Wil-liamson, 1975). Two of the four types of asset specificity are important to the analysis presented here:[4] (1) *Physical* asset specificity refers to highly specialized but mobile assets supporting a specific transaction. Due to the specialized features of such equipment or machinery, these assets have lower values in alternative uses. (2) *Dedicated* asset specificity refers to discrete investments in general-purpose assets in order to serve a particular customer, such as expanding plant capacity on behalf of one buyer. Although the asset itself may have common features, it cannot be redirected to another use without cost. The basic proposition is that firms will choose vertical inte-gration or some intermediate structure to replace external market contracts when high levels of asset specificity are present.

Before applying the concepts of transaction cost economics to the evo-lution of the Arizona project, the next section provides background infor-mation about the project.

THE ARIZONA DEMONSTRATION PROJECT

Prior to 1981, Arizona was the only state in the Union that did not have a Medicaid program.[5] Historically, individual county health departments had primary responsibility for providing medical care to their indigent res-idents. As the cost of providing indigent health care continued to escalate, Arizona turned to the federal government for help. To be eligible for federal matching funds, a state must obtain HCFA approval prior to implementing an innovative program. In 1981 HCFA and the state of Arizona reached an agreement to establish the Arizona Health Care Cost Containment Sys-tem (AHCCCS, pronounced "access") as a demonstration project (Senate Bill 1001).

The AHCCCS project has several unique features. All health plans pro-viding care to AHCCCS-eligible patients are capitated (receive a flat fee for each person enrolled). Unlike other states experimenting with capitation, Arizona does not include a fee-for-service reimbursement option; all AHCCCS clients are required to choose one of the approved AHCCCS plans. HCFA approved four other cost-containment features for AHCCCS that set it apart from traditional fee-for-service Medicaid programs in other states: a statewide competitive bidding system (the only one in the nation), nominal copayments by the client, primary care physicians as gatekeepers to the system, and capitated payments to the state by the federal government.

In an effort to encourage multiple bidders in the initial round of the competitive bidding system, the state of Arizona passed legislation providing two incentives to potential bidders. First, the requirements to participate as an AHCCCS plan were not very stringent. In 1982 Arizona had few managed care plans.[6] Only six health maintenance organizations existed, and there were no individual practice associations (IPAs).[7] The state encouraged the development of new managed care plans by making the bidding process open to virtually any organization that could provide or arrange to provide medical services regardless of previous experience with capitated financing. The financial constraints were very limited, particularly as compared to traditional insurance plans. There were no capitalization requirements and no financial performance standards.

Second, a stated goal of the program was to assist the winning bidders in becoming health plans for county and state employees as well as private-sector groups in the future. The intent of the state was to provide additional encouragement to the establishment of HMOs and IPAs. It was not clear, however, what form the state assistance would take. Some potential bidders were concerned that the state would allow only initial bid winners to be included as a managed care insurance option for state and county employees (Christianson and Hillman, 1986). Providers viewed the AHCCCS program as an opportunity to gain managed care experience prior to marketing health plans in the private sector.

With these incentives as encouragement, the entry of numerous competitors was expected to intensify competition to enter the lowest bid in order to win a contract to provide medical care to the AHCCCS enrollees. Arizona expected the increase in competition to result in a more efficient health care delivery system. If a firm won an AHCCCS contract, it was assumed that economies of scale and cost advantages would be gained over time as a plan gained a larger share of the overall managed care market.

The next three sections present a transaction cost explanation for why the AHCCCS system was unexpectedly dominated by vertically integrated participants and had a smaller number of bidders than anticipated. Then, after describing the importance of investments in specialized information systems, the structural responses of the plans and the participants in the competitive bidding are discussed.

IMPORTANCE OF INFORMATION SYSTEMS

Reliable information is required by each participating AHCCCS plan for three reasons. First, a plan needs reliable information as a basis for determining an accurate bid price. When bidding for capitated contracts, it is critical that costs are carefully understood, so the plan neither bids below costs (and loses money) nor bids too high (and loses the contract). Second, a plan requires information to monitor the performance of the subcontractors, primarily physicians and hospitals. Accurate information regarding utilization of services aids the plan in identifying practice patterns that deviate from standard practice and raise costs for the plan. Third, although initial AHCCCS reporting requirements were few in number and not well-defined, each plan was required to report information to AHCCCS administration. This information included financial data to aid administrators in assessing the financial strength of the plan as well as patient encounter data to aid the administrators in tracking utilization of services and the quality of patient care.

The importance of good information to the success of an AHCCCS plan means that the timely and accurate collection and analysis of data become critical. To assist the plans in this task, an investment in an information system is required. Due to the unique requirements of the AHCCCS program, an investment in an information system supporting AHCCCS transactions raises asset specificity. There are two reasons why an information system supporting a capitated system is transaction-specific. First, the information demands of any capitated or prepaid system are substantially different from the information demands of a fee-for-service system. In a traditional fee-for-service Medicaid program, providers must submit claims in order to be reimbursed. The administration of the program then takes utilization and cost information from the claim forms to use to monitor services, assess quality, and evaluate costs. In a capitated program, however, the providers have already received a capitated fee for each client and have no direct incentive to report timely information for administrative use. An information system for a capitated program must have special design features in order to collect adequate monitoring and quality assessment information.

The second reason for increased asset specificity is that the innovative and emerging nature of the AHCCCS program meant that some aspects of the program remained ambiguous or undefined. An information system designed to fit the idiosyncratic features of an evolving program would be worth less in alternative uses.

Even though the Arizona legislature wanted the project implemented within months of its approval, AHCCCS administration did not have its own information system in place or technical expertise to offer the plans in the designing of their own. At the time the program was initiated, information systems for capitated insurance programs were not available from vendors. For internal purposes, the administrator for the first year planned to use an existing Medical Management Information System (MMIS) from a fee-for-service program in the state of New York. Although it was expected that the system could be modified with "minimal development effort," the actual modification required was "grossly underestimated" (Stanford Research Institute, 1987:III–2). An existing information system could not costlessly or easily be modified to suit the unique features of AHCCCS.

The absence of adequate information meant that monitoring was low and the hazards of opportunism were high. For example, although some reporting requirements were in place, there were initially no financial penalties for not reporting; therefore, the plans did not have an incentive to comply with the requirements. Consequently, neither AHCCCS administration nor the plans had sufficient information.

Overall, the information system was the key to the viability of the innovative delivery system. There is no alternative use for this investment, because Arizona has the only capitated, competitive bidding delivery system for Medicaid in the United States. The question for participating health plans is: "What type of structural arrangement will minimize the transaction costs of safeguarding our investment from the hazards of opportunism?" With the importance of investments in specialized information systems to support AHCCCS transactions, transaction cost reasoning would predict the choice of vertical integration to organize these transactions. The next section discusses each category of health care plan and the structural arrangement chosen to organize its AHCCCS transactions.

STRUCTURAL RESPONSES OF THE PLANS

There are four key players involved in the delivery of medical care to the indigent who entered into the bidding. First, as anticipated, existing HMOs participated. HMOs took part in the bidding primarily for political reasons; they wanted to be eligible for participation when the state expanded the program to offer insurance coverage to private employer groups (Christianson and Hillman, 1986). Second, physicians also responded to the program's incentive of an expanded program and established IPAs. Third, several rural hospitals sponsored health plans and entered the bidding in the first year. At the time of the AHCCCS start-up, urban hospitals believed they were in the business of providing acute health care rather than of managing health plans, and they participated only as subcontractors. Fourth, several of the county governments, which were historically responsible for indigent health care, established plans.

Project designers assumed that the county programs were inefficient bureaucracies and expected that physician-sponsored IPAs and existing HMOs could more efficiently provide indigent medical care than the county programs. Presumably, price-based competition between multiple health plans would result in the closure of the county programs, and HMOs and IPAs would grow to hold the largest market share. This section describes the actual outcome, in which the relative importance of the types of plans is in direct contrast to the initial expectations.

Table 8.1
Relative Market Share by Plan Type by Year

Plan Type/Year	I 1982	II 1983	III 1984	IV 1985	V 1986	VI 1987	VII 1988
Existing HMOs	8.3%	5.6%	3.8%	---	---	---	---
Physician-Sponsored IPAs	39%	63.1%	56.8%	24.4%	22.5%	4.4%	4.9%
County-Sponsored	48.9%	21.9%	26.6%	30.1%	24.7%	22.9%	25.1%
Hospital-Sponsored	3.8%	9.4%	12.9%	45.5%	52.7%	72.7%	70%

Sources: Years I-IV: Stanford Research Institute (1987); Years V & VI: Peat, Marwick, Mitchell and Co. (1989); Year VII: Individual Plan Annual Reports.

Existing HMOs

In the first year, four existing HMOs were winning bidders. Their combined market share was 8.3 percent in the first year. By the start of the third year, three had withdrawn from the project, and by the end of that year the fourth experienced serious financial difficulties and its contracts were assigned to one of its major creditors, a nonprofit hospital. (Table 8.1 shows the relative market share of each category by year.) Thus, all participants in one category that was expected to dominate the system were out of the project within three years.

HMOs claimed that it took two to three times the amount of paperwork to process payment for an AHCCCS patient as for a private-sector patient. Although HMOs had information systems in various stages of development, further investments in changing the current systems were necessary due to unique program features and emerging reporting requirements. The HMOs did not believe there were economic benefits to AHCCCS contracting to make up for the bureaucratic costs. A growing concern was that participation in AHCCCS as a provider to the poor would alienate employed middle-class clients and limit the future gains from offering insurance to private employers and individuals. Although there have been 13 new HMOs in Arizona since the introduction of the AHCCCS project, none of them has participated in the competitive bidding.

Physician-Sponsored IPAs

In the initial round, physicians and, in some cases, other entrepreneurs created six IPAs as a direct response to the AHCCCS program and were awarded contracts. The IPA plans bid low, assuming this bidding strategy would rapidly gain market share and efficiency. IPAs had a 39 percent share of the AHCCCS market in the first year and grew to 63.1 percent in the second year. Even as their market share was growing, however, several IPAs were experiencing financial difficulties. They were unprofitable and insolvent. By the third year, the largest filed Chapter 11 bankruptcy and was acquired by a nonprofit hospital partnership, and two others were liquidated under Chapter 5 bankruptcy. When another financially troubled IPA was purchased by a nonprofit hospital in the fourth year, the combined market share of the remaining IPA plans dropped to 24.4 percent (refer to Table 8.1). By the fifth year, the largest of the remaining IPAs also withdrew. The IPA market share decreased to 4.4 percent by the first quarter of year six. Consequently, another category that was expected to be dominant has maintained only a minor market share.

The financial failure of the IPAs occurred in large part because they failed to develop information systems on a timely basis. It took longer than projected to develop these systems, so many were without them for two years (Kirkman-Liff et al., 1987). Without these systems, IPAs did not have the information necessary to identify high utilizers, to track financial data, or to estimate accurate bids. As newly created plans, the IPAs were also lacking the skills for managing a prepaid health plan. In an attempt to hire management expertise, one large plan employed a management consulting firm, a data management firm, and top managers. This directly increased their administrative costs and indirectly increased the costs of transacting because decision-making responsibility among the managers was not clear (Ibid.). For these plans, the economic benefits did not exceed the costs incurred.

County Systems

Four counties had experience in directly providing health care to the indigent and sponsored plans in the first year. Two of them, Maricopa and Pima, contain the only urban areas in the state (Phoenix and Tucson, respectively). During the first year, the county plans enjoyed a 48.9 percent market share of all AHCCCS eligibles. A rural county integrated its plan with a hospital-sponsored plan during the first year. The market share of the remaining three plans has declined but remains relatively stable at about 25 percent (refer to Table 8.1). Overall, county programs were more responsive than expected and retained a significant role in the delivery of medical care to the indigent in their respective counties.

The response of the county health departments was to establish a health plan as a separate division of the department. Three factors explain why the counties developed plans. First, in the initial round of bidding, the county health departments were the only participants with reliable information based on historical data about indigent health care costs and utilization of services. The county programs also had experience working under budget constraints. Presumably, some of this experience was transferable to the managed care constraints of the AHCCCS program.

Second, each participating county owns a hospital and has a salaried medical staff. Dedicated assets (hospital building and equipment) can not be costlessly reassigned to another use and, therefore, require safeguards. Vertical integration provides safeguards in the form of maintaining occupancy and utilization rates. A benefit of the salaried medical staff is that opportunistic physician behavior during recontracting negotiations can be restrained because the plan can require the physicians to cooperate through rules, policies, and executive order if necessary. Furthermore, because physicians are salaried and their fees do not fluctuate, costs can be predicted more accurately.

Third, the positions of many bureaucrats in the county health department and doctors and other county hospital personnel depend on continued county participation in delivering indigent care. Establishing a health plan as a separate division of the county health department protects these interests.

Hospital-Sponsored Plans

Three rural hospitals sponsored health plans in the first year and acquired a 3.8 percent market share of AHCCCS clients. These rural hospitals were located in counties that did not have a county-owned hospital and, therefore, had a high proportion of indigent patients. As owners of the plan rather than subcontractors, they could have more control over utilization decisions affecting their costs. In the first year, urban hospitals subcontracted with other plans rather than acting as primary contractors.

In the second year, four additional hospital-sponsored plans were created and awarded bids. As the IPAs began to experience financial losses and not pay hospital claims, hospital willingness to sponsor plans changed. Hospitals acquired several of the failed IPAs. The hospital-sponsored plans have experienced continued growth over the evolution of the system, with a combined market share exceeding 70 percent early in year six (refer to Table 8.1).

There are two primary reasons why hospitals sponsored plans. First, as indicated, major nonprofit hospitals increasingly realized they were at risk as subcontractors. Because subcontracting did not provide adequate safeguards for hospitals, it was necessary either to forgo serving the AHCCCS market segment or become primary contractors by developing or buying health plans. Community and religious-affiliated hospitals state that part of their mission is to provide some level of uncompensated care. As owners of AHCCCS plans and providers of indigent care, they could recover a larger portion of the costs of uncompensated care. As the original rural hospital-sponsored plans realized, by choosing vertical integration, a hospital can overcome some of the disadvantages of subcontracting. Whereas bankrupt plans in the past had not paid the hospital, the hospital-as-owner can ensure that it is paid the "capitated" amount as well as have more control over the utilization decisions that drive costs. A second factor influencing a hospital's assessment is its investment in dedicated assets. As owner or part-owner of a plan, a hospital can increase the flow of patients to its facilities and, therefore, increase the utilization of existing assets.

To summarize, hospital-sponsored and county plans made transaction-specific investments in specialized information systems to support AHCCCS transactions. In order to protect their specialized investments as well as their dedicated assets, both chose to integrate vertically. Through the use of bureaucratic policies and procedures, vertical integration can reduce the transaction costs of coordinating and monitoring the various health care providers involved in the delivery of health care. Vertical integration increases bureaucratic costs to impose controls, but it allows the hospital-sponsored and county plans to enjoy higher economic benefits as a result of maintaining hospital occupancy rates and utilization of other equipment. Contrary to initial program expectations, Table 8.1 shows that the relative market share of county and hospital-sponsored plans dominated HMOs and IPAs as AHCCCS providers.

PARTICIPANTS IN THE COMPETITIVE BIDDING

As previously discussed, a primary goal of AHCCCS was to increase the number of plans bidding for contracts each year. Table 8.2 shows the participating plans by year and the number of counties in which each plan participates. The county-sponsored plans are omitted from this table. From a high number of 14 plans in years two and three, 10 participated in year seven, and no new plans have entered the bidding since the second year. Plans showing an increase in the number of counties in which they participate have expanded through the acquisition of financially troubled plans previously serving those counties. Only three plans provide service in more than one county.

Table 8.3 shows the number of plans providing services in each county by year. From the perspective of the counties over the last five years of the project (years three through seven), 7 of the 15 counties in Arizona have experienced a decline in the number of plans providing services, 6 have maintained the same number, and 2 have increased from one to two plans. The general conclusion is that the goal of increasing the number of participants in the bidding has not been achieved.

The lack of growth in the number of participants in subsequent rounds of bidding can be partially explained by the differences in the availability and reliability of information between previous and new bidders. Infor-

Table 8.2
The Number of Counties in Which Each Plan Participated by Year

Plan\Year *	I	II	III	IV	V	VI	VII
Access Patients Choice	0	10	7	9	9	-	-
APIPA	14	12	13	12	12	12	12
Comp. AHCCCS	1	1	1	1	1	1	1
Coconino Health Care	1	-	-	-	-	-	-
Dynamic	1	1	2	1	-	-	-
El Rio Santa Cruz NHC	1	1	1	-	-	-	-
Gila Medical Services	2	2	2	1	1	3	1
Graham County Doctors Health Plan	0	1	1	2	1	1	1
Health Care Providers	2	2	2	-	-	-	-
Family Health Plan NEAZ	0	1	3	3	3	3	3
No. AZ FHP	2	2	1	1	1	1	1
Phoenix Health Plan	0	1	1	1	1	1	1
Pima Care	1	-	-	-	-	-	-
St. Joseph's Mercy Care	0	1	1	8	8	8	8
SHS Medical Care Systems	0	4	5	1	1	1	1
University FamliCare	0	1	1	1	1	1	1

*The county-sponsored programs are omitted from this table.
Sources: AHCCCS Demonstration Waiver Request (1987–88) and personal communication

mation asymmetry existing between previous and new bidders limits the number of bidders willing to risk. Once the participating plans make the investment in transaction-specific assets, they have an advantage over new bidders. With information systems in place, their bids are better informed about utilization patterns and the actual costs of delivering indigent care. New bidders do not have access to accurate information and cannot prepare accurate bids. At subsequent rounds of bidding, the initial bid winners can bid lower than new entrants who would have to include the start-up costs of an information system in their bid. For these reasons, as AHCCCS participants develop effective information systems, it becomes more difficult for new competitors to enter the market. In effect, the transaction-specific

Table 8.3
The Number of Plans in Each County by Year

County\Year	I	II	III	IV	V	VI	VII
Apache	1	1	2	2	2	2	2
Cochise	1	2	2	2	3	2	2
Coconino	4*	4	3	2	2	2	2
Gila	2	4	5	3	3	3	3
Graham	2	4	2	3	3	2	2
Greenlee	1	2	1	3	2	1	1
LaPaz	0	1	1	2	2	2	2
Maricopa	4*	7*	7*	5*	5*	5*	4*
Mohave	2	3	2	4	3	2	2
Navajo	1	3	3	2	2	2	2
Pima	4*	5*	5*	5*	5*	4*	4*
Pinal	4*	6*	6*	3*	3*	3*	2*
Santa Cruz	1	2	2	3	3	2	2
Yavapai	2	1	3	1	1	1	1
Yuma	2	2	1	3	3	2	2

*One program is a county-sponsored program
Sources: AHCCCS Demonstration Waiver Request (1987–88) and personal communication

asset becomes a barrier to entry and explains the unexpectedly small number of firms involved in the bidding process.

CONCLUSION

This chapter used transaction cost economics as the theoretical basis for evaluating health policy and the strategic responses of firms. Arizona implemented a competitive bidding system to encourage the entry of multiple health plans so that increased competitive behavior would drive down the price of delivering medical care to the poor. The importance of dedicated assets and specialized information systems was not recognized by either the program designers or some of the plans. As a result, the Arizona demonstration project has a small number of firms involved in the annual competitive bidding process and vertically integrated firms dominate the market.

Nevertheless, the Arizona program shows promise as an efficient health care delivery system. The Stanford Research Institute (1987) concluded that the AHCCCS program is less costly than traditional fee-for-service Medicaid programs, and HCFA has recognized the potential for efficient results. In 1988, HCFA approved the Arizona project for another five years.

The Arizona experience also suggests that efficient managed care plans developed in public Medicaid demonstration projects such as Arizona's have potential usefulness for addressing the problems of the uninsured in the private sector. AHCCCS plans in both urban counties in Arizona have recently offered health insurance to small employers having difficulty obtaining health insurance (Aleshire, 1990). Expertise gained by the plans through experience in Medicaid delivery systems can provide a basis for directly marketing health care services to small employer groups or individuals employed in the secondary labor market. Future research should evaluate the outcome of this expansion.

Lessons learned in Arizona can inform policymakers and program designers in other states. With HCFA's encouragement, there is interest in establishing similar systems as a cost-containment measure and as a partial solution to the uninsured problem faced by small employers and the secondary labor market in other states. Although AHCCCS administrators continue to believe that the absence of a standard information system encourages competitive behavior, the analysis here suggests that states might encourage a larger number of competitors (and less vertical integration) if the state removes the transaction-specific entry barrier by assisting in the development of a specialized information system that fits the key features of the program. Competition could then focus on improving the efficiency of medical care delivery rather than consuming time and resources to duplicate information systems. This action could potentially encourage more bidders and more competition to bring down the cost of health care for the poor and other uninsured Americans.

The policy implications of this analysis should be interpreted with caution. As contracting conditions change, the comparative efficiency of structural arrangements may also change. If the information needs of AHCCCS and similar programs are clarified and stabilized, vertically integrated providers may no longer be the most efficient structural arrangement. With stable information needs, software vendors and management companies can develop systems and expertise through contracts with current AHCCCS participants and then make their services available at a competitive price to new entrants. In the future, other structural arrangements such as long-term contracts or quasi-firms may replace the vertically integrated organization.

NOTES

1. The Medicaid program was introduced in 1966 as a federal-state matching program charged with providing medical care to the eligible indigent and administered by the Health Care Financing Administration.

2. Information from Employee Benefit Research Institute as reported in Faltermayer, 1990.

3. The most recent data show that Medicaid costs for medical services were $45.1 billion in 1987, up from $16.2 billion a decade earlier.

4. The other two types of asset specificity are site specificity and human asset specificity. Although human asset specificity can account for the choice of vertical integration to organize direct providers (Alchian and Demsetz, 1972; Jacobson, 1988), the analysis of the Arizona program does not show that it plays a role in the vertical integration of the financing function.

5. Information was collected from published description studies, articles printed in Arizona newspapers, and discussions with AHCCCS personnel.

6. Managed care plans are prepayment health plans. They are termed "managed" care because they intervene in the day-to-day management of medical treatment and provide treatment on a budget that has already been set.

7. An IPA is different from a group practice HMO in that the individual doctors remain in their own private practices. Also, as owners of the plan, the physicians are collectively at risk for the costs incurred.

REFERENCES

Alchian, Armen A. and Harold Demsetz. 1972. "Production, Information Costs and Economic Organization." *American Economic Review* 62 (December):777–95.

Aleshire, Peter. 1990. "Arizona Will Try Small-firm Insurance," *Arizona Republic*, March 5:C1, C2.

Christianson, Jon B. and Diane G. Hillman. 1986. *Health Care for the Indigent and Competitive Contracts: The Arizona Experience.* Ann Arbor, MI: Health Administration Press.

Christianson, Jon B., Bradford L. Kirkman-Liff, Teddylen A. Guffey, and James R. Beeler. 1987. "Nonprofit Hospitals in a Competitive Environment: Behavior in the Arizona Indigent Care Experiment." *Hospital and Health Services Administration*, November:475–91.

Doeringer, Peter B. and Michael J. Piore. 1971. "Theories of Low-wage Labor Worker." In *Readings in Labor Economics and Labor Relations*, L. G. Reynolds, S. H. Masters, and C. H. Moser, Englewood Cliffs, NJ: Prentice-Hall.

Faltermayer, Edmund. 1990. "How to Close the Health Care Gap." *Fortune*, May 21:123–34.

Jacobson, Carol K. 1988. "Strategic Linkages Between Hospitals and Physicians: A Transaction Cost Analysis." Unpublished doctoral dissertation.

Jones, Gareth R. and Charles W. L. Hill. 1988. "Transaction Cost Analysis of Strategy-structure Choice." *Strategic Management Journal* 9 (March–April):159–72.

Kirkman-Liff, Bradford L., Jon B. Christianson, and Diane G. Hillman. 1985. "An Analysis of Competitive Bidding by Providers for Indigent Medical Care Contracts." *Health Service Research* 20(5):549–77.

Kirkman-Liff, Bradford L., Jon B. Christianson, and Tracy Kirkman–Liff. 1987. "The Evolution of Arizona's Indigent Care System." *Health Affairs*, Winter:46–58.

Levitan, Sar A., Garth L. Mangum, and Ray Marshall. 1981. *Human Resources and Labor Markets*. New York: Harper & Row.

Luthans, Fred and Elaine Davis. 1990. "The Healthcare Cost Crisis: Causes and Containment." *Personnel*, February:24–30.

Office of National Cost Estimates, U.S. Department of Health and Human Services. 1990. "National Health Expenditures, 1988." *Health Care Financing Review* 11(4):1–41.

Peat, Marwick, Mitchell and Company. 1989. "Arizona Health Care Cost Containment System: Plan Operational and Financial Review Report," May.

Senate Bill 1001. 1981. State of Arizona, 35th Legislature, 4th Special Session.

Stanford Research Institute International. 1987. "Evaluation of the Arizona Health Care Cost Containment System." Prepared for the Health Care Financing Administration.

———. 1975. *The Economic Institutions of Capitalism*. New York: The Free Press.

9

Insuring Persons in High-Risk Categories

James Larson

A recent government report (GAO 1990a) indicates that health benefits in some large firms are beginning to erode, due to rapidly increasing health care costs. Companies are placing limitations on those covered, including retiree and dependent coverage, and are hiring more part-time workers. In addition, more companies are opting for self-insurance, in which the company itself is the health insurer of its employees. The principal benefit of self-insurance to the company is that it exempts them from state laws that regulate insurance companies. These laws may require insurance companies to provide coverage that is unprofitable but in the public interest (GAO, 1990a:14).

If cost containment is beginning to hurt gainfully employed individuals in large corporations, what about those who have difficulty obtaining insurance? What about the poor, the disabled, those with AIDS, and the elderly? How do the concepts of risk versus equity relate to the insuring of these individuals through public or private insurance? That is the subject of this chapter.

However, before turning to each of these groups and discussing their unique problems in obtaining adequate health insurance coverage, a brief examination of the private-public health insurance structure in the United States would be useful. About 60 percent of the U.S. population finance their health care either through private insurance or direct payment to health care professionals (Leichter and Rodgers, 1984:70). Private insurance accounts for about 35 percent of this amount and direct payments about 25 percent. Of those who purchase private insurance, over 90 percent do so through group insurance provided with employment. About 35 percent of private health insurance is purchased from Blue Cross/Blue Shield, 48 percent from other private insurers, 11 percent from self-administered and noninsurer third-party administrators, and 6 percent from HMOs (Pauly, 1988). The remaining 40 percent qualify for public health insurance, where about 17 percent receive Medicare, 10 percent receive Medicaid, and 13 percent other government assistance, principally Veterans Administration benefits (Health Care Financing Review, 1978).

Thus, approximately 25 percent of health care payments do not come from private or public insurance, but from direct payments by patients. A portion of these payments comes from deductibles and coinsurance (about 11 percent), and another portion from those who are uninsured. It is estimated that about 14 percent of the U.S. population is without any kind of health insurance. The uninsured in America tend to be young, poor (working and nonworking), minorities, and unmarried. In a recent study in Michigan, the uninsured included 30 percent with full-time jobs, 40 percent with part-time jobs, and 30 percent without jobs (GAO, 1990b:14–15). So the uninsured tend to be either unemployed or employed only part-time, if the Michigan data are representative of the national picture.

The U.S. government has failed to provide adequate health care for the disadvantaged and those in high-risk categories, such as AIDS patients, for the same reasons that private insurance companies have refused to provide coverage. High-risk means higher costs, and higher costs mean larger budgets and higher taxes. Since the inception of the Medicare and Medicaid programs, cost containment has been a problem. The poor and the elderly tend to use health facilities more than the general population, thus placing a greater burden on government. Government has become the insurer of last resort, taking on those who cannot afford private insurance or who cannot qualify for private insurance coverage. But, at the same time, government has limited coverage to the poor, elderly, and disadvantaged in order to contain costs.

The pressure of cost containment also has affected private health insurance and corporations. Health insurance premiums paid by employers doubled from 1980 to 1985, resulting in a significant increase in self-insurance plans within companies. But, along with self-insurance, companies are providing less-complete hospital coverage and higher deductibles (Jensen et al., 1987). Self-insurance has not led to better care, only cheaper care.

Higher insurance costs have affected not only corporations, but also physicians. A recent study found "positive statistically significant effects of insurance fees on physicians' prices" (Lee, 1989:705). The study concludes that insurers' fees are a primary cause of inflation in medical prices.

For the private insurance company, the concept of risk and profit motivate behavior. Each company selling health insurance attempts to maximize profits and minimize risks. This is accomplished by avoiding the insuring of individuals in high-risk categories. It is accomplished by spreading risk around: "Contrary to popular belief, insurance companies do not assume risk. Rather, they spread it, through a mechanism known as reinsurance" (Muzychenko, 1986:4). The company transfers a portion of the premium to another insurer in exchange for coverage of part of the risk, or higher levels of risk. Thus, insurance companies can avoid excessive risk without eliminating coverage. But this is not always possible, so persons in high-risk categories may be denied coverage.

Public health insurance policies are motivated by the concept of risk, but they also are concerned with the concept of equity. Government in the United States, and in most Western democracies, assumes the responsibility for maintaining the health of its citizenry. Government is the insurer of last resort for the poor, the disadvantaged, the elderly, and those who cannot afford health insurance. Individually, each citizen has certain "rights," including the right to "life, liberty and property," under law. Increasingly in the past decades, this right to life has included a right to good health and adequate health care. We, as Americans, are disturbed when we hear of someone being denied needed medical treatment for lack of money. Before the advent of Medicare and Medicaid, physicians routinely treated such patients as charity cases, and did not deny them care for lack of money. Our society has long assumed a right to health care, and the principle of equity assumes that we all have an equal right to basic care to preserve health and life.

Government policies in health care must balance the principles of equity and risk. They must insure a level of equity by providing health care or insurance to those who cannot afford private insurance. And they must regulate private insurance companies and corporations engaged in self-insurance of employees, to guarantee the rights of citizens to purchase health insurance without discrimination or denial of civil rights.

On the other hand, government must be cognizant of the element of risk in health insurance. Extended coverage of Medicaid and Medicare may take on too much risk, without fundamental changes in government policies to finance a more extensive system of health care. Also, it may be unfair to force private insurance companies and corporations to assume extreme risk, which may force companies out of business. Therefore, a balance is always needed. Nowhere is the need for balance more apparent than in the area of health insurance coverage for persons with AIDS.

AIDS AND INSURANCE COVERAGE

It is estimated that 44,000 cases of AIDS will be diagnosed in 1989; 56,000 in 1990, and 70,000 in 1991. The average lifetime treatment costs of a person with AIDS is $75,000, assuming an average survival length of 15 months. This figure reflects recent length of survival increases with AZT and other treatments. All in all, the national costs of AIDS treatment is estimated at $43.3 billion in 1989, $4.3 billion in 1990, and beyond $5.3 billion in 1991 (Hellinger, 1990). It is estimated that treating all HIV-related illnesses may cost the U.S. $50 billion in the 1990s, and the most likely scenario is that 40 percent of the costs will fall on Medicaid, and the remaining 60 percent on private insurers and individuals (Pascal et al., 1989).

Private insurance companies are financially threatened by the AIDS epidemic. If they were not regulated by state governments, they would not provide coverage for AIDS patients, because the risks for coverage exceed the benefits. According to a recent survey, all commercial health insurers included rated persons with AIDS as "uninsurable." But most insurance companies face some form of state regulation requiring coverage for AIDS patients. In 42 states, insurers may not question employees or applicants about the results of HIV tests. But in 35 states they may exclude HIV/AIDS conditions when they are "preexisting conditions" (Pascal et al., 1989). In other words, those with AIDS who are already employed are much more likely to be covered than those who apply for employment or who are newly hired and have AIDS.

Private insurers plan to use various tests to detect AIDS more in the future, despite the fact that existing tests are flawed. Recently, one insurance company used test results to deny an entire group policy, because one employee tested positively for AIDS (*The Economist*, 1988:14). Such abuses of testing are not currently the norm, but state regulation should be strengthened to prevent abuses of the testing policy.

State AIDS policies differ in how they are related to the incidence of AIDS in particular states. The highest rates of incidence of AIDS occur in California and New York, while moderate levels occur in Florida, Georgia, Illinois, Massachusetts, New Jersey, Pennsylvania, and Texas. The states with the most generous private insurance policies are the same as those listed above, with the exception of Illinois, Florida, and Texas, which have less generous policies (Pascal et al., 1989).

Despite these generous policies, state regulation of private insurance policies is relatively weak. Of the ten states reporting the greatest number of AIDS cases, four allow denial of coverage to group policy applicants because of HIV infection (Faden and Cass, 1988). There is every indication that insurance companies will continue to avail themselves of the opportunity to cancel policies of AIDS patients, if given the opportunity to avoid this "risk."

As persons with AIDS (PWAs) are excluded from private insurance coverage, the burden will fall increasingly upon the public sector and the Medicaid program. If 40 percent of the costs of treating HIV-related illnesses falls on Medicaid in the 1990s, it will consume 5 percent of the total budget.

To qualify for Medicaid, one must either be an AFDC or SSI recipient, or meet all the criteria except the income and asset maximum. PWAs meet federal qualifications for Supplementary Security Income (SSI), but must also qualify under state requirements: "Currently, all those with an AIDS diagnosis meeting the requirements established by the Centers for Disease Control are "presumptively disabled" and thus eligible for SSI. States typically impose income and asset maximums that govern qualification" (Pascal et al., 1989:94). States vary in eligibility criteria and in services provided—for example, reimbursement for AZT, hospice care, and such. The most generous states in terms of Medicaid benefits include California, Hawaii, Maine, Massachusetts, Michigan, New York, New Jersey, North Carolina, North Dakota, Ohio, South Dakota, Rhode Island, and Wisconsin (Pascal et al., 1989).

The average cost of treating a male Medicaid recipient with AIDS is about $75,000. In 1987 in the Michigan Medicaid program, there were twice as many men as women with the HIV infection, and their treatment costs about three times as much. The average cost of AZT treatment was $404.03 per month, or $4,848.36 on a yearly basis (Solomon, 1989).

In the latter stages of the disease, PWAs who come to nursing homes are young men who are homosexuals or intravenous drug users. They usually have only a few months to live and, as stated above, are very expensive to care for. PWAs place a great strain on most nursing homes, which lack the financial and staff capabilities to care for them. It is estimated that PWAs cost about three times as much as other patients in nursing homes (Kerschner, 1988). Therefore, nursing homes avoid the admission of PWAs if they are able to.

The potential future costs of AIDS and HIV infection are staggering, if projections are correct. And yet there is lack of agreement on these projections. For example, one study in California found that hospital expenditures for AIDS patients using Medicaid increased from 1982–83 but decreased in 1984. This decline in cost was attributed to several possible causes: more understanding of treatments and their usefulness, more use of local funding and volunteers, and a decrease in admissions of PWAs to save costs (Andrews, 1988).

As one researcher observes, "there is great uncertainty about the effects on cost of the changing nature of the HIV epidemic" (Scitovsky, 1989). Better data are needed to study the HIV epidemic. There is great need for studies on the cost of HIV-PWAs, support services available, and so on.

There is every indication that the cost of caring for persons with HIV-related illnesses will fall increasingly upon the U.S. taxpayer. It is simply easier for Congress to increase the Medicaid budget than to resist the private insurance lobby, which will fight for fewer regulations on exemptions for AIDS. As public policy, it makes sense to make private insurance bear its fair share of the costs of treating AIDS patients.

But the leadership for this initiative must come at the state level, where regulation of insurance policy occurs. At that level, state congresspersons are still under the pressure of the insurance lobby (and, in fact, many congresspersons are also in the insurance business). But the political will must be found at this level to say no to the insurance companies, and to avoid tax increases to expand the Medicaid program. The proper balance between equity and risk in insuring PWAs is found in a proper balance between private and public insurance coverage for the disease.

THE POOR, THE ELDERLY, AND INSURANCE COVERAGE

Insurance coverage for the poor is largely a public affair. The Medicaid program is a federal-state program of health care to the poor, and benefits under the program vary according to state regulations. In 14 states, only those who receive AFDC or SSI are eligible, while in the remaining states other rules govern eligibility. The federal government pays between 50 and 78 percent of the total cost, depending upon the state's per capita income (Cochran, 1990:279). It is estimated that only 45 percent of the poor receive Medicaid coverage. But within individual states, that percentage varies from 20 to 90 percent, as some states are more generous than others (Cochran, 1990:280). What about the remainder of the poor?

Much of the remainder consists of the "working poor"—those who work yet make below the Social Security Administration's standard for the poverty level. Surprisingly, a majority (60 percent) of the working poor have private health insurance coverage, but that coverage may be limited if policies are minimal. The remaining 40 percent of the working poor are largely ineligible for Medicaid and are unable to purchase private insurance. It is estimated that about 66 percent of the uninsured poor in America are among the working poor (Berk and Wilensky, 1987).

Fortunately, the lack of coverage for the working poor has not resulted in declining health. The working poor are at the same levels of health as the general population, and above the levels of health of the nonworking poor, according to a study conducted by the National Center for Health Statistics (1977). However, as this study is somewhat dated and the methodology for measuring health status is imprecise, consisting of perceived health status, activity limitation, and bed-restricted days (Berk and Wilensky, 1987), the results cannot be viewed as conclusive.

A large percentage of the Medicaid dollar goes to those who are genuinely unable to work. Nursing home care is financed largely through private payments (56 percent) and Medicaid (44 percent). Private insurance pays only 1 percent and Medicare only 2 percent. The average annual cost for nursing home care is $23,000, and patients must exhaust their own personal savings before they can qualify for Medicaid (Rovner et al., 1988).

What public policies are in the offing, particularly policies to aid the working poor? Senator Edward Kennedy is pushing for a bill based on the

Massachusetts law governing health care, which requires all but the smallest businesses to provide health insurance for their employees. President George Bush is reluctant to place such a burden on business and favors more conservative approaches to the problem. He proposes expansion of Medicaid benefits to more poor and near-poor women and children. Also, he favors a Medicaid-purchase program for the low-income, to allow them to receive Medicaid coverage for a modest price (Rovner et al., 1988). These appear to be stopgap measures to deal with immediate problems, without significantly increasing the cost of the program to government or business.

The insuring of the elderly is accomplished largely through the Medicare program. Medicare Part A is principally hospital insurance, which covers a wide range of services within and following a hospital visit, subject to limited deductibles and coinsurance. It is financed through the Social Security payroll tax (Cochran, 1990:277).

Medicare Part B pays for voluntary supplemental medical insurance, and the cost is so low (about $29 a month in 1989) that 98 percent of the elderly purchase it. It pays for physicians' services, outpatient hospital services, and other medical services (Cochran, 1990:277). In addition, many elderly purchase private insurance to supplement Medicare revenue.

The limited number who cannot afford to purchase Medicare Part B include the traditionally disadvantaged groups, those who have the following social characteristics: low income, low education, nonwhite, and single. Often, individuals in these groups are eligible for Medicaid, but only 44 percent of those who are poor and receive Medicare apply for Medicaid (Garfinkel et al., 1987). The elderly poor do not make full use of their Medicare benefits.

The total expenditures for Part A increased only 2 percent in FY (fiscal year) 1987, but outlays for Part B increased 10 percent for the same period. The success for limiting the growth of Part A expenditures is attributed largely to the success of prospective reimbursement at holding down hospital costs (Rovner et al., 1988). Prospective reimbursement provides for government reimbursement of hospital costs according to a prearranged schedule of prices for various services. The principal mechanism for accomplishing this is Diagnosis Related Groups, which is a scheme for classifying the costs of different services and procedures. Under the DRG program, government agrees to pay a certain price for particular surgical operations, or other medical services, but does not pay anything beyond that set cost. However, under the current system, physicians may charge patients above the Medicare limit and require payment from them for the difference. Thus, DRGs limit government expenditures, but they do not place a cap on private expenditures.

Currently, government is proposing mechanisms to limit the growth of Part B expenditures. One proposal is to narrow the gap in payments made to specialists in hospitals versus more general physicians, such as internists, who provide primary care. Regulation of these fees within the hospital would help to limit growth of expenditures. Another plan is to emulate the Canadian health care system, by imposing expenditure caps to control the price and volume of physician services. This would address the problem of physicians charging patients for costs above government reimbursement (Rovner et al., 1988). But such a plan would meet with significant resistance from the medical community. In the Canadian system, physicians were strongly opposed to expenditure caps, despite the fact that they were working under a national health insurance.

In sum, the elderly and the poor in the United States rely heavily on government programs to ensure health care. The principle of equity is dominant in this equation, because society has accepted the responsibility for caring for the poor and the elderly. The principle of risk comes into play only in the limited areas where private insurance has a role. Risk is not considered to be an acceptable value when discussing the welfare of those who are not earning a wage or cannot provide health care for themselves.

THE DISABLED AND INSURANCE COVERAGE

As the American population ages, it is plagued increasingly by chronic illness and disability. Most of the burden of paying for care is assumed by working people, through either private insurance contributions at work Federal Insurance Contribution Act deductions for Medicare, or taxes in support of Medicaid.

The burden assumed by private insurance companies is minimized by their unwillingness to assume great risk. Persons with certain chronic diseases or disabilities are considered high risks and are excluded altogether from insurance coverage. In a recent survey of insurance companies, 30 conditions were excluded from coverage, and most of them were chronic or disabling conditions (Fox, 1989).

Disabled persons are "often rejected by private insurers through medical underwriting criteria" or are discouraged from enrolling because insurance packages "limit the health related services they need most." Private insurers limit coverage by various methods: preexisting condition exclusions; by failing to cover certain equipment (e.g., wheelchairs); and by imposing deductibles and coinsurance (DeJong, 1989).

The alternative is public health insurance in the form of Medicare or Medicaid. It is easy enough for the elderly disabled to qualify for Medicare, but the working-disabled have greater difficulty. In a sense, they are discriminated against because of their ability to work and pay for private insurance, while being excluded from many forms of private insurance coverage.

One solution to this problem of the working disabled is a Medicaid buy-in program. For a modest fee, the working disabled would be able to qualify for the full benefits of Medicaid, without having to bankrupt themselves.

Another alternative would be to "mainstream" the disabled, instead of "targeting" them as a group for special consideration. One obvious method of mainstreaming the disabled is to enact a form of national health insurance, which would treat all citizens equally. Still another method is to require insurance companies to offer broader coverage through regulation. Then, the working disabled would be able to purchase their insurance along with other employees at work. This solution would place greater burdens upon insurance companies, and possibly on the disabled themselves, with higher deductibles and coinsurance.

Part of the problem in insuring the disabled lies in the cost of treatment, which is generally high. In most hospitals, the highest cost patients include those with AIDS, mental illness, or long-term chronic diseases. It has been suggested that better case management might help reduce the cost of treatment, but evidence suggests that it is not cost-effective in the short run. Case management is supposed to reduce costs by coordinating services to help patients, but the administrative overhead is higher and, hence, may be more costly in the short run (Henderson et al., 1988). But it may prove to be the solution in the long run, as services to the chronically ill become more complex and expensive.

Treatment of the disabled is complicated by the status of "rehabilitation medicine" in the medical community, where it has been limited by a lack of respect. It is controlled by orthopedic surgeons and physical therapy physicians, who do not enjoy high status among their colleagues. The organization of the medical profession, as well as the incentives provided by private insurance that reflect prevalent medical values, do not reward physicians who treat the disabled, or the patients themselves.

There is a further complication in that the disabled often desire to control their own rehabilitation services. The disabled believe that they have a unique understanding of their condition and of their needs and desire to have input into the rehabilitation process. This makes decisions and control by physicians more problematic (Berkowitz, 1989).

A surprising number of disabling conditions involve mental disability. In a recent study of Medicaid expenditures in California, Georgia, Michigan, and Tennessee, it was found that 37–58 percent of all expenditures were for SSI disabling conditions involving mental disability. Higher expenditures matched higher numbers of enrollees, and not higher expenditures per enrollee (the most expensive conditions were neoplasms and blood disorders). Mental disorders were a higher source of expenditure than mental retardation. The enrollees tended to be younger and, hence, unable to qualify for Medicare (Adams et al., 1989).

An important issue in providing care to the mentally disabled is the most cost-efficient method, as government must assume the lion's share of the burden. Private-sector contracting for mental health services is a relatively recent development, but it has the potential to provide more efficient and effective services. A recent article (Frank and Goldman, 1989) concludes that there is no optimal strategy for delivery of services, but that a flexible approach is needed. Competitive bidding for mental health services from private sources works best when markets are competitive and performance can be monitored. Contracting within government, or direct service provision, is better if markets are not competitive and performance is difficult to monitor. A voucher system may be best when patients are living with families or are geographically dispersed.

Coverage for alcohol and drug treatment has lagged behind coverage for other illnesses, because of the social stigma attached to the illness. But, by the end of 1985, 35 states required alcohol treatment coverage, or at least the option, and 18 required drug abuse treatment coverage in insurance policies. The only apparent restriction on the development of this form of coverage is the fact that self-insurance by companies exempts them from having to provide this coverage (Morrisey and Jensen, 1988).

Insuring the disabled is a combined public-private effort, but the greatest burden falls upon the public sector. Private insurance is helpful in protecting the working disabled, but insurance companies are placing more burden on those who are insured, with higher deductibles and coinsurance. As medical costs rise, the disabled are paying more for the same quality of care. And some of the disabled are simply excluded from private insurance coverage altogether by their conditions. The public sector must find better ways to control costs of care for the disabled, without diluting the quality of service. That will be a great challenge in the future, given the aging U.S. population and growth among the ranks of the disabled.

CONCLUSIONS

The health care industry was not called an industry 25 years ago (Miller, 1988). Since the advent of Medicare and Medicaid, health care has developed into a complex partnership between the public and private sectors. This relationship became more complicated with the advent of corporate medicine, in the form of group practice, HMOs, Preferred Payer Organizations, and other organizations. These new organizations created more competition within the health industry, with the promise of more efficient delivery of services.

Today, the American health care system is faced with an age-old problem. How does it care for those who are sick yet who are unable to afford their own medical care? The Medicare and Medicaid programs were designed to meet that need, but evidence clearly demonstrates that many poor, disabled, and chronically ill people fall between the cracks in the system. If they do receive care, a large number do so at great personal expense relative to their incomes.

Government regulation at the state level places some pressure on insurance companies to provide coverage, but that pressure is not sufficient to help all of those in need. There are many with AIDS, many who are poor, elderly, or disabled who can neither afford private insurance nor qualify for government benefits. Many must qualify by experiencing personal bankruptcy, and all of the indignities that accompany that condition, in order to qualify for Medicaid.

Our system of health care attempts to balance the insurance principles of risk and equity. The private insurance industry assumes risk and attempts to maximize profits by wisely choosing only acceptable risks. It cannot be blamed for attempting to minimize risks, for that is the lifeblood of the profession. But, at the same time, companies have public responsibilities to behave in ways that are morally acceptable to society. Companies must balance the profit motive with social responsibility. In the insurance industry, this means accepting certain risks that may not be profitable for the sake of conscience and good public policy. In other words, some degree of equity is required to maintain a reasonable policy with regard to coverage.

The public sector must concern itself primarily with equity, in terms of providing health care to all citizens. Most industrialized nations throughout the world have a national health insurance system, which provides universal coverage to all citizens. The United States is one of the few nations without such a system. Instead, we have a "segmented" system, in which government provides for certain segments of the population who are unable to provide for their own health services. Government programs take care of the poor, the elderly, and the veterans. It is assumed that other citizens are able to care for themselves.

Data indicate that American citizens do not have equal access to care, and that our segmented system overlooks many who need care or help in financing care. This has become even more of a problem as the cost of health care has risen. This is not just a problem in the United States, but is a worldwide problem. However, it is a special problem in the United States because cutbacks on costs are not cutbacks from a universal system of coverage, but from a segmented system. Citizens are already underserved by our system, and future cutbacks will threaten most those who can least afford treatment. From a public policy standpoint, this is unacceptable.

There are several solutions to the problem. Unfortunately, most of them are difficult to achieve and painful to some segment of the health care industry. One solution is to require insurance companies to assume more of the burden by state regulations protecting disadvantaged groups: the poor, disabled, and chronically ill, including AIDS patients. Another is to require companies who self-insure employees to conform to the same regulations to which private insurance companies must conform. Still another solution is to provide extended coverage through a Medicaid buy-in program.

The ultimate solution is to adopt a system of national health insurance.

150 Health Insurance and Public Policy

This would require significant public support as well as support (or acqui-
escence) from the medical community. But, with the rising cost of U.S. care
relative to nations with national health insurance, that option becomes more
probable.

REFERENCES

Adams, E. Kathleen et al. 1989. "Utilization and Expenditures under Medicaid for
Supplemental Security Disabled." *Health Care Financing Review* 11(1):1–
24.
Andrews, Roxanne. 1988. "Acquired Immunodeficiency Syndrome in California's
Medicaid Program, 1981–84." *Health Care Financing Review* 10(1):95–103.
Berk, Marc and Gail Wilensky. 1987. "Health Coverage of the Working Poor."
Social Science and Medicine 25(11):1183–87.
Berkowitz, Edward. 1989. "Allocating Resources for Rehabilitation: A Historical
and Ethical Framework." *Social Science Quarterly* 70(1):40–52.
Cochran, Clarke et al. 1990. *American Public Policy: An Introduction*, 3rd ed. New
York: St. Martin's Press.
DeJong, Gerben. 1989. "America's Neglected Minority: Working-Age Persons with
Disabilities." *The Milbank Quarterly* 76:311–51, Supplement 2, Part 2.
Economist, The. 1988. "The AIDS Clause." July 22: 14.
Faden, Ruth and Nancy Kass. 1988. "Health Insurance and AIDS: The Status of
State Regulatory Activity." *American Journal of Public Health* 78(4):437–
38.
Fox, Daniel. 1989. "Policy and Epidemiology: Financing Health Services for the
Chronically Ill and Disabled, 1930–1990." *The Milbank Quarterly* 67:257–
87, Supplement 2, Part 2.
Frank, Richard and Harry Goldman. 1989. "Financing Care of the Severely Mentally
Ill: Incentives, Contracts and Public Responsibility." *Journal of Social Issues*
45(3):131–44.
General Accounting Office. 1990a. *Reports and Testimony.* "Health Insurance: Cost
Increases Lead to Coverage Limitations and Cost Shifting." Washington, DC:
GAO, May.
———. 1990b. *Reports and Testimony.* "Health Insurance: A Profile of the Un-
insured in Michigan and the United States." Washington, DC: GAO, May.
Garfinkel, Steven et al. 1987. "Socioeconomic Factors and Medicare Supplemental
Health Insurance." *Health Care Financing Review* 9(1):21–30.
Health Care Financing Review. 1978. "National Health Expenditures, 1986–2000."
Summer 8(4):1–36.
Hellinger, Fred. 1990. "Updated Forecasts of the Costs of Medical Care for Persons
with AIDS, 1989–93." *Public Health Reports* 105(1):1–12.
Henderson, Mary et al. 1988. "Private Sector Initiates in Case Management." *Health
Care Financing Review*, Annual Supplement: 89–95.
Jensen, Gail et al. 1987. "Cost Sharing and the Changing Pattern of Employer-
Sponsored Health Benefits." *The Milbank Quarterly* 65:521–50.
Kerschner, Paul. 1988. "Caring for Persons with AIDS in Geriatric Nursing Homes."
Health and Social Work 13(2):156–58.

Lee, Robert. 1989. "Insurance and Medical List Prices." *Journal of Human Resources* 24(4):689–708.

Leichter, H. and H. Rodgers. 1984. *American Public Policy in a Comparative Contest.* New York: McGraw-Hill.

Miller, Frances. 1988. "Vertical Restraints and Powerful Health Insurers: Exclusionary Conduct Masquerading as Managed Care?" *Law and Contemporary Problems* 51(2):195–236.

Morrisey, Michael and Gail Jensen. 1988. "Employee Sponsored Coverage for Alcoholism and Drug-Abuse Treatment." *Journal of Studies on Alcohol.* 49(5):456–61.

Muzychenko, Jay. 1986. "Where Did All the Insurance Go?" *Public Management* 68(11):3–5.

Pascal, Anthony et al. 1989. "State Policies and the Financing of Acquired Immunodeficiency Syndrome Care." *Health Care Financing Review* 11(1):91–104.

Pauly, Mark. 1988. "Competition in Health Insurance Markets." *Law and Contemporary Problems* 51(2):237–72.

Rovner, Julie et al. 1988. "Legislative Outlook: Bush, Congress Face Some Familiar Problems." *Congressional Quarterly Weekly Report*, December 24:3569–71.

Scitovsky, Anne. 1989. "Studying the Cost of HIV-Related Illnesses: Reflections on the Moving Target." *The Milbank Quarterly* 67(2):318–44.

Solomon, David. 1989. "Analysis of Michigan Medicaid Costs to Treat HIV Infection." *Public Health Reports* 104(5):416–24.

10

The Codification of Compassion: Impact of DRGs on Hospital Performance

Miriam K. Mills

INTRODUCTION

The traditional view within the health industry has been that the interest of the patient or client is the key concern of the field. This view has now become adapted to state that the interest of the patient or client is paramount, but within defined fiscal constraints. In 1965 Medicare was established, representing a significant change in the financing of health care. In 1983 another important modification was enacted: Congress approved a system of prospective payments for hospital inpatient services, whereby hospitals received a fixed sum per case according to a preestablished schedule of Diagnosis Related Groups (DRGs). The hospital economically benefits when the patient's stay is within the low range (in this case, 4 to 9 days) and loses when the stay falls in the high range. Once the hospital stay exceeds the day outlier limit or trimpoint, the hospital is reimbursed on a per diem basis according to a formula devised by HCFA (Maurer, 1987). The program that began in October 1983 has been phased in over a four-year period. The goal was to stem the rise in hospital costs, promote the financial solvency of New Jersey's hospitals, and to maintain if not improve the quality of care delivered throughout the state (Wasserman, 1985).

The data used to calculate the rates were published in September 1983 as part of the interim final regulations. The implications for most hospital services is to put greater emphasis on reduced hospital length of stay, increased outpatient care, increased productivity, and much more detailed documentation and accounting, which is now expedited through the use of technology (Davis, 1984).

In their most favorable definition, DRGs combine to provide a clinically coherent breakdown of patient classification. These are related to the hospital's case mix of resource availability and costs experienced. These DRGs are based on the principal diagnosis, secondary diagnosis, type of surgical intervention, age, and discharge status. Hospitals ideally can begin to have a better grasp of the costs incurred and benefits to be realized by the services anticipated. The initial design was clear. Norms for various illnesses could be established, as well as time schedules for discharge. Sophisticated data collection and analysis were made possible by computers. One might question whether perhaps the zeal for accuracy in data may call for greater investments in recording equipment, rather than in curative technology. "The system has been praised widely for its payer equity, an awkward term used to stand for the principle of equal prices charged for treating clinically similar cases" (Wasserman, 1985).

When unions first entered health facilities, there was anxiety and apprehension that the power shift from administration and medicine to subordinate health professionals would have dire consequences for patient care. Perhaps it was the exposure and familiarity that has now persuaded some administrators that this intrusion ultimately became an opportunity for better management. So, too, DRGs can be regarded as onerous record keeping or an opportunity for organizational efficiency. If anything, DRGs are steadily beginning to make the practice of medicine considerably more of a science than an art, requiring the practitioner to state his or her diagnosis swiftly, and then to definitively assign a treatment plan that will conform to norms for the particular sequence of illnesses. For many hospitals, failure to monitor costs and plan judiciously could well lead to their demise.

One thing is certain. This method of reimbursement has done much to foster organizational interaction between physicians and administrators within hospitals. It may also well have the secondary impact of accelerating the trend toward full-time salaried service chiefs within community hospitals. Most significant, from the physician's point of view, is that this financing mechanism now permits, almost compels, intense scrutiny of physician activities, not always a welcome benefit to some practitioners (Vladeck, 1984).

Hospitals can now compare their data with the standard for the average hospitals in their own peer group. Whether they are major teaching, minor teaching, or nonteaching, variations can be established between a hospital's cost and length-of-stay performance. Failure to meet the standard becomes an indicator of potential organizational problems. President Bush (1988) has said "the less that government is involved in the day-to-day administration of the health care system, the more efficiently it will run...I am skeptical of regulatory schemes that could have the unintended effect of lowering the quality of health." Cost and performance are inevitably linked together.

IMPACTS OF DRGs ON HOSPITAL ORGANIZATION

Administration

Hospitals will see their roles becoming more like a chief operating officer in a corporation. There will be increased staffing in the administrative units of large hospitals to deal with the negative impact of DRGs and to bring about a happy reunion of medicine and management (Mehra, 1981b). What is called for here is a more reasonable long-term evaluation of cost effectiveness. DRGs are not static. They change over time. As education permits more preventive action, some illnesses may be diagnosed earlier and, thus, not require as much intervention at a later and more costly stage.

The DRG system has provided hospital management with an incentive to restructure its practices. It also provides important data for both administrators and physicians to identify, analyze, and monitor superfluous or inefficient patient care services. The array of such data permits more accurate and precise decisions. Administrators have been obliged to go to extraordinary lengths to minimize the costs of direct patient care, while still making efforts to preserve quality. Questions were raised about the necessity for specific services, for admissions, for overlong stays, for overtesting and excessive treatment. Slowly, these questions will begin to narrow the discretionary powers of health professionals who formerly were able to rely upon justification of performance solely on the basis of expert opinion.

Long-standing committees now have even greater influence and impact. Utilization review monitors length of stay. The laboratory committees examine suspected overutilization of laboratory tests. What was formerly regarded as defensive medicine with extraneous efforts taken to fend off potential malpractice suits now becomes more limited. Transfusion committees monitor blood, and cardiologists review the use of pacemakers.

Many hospitals have found it appropriate to establish new organizational positions to supervise the DRG process. Such positions normally are instrumental in developing, coordinating, and integrating revenue and cost-related activities of the patient management system. This position can be said to close the gap between the clinical and administrative financial sectors. Data processing capabilities of medical records and finance departments are now developed for maximum compatability.

If nothing else, a DRG has come to require collaboration between clinical, financial, and administrative sectors of the hospital. While this has always been an ideal of the health industry, now the penalties for failure to establish this responsible triad can have detrimental effects on hospital fiscal stability.

Overall patterns of care in public as well as private hospitals can be differentiated. Although about half of the 20 most prevalent DRGs are similar in both institutions, there are still clear case mix differences. The higher percentage of abortion, psychiatric, and chemical dependence discharges and the lower prevalence of surgery in public hospitals contribute to the difference. In New York's Health and Hospital Corporation, (HHC), for example, the caseload is more concentrated in fewer DRGs. HHC hospitals treat more patients in DRGs with shorter lengths of stay, but on the average, patients in the same DRG stay more than a day longer. To some extent, this long length of stay can be explained by differences in payer type, primary diagnosis within a DRG, and, most important, in the percentage of outlier patients. There tend to be greater problems of discharge planning for unaffiliated urban individuals who may not be able to have familial resources available to them. Thus, the constraints on administrators, no matter how cautious, will, to a large extent, be modified by the setting. Further refinement and adjustment of DRGs and case mix within such different locations will yet have to be achieved (Schwartz, Merrill, and Blake, 1984).

Hospital care for the poor and medically indigent (i.e., people who are not considered to be impoverished in the general sense, but are unable to meet their medical expenses) were paid for by a variety of sources. State Medicaid programs, charitable gifts, charges to other payers, and care provided by public hospitals all contributed to meeting the health care needs of those who were not in a position to pay for the medical goods and services they required. The consequence of this was to create high deficits in those hospitals that refused to turn the poor away from their doors. Large increases in hospital care prices have brought the question to a boil now. The patchwork system of responsibility for the care makes it too easy for people to fall through the cracks. This includes economic recession, declines in private insurance coverage, Medicaid cutbacks, and limits on the growth of government spending.

Physicians

Clearly, the physician is key to any management strategies geared toward cost containment. Since the medical record is the source of the patient characteristics required to assign a person to a DRG, a complete and accurate record is necessary to assure a valid DRG classification for each patient. While this is the prime responsibility of the physician, this function cannot be carried out without a strongly developed medical record department.

Some physicians may argue that DRGs do not satisfy basic management controls or principles. They contend that a more appropriate hospital control system would have physicians directly incorporated into the hospital's management structure. To ensure that the new control system is medically and financially appropriate, some have argued that physicians must seize the initiative in determining the standards against which their performance will be measured. While peer review has always existed, as well as the in-house tissue committee and utilization reviews, now performance is being monitored and communicated by nonphysicians, surely an unwelcome proposition (Young and Saltman, 1982).

Most physicians are unaware of the cost effect of their patient management decisions. In fact, such considerations have always appeared somewhat callous or unfeeling. Cardiologists and pacemaker surgeons become cruelly aware of the significant price differentials among pulse generators in reviewing costs for DRG 116, implementation of permanent pacemakers. (An ironic observation made during early moon flight days was that it was reassuring for the astronauts to know they were being transported to the outer regions of space by the lowest bidder.) Cost is a curious thing. In the abstract, no one supports excessive expense. In the individual case, however, one prefers to see no expense avoided if it could make the smallest difference in curative impact. Hospitals have come to recognize that it is the physicians' behavior that is the key determinant of the costs and quality of hospital care. Supervision and monitoring have to be rigid enough to permit hospital survival, but not so stern that they discourage effective physicians from practicing at the institution altogether.

The profits appear to have resulted from several factors: the success demonstrated by hospitals in controlling costs; a dramatic reduction in the length of hospital stays, perhaps in some cases reflecting premature discharge of patients; and projections used in setting the Medicare payment system. Under the DRG system, a hospital can retain the surplus payment if the costs of treating a patient are less than the reimbursement from government. The American Hospital Association (AHA) maintains that the hospitals must earn a surplus if they are to be protected against unpredictable fluctuations in revenue from other sources. Further, the AHA argues that Congress provided an opportunity for hospitals to earn a surplus in the hopes that they would become more efficient and productive. "It would be patently unfair to penalize them for responding to those incentives" (*Rhode Island Medical Journal*, 1987).

While physicians are the key component of cost containment, they are also the ones with the most to lose from this rigorous examination of their practices. Accurate, timely physician documentation of all diagnoses and procedures is essential. In many cases, this may call for a reeducation of physicians. There will be occasions when more teamwork is called for between individual medical practitioners. For one example, DRG 165 has created such discussion with respect to the clinical findings during the operative procedure as opposed to the pathological findings of the specimen submitted. The surgeon may record the principal diagnosis as acute appendicitis, if there is no clinical evidence of peritonitis. However, the pathologist must record peritonitis if there is a break in the mucosal wall of the intestine. It is the responsibility of the physician to document this complication, as stated by the pathologist, of the acute appendicitis. The difference between the two DRGs represents a financial loss to the hospital of $1,000 per patient.

The principal diagnosis by the physician determines the major diagnostic category. The various secondary diagnoses can impact DRG assignment if they are classified as substantial complications. Each complication is coded by the Medical Records Department, and computer software—such as GROUPER—automatically looks at the most resource-intensive diagnosis in the assignment process. Here again, if there are incomplete listings of seconding diagnoses or procedure, there may well be a negative impact upon the classification.

There are some devilish capabilities to software in this area. Some researchers have been able to predict acute care hospital bed needs based upon physician characteristics. Ratios of physician inpatient activity by specialty from one age decade to the next were computed from the researchers' data base of 1.2 percent of all admitting physicians (Hughes, Daley, and Patterson, 1983). Physicians now become quite vulnerable to observation, not only of individual cases, but to overall performance. The various individual segments of judgment get woven together and become the criteria for total judgment. What is worse, from the physician's point of view, is that he or she may well be judged against the anticipation of what their performance is supposed to be, based on their demographic profile. There may, indeed, be real problems involved in securing the wholehearted participation of physicians, if there is too relentless a scrutiny of their behavior.

Nurses

One of the major underestimated forces within hospitals is the vital contribution of nurses toward facilitating the greater self-sufficiency of patients and their ability to fend for themselves outside of the hospital environment. While the physician establishes the diagnosis, it is the full spectrum of nursing care planning that can make the difference between a timely or delayed discharge.

Nursing administrators are obliged to deal with effectively working within set reimbursement limits. Nurses are encouraged to utilize the unique aspects of prospective pricing in a program that maintains professionalism while improving bottom-line outcomes. Thus, the degree to which nursing administration can portray itself as being a profit center rather than a cost center, so much stronger will be its negotiating position vis-a-vis management. Patients can be released only when they have the understanding and ability to fend for themselves. It is this educational component of nursing that will do much to permit the hospital to remain within its constraints. Determining nursing costs and revenues by diagnosis can be a method to validate both the cost effectiveness of a nursing staff and a high professional standard of practice (Olsen, 1984).

Patients

Not to be overlooked in this overview of DRG impacts is the patient. Preadmission testing and patient education become important components in eliciting patient cooperation. The patient needs to be able to plan for discharge as soon as he or she is admitted. The patient needs to have a clearer understanding about early discharge and the resulting effects on reduced length of stay. More important, the patient needs the supportive rehabilitation and guidance to continue the curative process after discharge. The goodwill of patients can easily be undermined if there is precipitous and insensitive urging of them to the exit. A proper balance needs to be struck between meeting the hospital's needs for cost containment and the patient's emotional well-being that they are not being discharged before they are emotionally ready. Much of the discussion has been focused on measuring cost and documenting excesses. Not to be lost in this review is the sense of satisfaction that the patients must feel, that they have received considerate care, that they will be able to manage for themselves, and that their needs are not subordinated to fiscal solvency alone. Hospital administration needs to develop strong general public education so that the various constituencies understand the restraints placed on hospitals under the new payment system.

The diminishing prohibitions against medical advertising also serve a salutary effect. The removal of these impediments permits, it is hoped, informed patient choice. This unfettered dissemination of advertising has not been uniformly applauded.

There was fear that advertising would reduce the health professions' status to that of a trade, while others despaired that the advertisers among us with their ridiculous claims of superiority or gimmickry are coming out of the woodwork. Whether these fears are overstated will not be known for several years (Cole, 1984).

NEW MEASURES OF PERFORMANCE

Economy

Now more than ever before, hospitals are obliged to quantify the costs of operation. Traditionally, many hospital costs were allocated to patients using indirect measures that did not always reflect the value of the resources used to provide care. Costs are generally allocated by multiplying the patient's charges by the hospital's ratio of costs to charges. Yet this allocated cost does not reflect actual cost because the hospital does not uniformly charge for services in proportion to their cost. The choice of method for cost allocation will be quite important for the newly developed case mix cost accounting systems. Hospitals will have to develop ever more inventive ways of truly isolating charges. Thus, quantification of what was before a rather fuzzy idea now becomes critical. As noted earlier, hours of nursing care per diagnosis begin to tap the concept of true allocation. It also has the happy side benefit of indicating precisely which area has generated what portion of profits retained (Williams et al., 1982).

All functions within the hospital now become focused upon supporting the DRG system. Medical records, utilization review, quality assurance, discharge coordinators, and others now become vital components of the new emphasis on economy. Hospital management needs to monitor operational costs frequently and compare to prior years. The emphasis turns to cost per admission rather than cost per patient day. Another economic factor is the start-up costs of changing into the prospective payment mode. One begins to look for those forms of treatment, medication, and support services that will yield the most effective result most economically. The range of choices is now considerably circumscribed because of the many observation sites that now begin to monitor almost every aspect of the hospital operation. A hospital's success is now measured by its fiscal austerity rather than predominantly by its technological innovation. These trade-offs will be considered in the section dealing with some of the unintended consequences of this new financial emphasis.

The Health Care Financing Administration, which developed this system of patient reimbursement limit setting, had built upon the quantification of hospital case mix through the AUTOGRP DRGs developed at Yale. The reliability of the method was dependent on diagnosis.

One experiment examined the billing data for a large teaching hospital with respect to medical records data. In that instance, data were evaluated based on the diagnosis and procedure codes and on the DRG groupings used by HCFA. Concurrent and retrospective data were found to be widely divergent on both measures. An apparent difference in complexity of extent of resource use was noted. This suggests that the data being used in the HCFA's development may not have fully represented the level of complexity of cases being treated and that reimbursement based on those data may not be completely accurate. As experience with use of the DRG mechanism continues, there will undoubtedly be greater disagreements with the norms against which institutional economics are measured (Barnard and Esmond, 1981).

One wonders if the cost of these added layers of bureaucracy will exceed the medical saving. The present method of in-hospital concurrent review, combined with a retrospective review, would accomplish much more at less expense than the arbitrary DRG system. Physicians could then return to a system that stresses finding the proper treatment and care for their patients, rather than the current quest for finding the diagnosis with the highest rate of DRG reimbursement.

The central theme is that the hospital should locate money-losing DRGs and either make them cost-effective or find ways to deemphasize them from its operations in this respect. Cost-effectiveness should be a hospital-wide goal and should not be confined only to certain measures. A profit-making DRG and a cost-effective DRG may not have much correlation at all. A cost-effective DRG would eventually turn profitable for the hospital in the long run (Mehra, 1986).

Efficiency

Too earnest attention to economy might result in a case where the health team in a poor urban hospital might also argue that the costs and demands of professional time would be better utilized for other patients who might be restored to health. This is in relationship to the problem of total parenteral nutrition, which might provide but slight benefit to a terminal patient (Mehra, 1986).

Some consideration should be given to the concept of marginal cost, which is the additional cost incurred for an additional unit of output. The importance of health care organizations knowing marginal costs in a DRG environment will increase due to greater competition and falling occupancy and payment rates. "The marginal cost of the case is an extremely valuable tool. It allows hospitals to assess the impact of relatively small changes in case loads" (Marty, Bridges, and Jacobs, 1986). Although marginal cost estimates have been used in reimbursement for some time, little is known about how marginal costs vary across DRGs. Such information would allow hospitals to better assess the financial impact of expanding or contracting in specific areas.

Efficiency becomes a relevant secondary factor. All components of hospital care need to be cautiously interlocked so that no oversight results in burdensome costs. Thus, greater demand for efficiency are made on those departments who did not previously have such significant impact in the financial health of the hospital. Social service was always involved in discharge planning, and it was, parenthetically, for many social workers one of the least desirable aspects of their work. Medical records now have to precisely monitor the medical diagnoses to make sure that the sequence of diagnoses is so organized as to generate the best hospital reimbursement. Utilization review is now charged with the responsibility of closely monitoring utilization patterns and reporting deviations to upper management.

While the DRG system provides hospital administrators with a strong economic incentive to curtail the amounts of resources used to treat individual cases, it does not follow that this will cause quality of care to decline. In fact, decreases in the quantity of care offered may lead to quality improvements by reducing the chances of iatrogenic illnesses through cutbacks in length of stay, unnecessary tests and procedures, and so on. Quality of care may be further enhanced if the system is successful in stimulating hospitals to specialize in treating particular types of cases, since there is convincing data that suggest there is a positive relationship between quality of care and volume of cases treated (Wasserman, 1985).

The concern for efficiency also causes the hospital to look for less costly alternatives of skilled manpower. A congressional study of health care for the elderly, for example, concluded that one important goal should be to encourage the use of more nurse practitioners and physician's assistants to perform routine procedures that do not require a physician's expertise (Molotsky, 1984). The question now posed by hospitals is what is the least professional, and hence most economical, level of care that can be provided that gets the job done. Up to now, the cost of procedures was determined by the level of the practitioner. Thus, if a nurse did temperature, pulse, and respiration, that was more costly than having a nursing aide do so. Yet, with proper training, the results of that activity performed by an aide would be equivalent. DRG should propel the movement of shifting tasks down the occupational ladder to where it can be done most efficiently and economically.

Other proposals that have been made to reduce the cost of care and also to improve the efficiency include discouraging physician specialization and urging more to enter family practice. Now for those with obscure ailments that urgently require the need of distinct specialties, this is not a welcome proposal. Yet, in the larger picture, more are served more economically by having all-purpose physicians, rather than specialists whose additional training and need for supportive technology increase their charges.

Another proposal has been to emphasize the delivery of more treatment in smaller facilities and reducing the proportions done at large complex medical centers. Again, this will ultimately lead to the increased cost of care in the major medical centers, because they will be left with the most costly DRG groupings that could not receive care elsewhere.

Equity

This payer equity is really misleading because the true equity is to arrive at a state of health. The person frequently does not have control over which ailments he or she will present and is concerned more for the specific costs of the care received, rather than the fact that the cost for tonsillectomy is the same as for someone else's tonsillectomy.

One has to question the wisdom and rationale for requiring those who are without insurance, and perhaps just barely being able to meet their own bills, to assume a share of the costs incurred by indigent patients and/or patients who choose not to pay their bills, even through they are able to afford them. The idea of renegade bill payment avoiders is a kind of straw person. When the outcomes have been good, I would suspect that those who could afford to, would pay. What is more likely is that when the outcomes have been negative, those who are marginally able to pay choose not to. The American marketing system tends to suggest that people receive satisfaction for their expenditures in the products they purchase. The reluctant bill payer may, in fact, be saying that since the outcomes were not as expected, she or he has no obligation. Perhaps we need to reemphasize the point that there are costs incurred that must be paid, even when the outcomes are not as one would wish.

All payers can potentially suffer a loss in terms of higher charges if the system causes an increase in the overall caseload. Although it may be an intended and socially desirable effect, if the system succeeded in improving access to care for the medically indigent, it is entirely possible that concomitantly the program may reduce the level of rigor that hospitals apply to their debt collection efforts. This, in turn, may prompt people to question the need to purchase appropriate insurance coverage, which will exacerbate the problems of the bad debt.

In an increasingly competitive health care environment, business and consumer groups are likely to use information to steer prospective patients to those providers with comparatively low uncompensated care cost factors built into their rates.

The more prosperous suburban hospitals that tend to have less uncompensated care are already having individuals steered to them. The needy or marginal hospitals that would benefit from a mix of perhaps more elective surgery, as compared to emergency surgery, are already finding that they receive the more difficult cases with the poorer patients.

UNINTENDED CONSEQUENCES OF DRG

With any major change in reporting activities within an institution, there are bound to be a number of unexpected impacts. These can range from an overemphasis on quantification to the discouragement of technological innovation. The most frequent criticisms leveled against the DRG system are that it is unduly complex, and that there was inadequate analysis prior to implementation. In addition, the system has generally been fairly inflexible in adjusting for varied service utilization patterns of patients covered by different payers. The impact on insured patients has also not been fully assessed.

Technology Trade-offs

Given the severe penalties to the hospital for inaccurate or incomplete information, greater emphasis has been placed on computerized data information systems. These costly software programs generate information regarding problematic patient care decisions. Such expenditure choices will inevitably curtail expending for more sophisticated diagnostic equipment, where the cost-benefit ratio may not be as favorable. The concern for measuring the activity rendered may begin to undercut resources for the activity itself.

One study has examined the impact of rate-setting regulation on technology, and it was indeed found that such regulation did reduce the prevalence in the late 1970s and early 1980s. That study cites findings that new health care technology is frequently a major cause of rising medical expenditures. Regulation of investment in medical technology has been justified on the grounds that hospitals have incentives to overinvest in technology. The training and preferences of physicians, the competitive positions of hospitals, and the third-party payment system allegedly jointly facilitate overinvestment (Fuangchen and McCaffrey, 1984).

It was developments in medical education that permitted the expansion of specialty training. These specialties, in turn, began to call for more sophisticated technology for both diagnosis and treatment. The technology examined by the researchers included CT scanners, cobalt therapy, inpatient hemodialysis, and open-heart surgery. The variables represented the number of hospitals in the state in a given year using such technology. The greater emphasis on cost accounting may well cause limits in the use of complex treatment modes.

Precision versus Hunches

Indecision as to prime diagnosis is penalized. The physician will have to precisely make his or her diagnosis so as to avoid costly repercussions. Yet sometimes intuitive hunches can give the key insights for dealing with a specific malady. The physician is now obliged to get the patient out as fast as possible. His or her thoughts can now be directed as much to cost as to care, and delay is too costly to support. There has been a kind of schism between the general societal view that health care is too costly as contrasted to the personal view that no cost should be spared in dealing with an individual case. One would vastly prefer an uncertain diagnosis with time to consider alternative forms of treatment rather than to be faced with a definitive conclusion that is reached prematurely because of penalties for delay. There are also differences between the layperson's conventional impression that physicians are paid too much to the individual view that good physicians performing risky procedures should be appropriately compensated.

One may have certain hunches about outliers, but they should be checked against medical review of outliers. This is informative for evaluating the quality of hospital care. There are four ways that a patient becomes classified as an outlier: (1) miscoded record, (2) undetected clinical signs could explain the pattern of resource use, (3) administrative medical mismanagement could result in prolonged treatment (this includes failure to schedule tests in a timely fashion or process them), (4) a patient could be a true outlier who doesn't fit the normal pattern (McMahon, 1984).

There is extensive new technology available that, coupled with pharmaceutical research and findings in biomedical research, has led to a more profound understanding of disease processes. In earlier years, the federal government under Hill Burton legislation supported hospital construction and increased bed capacity so as to upgrade medical care. Today, with strains on the economy, hospitals are forced to change to ambulatory, low-tech services making the increasing improvement of health care questionable. This is not to suggest that only high tech can make the difference, but the current cost emphasis tends to bring the total system back to an earlier era of care. The familiar general practitioner, the distrust for technology, the underlying suspicion that some were profiting excessively have led to what can be regarded as an overemphasis on cost.

As the costs of the American health care system escalate, there is a tendency to identify the biggest cost item and attempt to reduce it to a manageable size. However, since that biggest cost item, the hospital, is a creation of uncontrolled forces within the system as a whole, attempts to manage costs will be limited in effectiveness. The hospital is the end product of an uncontrolled system, a product that displays little understanding of the economic principles of tradeoff, efficiency, and productivity. To limit spending in the hospital care system, controls must be rooted in an analysis of the forces that have shaped the hospital's present form and structure (Reilly and Legge, 1982).

Science versus Art

One expects the physician of today who functions within the DRG environment to make cost-effective decisions. His or her ability is measured by the clarity of the budgetary choices. Codification becomes the byword. Where the boundaries become somewhat fuzzy within DRGs is in the area of mental illness. Under the new DRGs, 15 of the 467 DRGs cover mental disorders. Some observers have found them insufficiently homogeneous within categories. Variables such as age, marital status, and type of treatment can dramatically impact on diagnosis (Taube, Lee, and Forthofer, 1984).

Decision processes of the physician become subject to greater scrutiny. The medications prescribed, the length of hospitalization, the procedures used are all evaluated against rigorous norms. Variation in performance is discouraged so that the great golden mean can be sustained. This tends to minimize the creative leaps of insight that earlier physicians may have espoused.

Implicit in the data generated for fiscal purposes is that the same material can also be used for monitoring physician performance. The erstwhile inviolability of physicians' autonomy from the review of nonphysicians has now become seriously challenged by a greater reliance on codification.

In considering the DRG reimbursement patterns, there is a demand for greater system sensitivity. Not all patients should be charged the same payment rate. As there are shifts within the intra-DRG, mechanisms should exist to cover them. Yet the emphasis on rapid quantification tends to undermine the need for greater responsiveness to real-life situations.

Codified Compassion

The underlying assumption is that all wish to be treated equally. Equality in medical terms means that we all wish to be treated as specially as possible. The emphasis on cost and codification may have the unhappy consequence of minimizing medical compensation. Unless one can show that demonstration of human regard and time-consuming interest in the patient's feelings and reaction can have a payoff in faster discharge or recovery, then that sensibility can be given short shrift with impunity. This may, of course, paint an altogether too bleak a picture. I prefer to think that this will not necessarily be the result.

Like most people, doctors are motivated by a mixture of values. Pride, dignity, and moral sensitivity also enter into people's makeup, and the health professionals have attempted to emphasize these characteristics in consideration of their members' activities. If the behavior of individuals fails to match the ideals of their profession, this does not lessen the importance of the ideals (Cole, 1984).

If Hippocrates said at first do no harm, the proverb could now be restated first do some good but don't go overboard.

While the symbolism of competition may make DRG price regulation widely acceptable, the real world of DRGs is a good deal more Calvinist—redemption or perdition turn on a number of factors entirely beyond a hospital's control. Even a great deal of efficiency will not bring financial success to hospitals with the wrong types of patients or be competition for the right mix of patients. Winning and losing will be less a consequence of efficiency than of who is paying the bills.

In short, Medicare DRGs are likely to be difficult on hospitals that rely on Medicare, devastating for those full of poor Medicare beneficiaries and unsponsored indigents who cannot pay their bills. They will threaten the commercial health insurance, constitute a growing problem to corporations who ultimately pay the insurance premiums, and prove only marginally successful to Medicare and federal budget (Morone, 1985).

There is also within this entire DRG system a fundamental shift of power from the physician to the monitors of physician activity. What propelled many young people initially into medicine was the aura of omniscience attributed to the profession and the combination of power of position and the ability to make major changes in relief of human suffering. Cost constraint was not taught within medical schools (although doubtless this will now become incorporated within curricula). Inexorably, the physician becomes a deliverer of care according to formula. Similar to completing one's very own oil painting with the numbers, giving even the most untalented a sense of "creativity," so too the physician's area of independence becomes steadily more circumscribed. Those who monitor the performance become as vital, if not more so, to the hospital stability as those who provide the treatment.

CONCLUSION

Oregon health officials have overhauled the rankings and produced a list that is far more reflective of popular sentiment, a kind of health care by democracy. Medicaid, the federal-state health care program for the poor, will finance treatments only for those procedures in the upper part of the list. "The money saved by eliminating costly procedures at the bottom will be used to provide treatment for many more people. To spread the money around to every Oregonian who is without health insurance, fewer options for treatment would be available to the 190,000 who are receiving Medicaid now" (Egan, 1991).

Included among the highest benefits are several types of pneumonia, tuberculosis, peritonitis, appendicitis. Listed among the lowest are terminal HIV disease, chronic pancreatitis, superficial wounds, and encephaly where a child is born without a brain. The cutoff—the line below which no public financing would be provided—will be after actuaries determine the full cost of the operations in the budget. Representative Henry Waxman, the California Democrat who is chairman of the House Health and Environment Committee, said the plan set up a two-tier medical system—one for those with access to costly miracles and modern medicine and one for those without. Some see this as a model for a national health care system. The existing system already amounted to health care rationing by default, because it deprived so many of any health insurance.

This plan is an example of the ultimate implication of a DRG approach. In addition, there has been the activity of health evaluation services that review physicians' treatment plans. Many doctors do not like these. About 10 percent of all proposed tests or operations reviewed proved clearly unnecessary when subjected to careful scrutiny. The year-long study on the efficacy found that 34 percent of the cases failed the first screening. After a further investigation, a total of 11 percent of the cases reviewed were deemed inappropriate. In some cases, the doctors agree not to perform procedures after talking with reviewers. In others, they go ahead anyway.

For now, some insurers will pay for the procedure as if it had been approved, but others will pay nothing. Insurers say the day is coming when denial of payment will be far more common (Kramon, 1991). Ultimately, an uneasy balance must be struck between government and health positions. The use of DRGs is, for all its limitations and biases, an important first step to nationalizing health care.

REFERENCES

Barnard, C. and T. Esmond. 1981. "DRG Based Reimbursement: The Use of Concurrent and Retrospective Clinical Data." *Medical Care* 19(11):1071–82.

Bush, George. 1988. "Campaign 88: More Efficient Health Care Delivery Needed." *Modern Health Care* 18(20), May 13.

Cole, L. A. 1984. "Public Policy on Health Care and the Attitudes of Practitioners: The Case of Dentistry." Paper presented at 1984 Annual Meeting American Political Science Association. Washington, DC, August.

Egan, Timothy. 1991. "Oregon Shapes Up Pioneering Health Plan for the Poor." New York Times, February 22: A12.

Fuangchen, S. N. and D. P. McCaffrey. 1984. "The Impact of Certificate of Need and Rate Setting Regulation on Complex Medical Technology, A Nine Year Evaluation." Paper presented at IASIA Conference. Bloomington, Indiana, July.

Hughes, K. E., H. L. Daley, and W. M. Patterson. 1983. "Predicting Acute Care Hospital Bed Use Through Physician Inpatient Activity Modeling: First Steps." *Health Care Strategy Management* 1(1):8–11.

Kramon, Glen. 1991. "Medical Second Guessing in Advance." *New York Times*, February 24:12.

Marty, J., L. Bridges, and Philip Jacobs. 1986. "Obtaining Estimates of Marginal Cost by DRG." *Health Care Management*, October: 40–46.

Maurer, Robert. 1987. "The DRG System: An Exercise in Illogic and Frustration." *Osteopathic Hospital Leadership* 1(6):20.

McMahon, L. F., Jr. 1984. "Diagnosis Related Groups Prospective Payment." *Evaluation and the Health Provisions* 7:25–41.

Mehra, Satish. 1986. "Prospective Pricing System: DRGs and Their Impact on Health Care Operations." *Journal of Health and Human Resources Medicine* 9(2):232–45.

Molotsky, Irvin. 1984. "Study Urges Use of Health Aides." *New York Times*, May 6:35.

Morone, James A. 1985. "The Politics of DRGs: New Jersey to New Hampshire." Unpublished paper presented at Seton Hall Conference.

Olsen, S. M. 1984. "The Challenge of Prospective Pricing: Work Smarter." *Journal of Nursing Administration*. 14(4):22–26.

Reilly, B. J. and J. S. Legge. 1982. "The Embattled Hospital Care Control Measures versus Imperatives for Expansion." *Journal of Health Politics Policy and Law* 7(1):254–70.

Rhode Island Medical Journal. 1987. Editorial 70:203–4.

Schwartz, M., J. C. Merrill, and L. K. Blake. 1984. "DRG Based Case Mix and Public Hospitals." *Medical Care* 22(4):283–99.

Taube, C., E. S. Lee, and R. N. Forthofer. 1984. "Diagnosis Related Groups for Mental Disorders, Alcoholics and Drug Abuse Evaluation Alternatives." *Hospital Community Psychiatry* 35(5): 452–53.

Vladeck, D. C. 1984. "Medicare Hospital Payments by Diagnosis Related Groups." *Annals of Internal Medicine* 100(4):576–91.

Wasserman, Jeffrey. 1985. "Unfinished Business: Issues and Empirical Findings on the New Jersey DRG System and Uncompensated Care." Paper presented for Seton Hall University/UMDMJ Conference, June 20.

Williams, S. V., S. A. Finkler, C. M. Murphy, and J. M. Eisenberg. 1982. "Improved Cost Allocation in Case Mix Accounting." *Medical Care* 20(5):450–59.

Young, D. and R. Saltman. 1982. "Prospective Reimbursement and the Hospital Power Equilibrium: A Matrix-Based Management Control System." *Inquiry* 29:20–53.

PART IV

PREVENTION AND RISK

Part IV assesses prevention and risk within health insurance. Both concerns impact on health financing and ultimate access. If the goals of prevention can help limit costs, then more attention must be paid. Yet costs saved in this area will be squandered unless there are accompanying reductions in the cost of mounting risk.

In Chapter 11 Saint-Germain and Longman examine preventive health. Even when breast self-examination training was provided free (particularly among older, widowed women with less education and income and with poorer general health) there was a general refusal to participate. While a dollar spent in prevention may generate much more dramatic outcomes and benefits than a dollar spent in primary care, the social stereotypes that undervalue older women limit their willingness to take preventive action.

In looking specifically at Hispanic women, Saint-Germain and Longman note that Hispanics are more likely to receive late-stage diagnosis, with its accompanying poorer success rate, because of irregular screening and the failure to respond to symptoms. Their study examines 400 Hispanic women in Arizona to determine reasons for noncompliance. The importance of social tradition and family structure is highlighted here, and the authors conclude that any activities geared at challenging traditional social norms must recognize limits. Since earlier detection could reduce mortality by 30 percent, the authors stress the need for more research on cultural variations in responding to breast cancer.

Miller in Chapter 12 examines the costs contributing to increased medical charges from high medical malpractice premiums that have affected health care. The frequency of claims, as well as the amounts awarded, have led to very high malpractice charges. Miller points out that, in contrast to health insurance and workmen's compensation, malpractice insurance returns less of the premium dollars. While general societal litigiousness has contributed in part to the growth in malpractice suits, it is not the sole reason.

The specter of malpractice suits has led to increases in the costs of medical care delivery. Among the reforms that are suggested is a cap on the damages that can be covered. Another approach is to permit juries to receive information on other sources of compensation, without necessarily mandating a reduction in awards. Establishing a statute of limitations on most actions, as well as trying to limit frivolous suits, might also be helpful. Arbitration has also been recommended as a way to deal with conflict. The contingency fee also can be a worrisome factor, since the attorneys benefit in proportion to damages recovered. There are several insurance reforms noted, such as patient compensation funds, experience rating, and class rating. The goal of the tort system is to compensate victims of malpractice and to deter its commission. Malpractice serves, despite all its shortcomings, as a modifier and monitor of the medical care market, but improvements are necessary.

11

Preventive Health Care for Older Women: The Case of Breast Cancer Screening

Michelle A. Saint-Germain and Alice J. Longman

INTRODUCTION

Breast cancer is a leading killer of women over 50 years of age (Leslie and Swider, 1986). All older women are considered to be at risk as 75 percent of breast cancers occur after age 50, and more than half of all breast cancer deaths occur after age 65 (American Cancer Society, 1990; Gilbert and Low, 1986; Fernandez et al., 1986; Byrd, 1989). Despite two decades of research on treatment and prevention, the incidence of breast cancer is increasing (American Cancer Society, 1990; Shingleton and McCarty, 1987). One in nine women will eventually develop breast cancer (Anstett, 1991). More than 150,000 new cases are detected and more than 44,000 women die from breast cancer in the United States each year (American Cancer Society, 1990). Because many women from the "baby boom" generation are now turning 40, these numbers may substantially increase over the next 40 years (U.S. Preventive Services Task Force, 1989).

While nothing can prevent the disease, breast cancer screening—when combined with early treatment—has been shown to be effective in reducing mortality rates, especially for women over 50 (O'Malley and Fletcher, 1987). Discovery of breast cancer occurs nearly two years earlier for women age 35–49 and nearly three years earlier for women age 50 and over when they participate in screening tests than it would have without the tests (Moskowitz, 1986). Startling differences in five-year survival rates are found for those who detect the cancer early (90 percent), after some spreading (68 percent), or late (18 percent) (American Cancer Society, 1990). Screening and treatment are both important, as long-term survival depends on the state of the disease at the time of diagnosis and the interval until treatment begins (Farley and Flannery, 1989). Up to 50 percent of those with no delay in seeking treatment after finding breast cancer were alive after ten years, versus only 25 percent of of those who waited six months or more before seeking treatment (Neale et al., 1986).

The three main breast cancer screening tests are mammography—a type of X ray of the breast; clinical breast exam—a manual examination of the breast by a health care professional (doctor, nurse); and breast self-examination—a monthly screening routine for women to practice on themselves. Guidelines have been developed that outline the recommended frequency of use of these tests for women in different age groups:

Age Group	Recommended Screening Tests
20–39	Monthly Breast Self-Examination (BSE)
	Clinical Breast Examination (CBE) every 3 years
	Baseline mammogram between ages 35 and 40
40–49	Monthly BSE
	CBE every year
	Mammogram every 1–2 years (if indicated)
50 and over	Monthly BSE
	CBE every year
	Mammogram yearly

Evidence of voluntary utilization of breast cancer screening tests is scarce, but most studies show that actual rates are substantially lower than recommended levels. In the case of mammograms, a study based on clinic records showed that only 8 percent of women age 45–65 in a health insurance plan had at least one mammogram over a three-year period (Lurie et al., 1987). A recent national telephone survey found that while 85 percent of women over 40 had heard of mammograms, only 26 percent reported obtaining one yearly (American Cancer Society, 1988). A study of nearly 12,000 retirement community residents found only 10 percent of the women reported yearly mammograms (Chao et al., 1987).

Less is known about clinical breast exam. In the 1988 American Cancer Society survey, 88 percent of women knew about CBE and 67 percent of women over 40 reported retrospectively that they obtain this service every one–three years. In other studies, obtaining a Pap smear (a screening test for cervical cancer) is used as a proxy for obtaining a CBE, since women often receive CBE as part of the same office visit. In the health insurance study cited above, 57 percent of women age 45–65 received at least one Pap smear in three years, based on clinic records (Lurie et al., 1987). In the retirement community study, 60 percent of the women reported yearly Pap tests (Chao et al., 1987). But use of the Pap smear as a proxy for CBE does not provide accurate information, since older women—especially those past the menopause—may not receive CBE during routine gynecological examinations. Health care practitioners may not perform CBE on older women due to ignorance of the recommendations, disagreement with the recommendations, forgetfulness, dislike of the procedure, or lack of time. Pressures to reduce health care costs may also create incentives to reduce preventive services such as CBE (Lurie et al., 1987).

A large volume of literature has been generated concerning breast self-examination in relation to cancer detection, but little evidence exists as to whether women actually perform BSE and, if so, in correct fashion. One study found only 27 percent of women report doing BSE during a given year and 20 percent report never attempting BSE at all (Grady et al., 1983). Another study found that only 1 in 200 Mexican women reported performing BSE correctly and at the proper time of the month (Sheley and Lessan, 1986). The 1988 American Cancer Society survey found that 82 percent of women over 40 report that a doctor has explained BSE to them, but only 23 percent perform BSE monthly, and less than half practice it three times a year. Only 37 percent of women retirement community residents reported practicing BSE "on a regular basis" (Chao et al., 1987).

Reasons for lack of compliance with recommended frequency of screening tests are not well understood. The three major types of barriers are lack of services (infrastructure), lack of access to services, and lack of utilization of accessible services. Much of the research on screening has focused on characteristics of individual women associated with compliance or noncompliance, ignoring whether the infrastructure is in place and/or women have access to it. Lack of infrastructure includes lack of mammography equipment, technicians, and radiologists; long waiting periods for appointments; and reluctance of health care providers to recommend or perform screening.

Lack of access is another significant barrier, since all three modes of detection—mammogram, clinical breast exam, and breast self-exam—depend heavily on access to the formal health care system (American Cancer Society, 1990). Mammography requires complex equipment; clinical breast exam is performed by a trained health professional; and proper breast self-exam relies on initial instruction and ongoing feedback from a knowledgeable health practitioner. Access to formal health care is important both for early detection and for treatment of breast cancer. Studies show that women who live in lower SES (socioeconomic status) census tracts are likely to have more advanced disease at the time of diagnosis and to have higher death rates from breast cancer than women who live in higher SES census tracts, regardless of race (Farley and Flannery, 1989). In a study of breast cancer patients, those with more advanced disease at the time of diagnosis had lower mean incomes (Walker et al., 1989).

Having access to health care services, however, does not ensure that a woman will be screened. Even with free or low-cost screening, not all women will choose to participate (Grady et al., 1983; Lurie et al., 1987; Rimer et al., 1988; Taplin, Anderman, and Grothaus, 1989). Some of this is due to the difference in the quality or type of services offered to the poor. Funch (1981) found that women most in need of these services are often least likely to receive them. For example, in a national survey, 35 percent of women in the lowest income level had never received a clinical breast exam, compared to only 13 percent of women in the highest income group. Other research—mostly with Anglo-American women—has found that some women do not participate in breast cancer screening because of fear of finding cancer; fear of mutilation, of losing one or both breasts; fear of radiation or other technology; and embarrassment from exposing their breasts (Crooks and Jones, 1989). But Kagawa-Singer (1987) points out that "consideration of cultural differences" has been largely ignored in the field of cancer research.

Hispanics are an important ethnic group in the United States, forming the sixth largest concentration of Hispanics in the world (16.9 million), whose numbers are expected to double every five years (Texidor del Portillo, 1987).[1] Breast cancer occurs less frequently in women like Hispanics who have comparatively low levels of socioeconomic status, but such women are also more likely to be diagnosed at a later stage, with poorer prognosis for survival (Farley and Flannery, 1989; Funch, 1986; Newell and Mills, 1986). Hispanic women are more likely than Anglo women to have low socioeconomic status and to have late-stage diagnosis due to irregular screening and the inability to detect and respond to breast cancer symptoms (Richardson et al., 1987). Much of this difference, however, is attributable to lower SES than to racial or ethnic factors. When breast cancers are detected at the earliest stage, the survival difference between the races is minimal or nonexistent (Funch, 1986).

The fact that Hispanics over age 65 are the fastest-growing segment of the elderly, and that women in this age group greatly outnumber men (Cubillos, 1987), may result in an increase in breast cancer deaths among older Hispanic women in the future, if nothing is done to encourage higher rates of breast cancer screening. Yet the health care beliefs and practices of older Hispanic women are largely unknown to most health care professionals (Kosko and Flaskerud, 1987). Although it has been posited that there are ethnic differences that influence rates of breast cancer screening, most research on this subject has found socioeconomic factors to be more important than cultural or other factors in access to health care (Lee, 1976; Marks et al., 1987; Saint-Germain and Longman, 1990). For Hispanics health care is often a luxury, as food, clothing, and shelter come first. To ascribe lack of utilization of health care services to cultural eccentricities is often just another case of blaming the victim (Giachello, 1985).

Breast cancer is a serious disease affecting thousands of American women each year. Despite recommendations to obtain regular screening for this disease, actual rates are low. In order to recommend policy changes, a model of breast cancer screening behavior must be developed that recognizes the voluntary nature of preventive care and can identify key points at which interventions could be made. It is necessary to ascertain whether the required infrastructure is in place, whether women have access to it, and, given the first two, whether women are using available and accessible screening services.

METHODOLOGY

In order to address these concerns, a study was made of 409 Hispanic and 138 Anglo women over age 50 living in Tucson, Arizona.[2] The sample was selected using random cluster sampling from ethnically heterogeneous as well as ethnically homogeneous neighborhoods and with a wide range of income levels. A structured interview guide was developed and pretested on a pilot sample that resembled the target population. The instrument was translated into Spanish and back-translated into English to ensure comparable meaning in both languages. A group of trained bilingual women from the community with previous experience in health surveys conducted interviews lasting from 30 to 90 minutes in the respondents' homes, in the language of their choice.

Each respondent was asked a series of questions on social and demographic characteristics, acculturation, access and barriers to health care, knowledge and beliefs about breast cancer, past medical history, and what it would mean to get breast cancer. The following pages report on what the women in this sample say they know about breast cancer and breast cancer screening tests, their attitudes toward the disease and the tests, and how often they use these tests. Also reported are the barriers they encounter, as well as the positive cues they receive, in relation to screening. A preliminary model of the factors that influence utilization of breast cancer screening is developed. Finally, some conclusions are drawn, with implications for health care policy and for further research. The findings are shown in Tables 11.1–11.6.

DISCUSSION

Based on the results of our study, we have identified a preliminary model to describe the factors that influence breast cancer screening utilization. We hypothesize that the two independent variables, socioeconomic status and culture, influence breast cancer screening practices through five mediating variables: access, barriers, beliefs, cues, and knowledge (See Figure 11.1).

SES influences utilization of breast cancer screening services through several paths. SES (measured by level of education and level of income) largely

Table 11.1
Demographic Characteristics

DEMOGRAPHICS (percentages)	HISPANICS (N=409)	ANGLOS (N=138)
AGE		
50-64	61.8	41.6
65+	38.2	58.4
FINISHED HIGH SCHOOL	25.2%	68.1
MARITAL STATUS		
Never Married	3.7	5.8
Currently Married	56.9	47.1
Separated	2.2	0.7
Divorced	11.0	10.1
Widowed	26.2	36.2
CURRENTLY EMPLOYED	25.1	14.5
AVERAGE NUMBER IN HOUSEHOLD	3.5	2.3
MONTHLY INCOME IS BELOW $1,000	63.4	50.9
BORN IN U.S.	68.0	94.2
CATHOLIC	89.0	31.2
LANGUAGE PREFERENCE		
Only or Mostly Spanish	34.7	0.0
Spanish/English Equally	38.6	3.6
Only or Mostly English	26.7	96.4

determines a woman's level of access to the formal health care system (for example, having a private physician, having health insurance, and having transportation). Women with greater access (or exposure) to the formal health care system have more knowledge about breast cancer and screening, and have more positive beliefs about the ability of the formal health care system to detect and treat breast cancer. SES is inversely related to experiencing barriers to breast cancer screening; the experience of barriers reduces one's positive beliefs.

SES also influences utilization through the mediation of positive cues in the environment. Women with higher levels of SES are more likely to be English-speaking and to receive more positive cues for breast cancer screening, from reading, radio, and TV. This may be due both to a higher number of media messages aimed at more affluent women, the larger number of

Table 11.2
Access to Health Care

ACCESS VARIABLES (percentages)	HISPANICS (N=409)	ANGLOS (N=138)
HAS HEALTH INSURANCE	74.6	84.1
HAS A REGULAR DOCTOR	74.6	69.6
IN PAST YEAR,		
Saw a Doctor	81.9	81.2
Had a Physical	54.3	57.2
Saw a Gynecologist	35.7	33.3
Saw a Dentist	41.8	50.0
USUAL SITE OF HEALTH CARE IS		
Private Physician	30.4	54.4
HMO	15.2	8.8
Community Clinic	31.9	16.2
Hospital Clinic	15.7	16.2
Other	6.8	4.4
USUAL TRANSPORTATION IS		
Drive Own Car	45.1	65.7
Family or Friends Drive	40.6	24.1
Public Transportation	11.8	8.7
Other	3.5	1.5
MEDIAN TRAVEL TIME (MINUTES)	18.5	15.0
WILL SEE A DOCTOR WHEN NOT SICK (Preventive Care)	46.5	55.8
CURRENT HEALTH IS		
Very Good	29.6	44.5
Fairly Good	40.6	41.6
Somewhat Poor	24.7	9.5
Very Poor	5.1	4.4

English-language media outlets (and thus the larger number of messages aired in English), or the difference in content of messages that are aired in English versus Spanish. Higher SES results in higher levels of knowledge both directly (e.g., through higher educational levels) and indirectly (through having more cues in one's environment about breast cancer and screening).

From this model it can be seen that utilization of breast cancer screening services is not merely a function of access or knowledge, and that purely informational campaigns (i.e., targeted only at the knowledge variable) will have limited effects on utilization of breast cancer screening. Also, merely increasing the level of access will not ensure utilization without a multifa-

Table 11.3
Barriers to Health Care

BARRIERS EXPERIENCED (percentages)	HISPANICS (N=409)	ANGLOS (N=138)
COULDN'T AFFORD TO PAY	29.4	16.8
NO HEALTH INSURANCE	23.5	17.5
TOO LONG A WAIT TO SEE THE DOCTOR	17.4	11.0
DIDN'T KNOW WHERE TO GO	14.4	9.4
DIDN'T SPEAK THE LANGUAGE	11.9	0.7
DIDN'T HAVE TRANSPORTATION	11.5	5.1
COULDN'T TAKE OFF FROM WORK	6.6	5.1
SITE WAS NOT OPEN	5.4	4.4
COULDN'T GET A BABYSITTER	3.7	2.9

ceted strategy that also reinforces positive cues and eliminates barriers in the environment as well, increasing the level of positive belief in the ability of the formal health care system to detect and treat breast cancer. Finally, although touched on only briefly by our research, none of these efforts will be successful if the necessary infrastructure (mammography equipment, technicians, radiologists, and health care professionals who perform screening and make referrals) is not in place.

As found in other studies, culture (in this case Hispanic ethnicity) is not significantly related to access when SES is controlled. Culture is positively related, however, to the experience of barriers to breast cancer screening. Women from the lowest SES groups experience the most barriers, and Hispanic women experienced more barriers than Anglo women, even controlling for SES. Some of these barriers were common to both Hispanic and Anglo women, such as lack of health insurance or transportation, but others, such as language problems, are more keenly felt by Hispanic women. The experience of barriers leads to lower levels of positive belief in the ability of the formal health care system to detect and treat breast cancer, which in turn reduces the likelihood of participating in screening.

Table 11.4
Knowledge of Breast Cancer and Screening Tests

KNOWLEDGE VARIABLES (percentages)	HISPANICS (N=409)	ANGLOS (N=138)
KNOWS SCREENING TESTS		
Breast Self-Exam	46.9	70.3
Clinical Breast Exam	44.7	46.4
Mammography	37.7	37.7
Doesn't Know Any Tests	16.9	6.5
HAS HEARD OF MAMMOGRAMS		
(When prompted)	77.5	86.2
KNOWS SIGNS OR SYMPTOMS		
Lump	84.1	85.5
Ache	42.5	31.2
Discharge	17.1	25.4
Doesn't Know any Signs	7.4	6.5
Names Erroneous Signs	12.5	10.9
KNOWS RISK FACTORS		
Family History	38.4	57.2
Age	10.8	7.2
Doesn't Know Any Risks	26.6	15.2
Names Erroneous Risks	43.0	50.0
KNOWS PRIME RISK AGE		
(Age 50 and older)	22.0	23.2
KNOWS INCIDENCE OF BREAST CANCER		
(1 in every 10 women)	26.2	35.4

Health is often measured by a person's ability to carry out normal duties. Illness is doubly unpleasant because it is both personally painful and is accompanied by the fear of loss of certain social privileges and respect from family and friends, who will be required to fill in for the ill person. The individual is not free to make independent decisions about treatment for illness (Clark, 1970), since treatment in the case of breast cancer (such as surgery or chemotherapy) will require substantial commitment from the extended network. An acceptable treatment regimen must address not only the personal sickness but also the disruption in the family network. Some Hispanic women in our sample expressed great concern about the treatments prescribed for breast cancer, such as surgical breast removal, chemotherapy, radiation therapy, male hormone therapy, and such, because of the problems they cause both for the woman undergoing them and for her relationship with her family and relatives.

Table 11.5
Breast Cancer Screening Practices

PRACTICES (percentages)	HISPANICS (N=409)	ANGLOS (N=138)
EVER HAD A MAMMOGRAM	51.3	55.1
MAMMOGRAM IN PAST YEAR	31.8	35.5
EVER HAD TWO MAMMOGRAMS	20.0	25.4
TWO MAMMOGRAMS IN TWO YEARS	12.0	17.4
EVER HAD THREE MAMMOGRAMS	9.0	13.8
THREE MAMMOGRAMS IN THREE YEARS	5.9	8.7
EVER HAD BREASTS EXAMINED	84.4	94.2
BREASTS EXAMINED IN PAST YEAR	55.7	54.3
EVER DONE BREAST SELF-EXAM	72.1	79.0
BREAST SELF-EXAM IN PAST YEAR	61.1	71.0
DOES BREAST SELF-EXAM CORRECTLY	14.9	27.5

CONCLUSIONS AND RECOMMENDATIONS

The cost in terms of years of life lost due to cancer is greater for women than men, and the most costly cancer for women is breast cancer. In 1984, 760,000 years of life were lost among the 39,470 women who died of the disease in the United States. If mortality could be reduced by 30 percent through the use of breast cancer screening, early detection, and prompt treatment, 11,800 deaths could be avoided each year and 227,000 fewer years of life would be lost (Horm and Sondik, 1989). The age-specific incidence of breast cancer continues to increase with increasing age, into the 80s; even in women over age 75, breast cancer shortens life expectancy (Rybolt and Waterbury, 1989). Thus breast cancer remains a serious challenge to older women's health and quality of life.

Concerns for identifying policy-relevant aspects of this problem have oriented our research. The first area we address is the structure and organization of the health care system. One important component of this system is the supply and placement of mammography equipment.

A recent analysis of the number of operating mammography machines concluded that there is an oversupply of these machines, and that this oversupply is keeping the price of mammography artificially high (Brown, Kessler, and Rueter, 1990). The authors estimated that there would be 10,000 mammography machines operating in 1990, which at a reasonable rate of 25 mammograms per day—or 6,000 per year—per machine, would yield a capacity of 60 million per year. Of the 40 million women eligible

Table 11.6
Cues and Barriers to Breast Cancer Screening

PRACTICES (percentages)	HISPANICS (N=409)	ANGLOS (N=138)
REASONS FOR MAMMOGRAPHY		
Doctor's Recommendation	39.4	37.0
Found Signs or Symptoms	26.1	21.0
Routine Preventive Care	24.7	19.0
Know Someone With Breast Cancer	3.2	11.0
Family or Friend Suggested	1.4	6.0
Other	5.2	6.0
CUES FOR MAMMOGRAPHY FROM		
TV	53.1	76.8
Reading	40.1	60.9
Radio	21.3	32.6
Family or Friends	17.3	17.3
BARRIERS TO MAMMOGRAPHY		
No Signs or Symptoms	38.4	48.0
No Access to Services	23.2	11.9
Doctor Didn't Recommend	20.0	20.0
Don't Like It or Don't Want To Know	14.8	17.3
Other	3.6	2.8
BARRIERS TO CLINICAL BREAST EXAM		
No Signs or Symptoms	45.5	-
Doctor Didn't Recommend or Do It	21.2	-
Don't Look For Trouble	19.7	-
Not Proper	9.1	-
Other	4.5	-
BARRIERS TO BREAST SELF-EXAM		
Don't Know How/Won't Find Anything	27.5	19.5
Don't Look For Trouble	18.1	19.5
Too Embarrassed	17.4	9.8
Put It Off or Forgot	13.4	17.1
Doesn't Apply to Me	12.8	17.1
Mammography and/or CBE Is Enough	7.3	9.8
Other	3.5	7.2
HEALTH INSURANCE COVERS MAMMOGRAM		
Yes	37.2	39.1
No	18.1	21.0
Don't Know	44.7	39.9

Figure 11.1
Factors Affecting the Use of Breast Cancer Screening

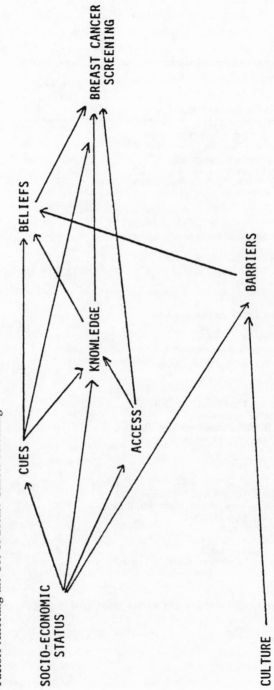

for yearly mammograms in 1990 (according to recommended screening guidelines), less than one-fourth would probably obtain them, or about 10 million. The oversupply of mammography machines thus ranges from about 6:1 in actuality to about 1.5:1 if guidelines were strictly followed. This oversupply has not resulted in lower prices for mammography. Most installations are operating at reduced capacity, but high fixed costs of equipment and space result in high charges to break even. At one-sixth capacity or 4 mammograms per day, operators charge $135 apiece; at one-fourth capacity or 6 mammograms per day, $100 apiece; but if recommended guidelines were followed and each installation did about 18 mammograms per day (about 75 percent of capacity), the price could fall to $50 apiece. These calculations assume that mammography equipment is distributed in such a way that all women who should be screened have access, but the actual location of mammography equipment in relation to neighborhoods of more and less affluent women remains to be explored.

Convincing physicians to recommend breast cancer screening for their older patients is another structural problem that must be overcome (Cohen et al., 1982; Fox, Klos, and Tsou, 1988). One survey found that while 68 percent of primary care physicians agreed with screening guidelines, only 11 percent adhered to the recommendations, mostly because they thought it was too expensive (American Medical Association, 1989). If all 40 million women age 40 and over had annual mammograms at $50 apiece, $2 billion would be added to the national health care bill (Dodd, 1987). While there is some disagreement about the benefits of mammographic screening for women aged 40–49, most professional health care groups endorse annual screening for women age 50 and older. But few studies have attempted to calculate a cost-benefit ratio for mass screening. The Health Insurance Plan study begun in New York in 1963 screened over 20,000 women and averted 37 deaths that otherwise would have occurred from breast cancer. The cost for screening was estimated at $4,072,200 and the savings $1,497,960. The cost per breast cancer found was estimated at $23,403, and the cost per death averted $123,400 (American Medical Association, 1989).

The second area we address concerns factors that limit women's access to preventive breast cancer screening services. Action is needed because the outlook for older women is not bright. The majority of people over age 65 are women, half of whom have incomes under $5,000 per year (Leslie and Swider, 1986). Government health programs do not cover the full cost of health care, so the elderly may spend up to half their income on health (Sidel, 1986). Older and poorer women have less knowledge of health matters than similarly situated men, and much research on health consumption has excluded older women (McCall, Rice, and Sangl, 1986). Even employed women are not guaranteed access, as many work part-time or in jobs in the service sector that offer few if any health benefits. More than 41.5 percent of all women are not covered for health care as dependents or spouses

(Leslie and Swider, 1986), and noninsured rates of as high as 34 percent have been found among Hispanics in the Southwest (Andersen et al., 1981). The increasing feminization of poverty may seriously affect older women's access to health care. Public policies to deal with changes that may affect older women's health, for example, the impact of retirement (Rathbone-McCuan, 1985), are lacking.

The situation is even worse with respect to older women's access to preventive care. Fewer of women's visits to physicians are considered "elective" compared to men's (Aday and Andersen, 1975); other studies show delayed access or reduced use of health care for older women (Grady et al., 1983), unmarried women (Keith, 1987), and widows (Neale et al., 1986). Older women tend to postpone needed health care, including preventive care, at twice the rate of the general population, citing both economic and other barriers, such as distress over standard of living (Keith, 1987). In fact, health care providers are contacted infrequently in relation to actual symptom episodes (Menninger, 1986).

By 1989, 21 states had some form of legislation, with 18 states mandating third-party payment (Thompson, Kessler, and Boss, 1989). In our study in Arizona, however, many women didn't know whether their health insurance would cover a mammogram, despite the existence of legislation requiring third-party coverage of screening mammography (See Table 11.6). One problem is that federal law prohibits states from mandating coverage by self-insured health programs, which amounted to half of all employer-sponsored health insurance plans in California (Thompson et al., 1989). Another problem is that often there is no budget in the legislation for dissemination of information about coverage to health care providers or consumers. At the federal level, the Medicare Catastrophic Coverage Act passed in 1988 would have provided up to $50 in coverage every two years for screening mammograms for women over age 65, and some coverage for disabled women over age 35. This coverage disappeared when the Act was repealed in 1990 (National Women's Health Resource Center, 1990). Thompson et al. caution that increasing the use of mammography through legislation will have implications for public health officials. Adequate infrastructure will have to be in place, including mammography equipment, trained technicians and radiologists, and a quality assurance system to follow up abnormal results. Avoiding false positives will be important, as the cost of confirmatory tests (e.g., biopsies) can run as high as $900 (Bishop, 1988).

The third area we address concerns the knowledge and belief barriers to utilization of available care. We found that many older women—Anglo and Hispanic—are not convinced of the benefits of prevention and have only vague notions of the warning signs and risks for breast cancer. Most do not appreciate their own risk of developing this disease. In addition, they have erroneous notions about the causes and manifestations of breast cancer that affect their decisions about screening behavior. For most women, breast cancer screening is perceived as risky behavior, as the fear of finding something predominates over the fear of not finding cancer if it is present (Meyerowitz and Chaiken, 1987). But prevention should remain an important goal for older women, as more women over 55 have late-stage diagnosis than younger women (Welch-McCaffrey and Dodge, 1988). Educational and outreach programs should be tailored for specific groups of older women, such as widows.

For the Hispanic population, educational materials are needed in Spanish for distribution through the print, radio, and TV media. Videos of breast self-examination made with culture- and age-appropriate models are sorely lacking. Educational programs to address the underrepresentation of Hispanic women in breast cancer screening, however, must not merely translate materials from English but must in addition take note of the meaning of cancer within this culture. For Hispanic women, breast cancer represents a threat to the sense of balance of the individual woman (through loss of a breast) as well as her equilibrium in relationships with significant others. Most Hispanic women we interviewed who had not been screened for breast cancer reported that no one in their family had ever discussed it with them; that is, it had not been validated within their social circle. The family is an underutilized resource for promoting preventive breast cancer screening for older Hispanic women. For example, a woman's siblings or adult children could play a role in convincing her that screening for breast cancer would be good both for her and the family (Markides, Boldt, and Ray, 1986).

Educational programs should incorporate traditional values such as respect, *sacrificio* (sacrifice), and *ejemplo* (exemplary behavior), in novel ways (Solis et al., 1985). For example, older, well-respected members of the Hispanic community could set an example for other women by getting breast cancer screening themselves. The embarrassment or indignity of breast cancer screening could be acknowledged as a short-term sacrifice on the woman's part in order to safeguard her health for her family's sake in the long run. New studies on social networks suggest that education campaigns about breast cancer are well received when undertaken in small, kin-based or church-based groups (Eng, Hatch, and Callan, 1985; Gottlieb, 1985; Israel, 1985). Another study shows that among working Hispanic women, close social networks that approximate the kinship model can develop (Zavella, 1985). These networks could provide the basis for a work-based intervention program. Ideally such campaigns would be conducted by older women who have had first-hand experience with breast cancer and who tend to have more positive attitudes, such as the woman who said: "My aunt did OK with the treatment." It would be imperative to give Hispanic women ample opportunity to work through the illness (interpersonal) aspects of breast cancer, as well as to deal with the technical (disease-related) aspects, manifestations, and treatment. Giving women the knowledge that they can detect breast cancer, that it can be treated, and that there is life after breast cancer is one important part of the message. It is also important to pay attention to the interpersonal feelings that the possibility of breast cancer arouses, especially in relation to significant others, where it is easier to deny that one will get the disease than to contemplate the perceived disaster it would create in a woman's social life. Policies that are sensitive to age and culture that will enable and encourage older Anglo and Hispanic women to get screening for breast cancer are needed in order to break down the barriers of myth, silence, and resignation that surround this disease, and to encourage resilience and resourcefulness as acceptable responses to the challenge of conquering breast cancer.

NOTES

1. The authors recognize that the term "Hispanic" is an artificial construction, embracing many different people of Spanish, Latin American, and Caribbean origin.

2. The respondent was asked how she identified herself, and read a list of pre-defined choices. In a few cases the respondent's self-classification did not appear to be consistent with observations made by the interviewer; however, in all cases the respondent's selection was respected.

REFERENCES

Aday, L. and R. Andersen. 1975. *Access to Medical Care*. Ann Arbor, MI: Health Administration Press.

American Cancer Society. 1988. *The 1987 Survey of Public Awareness and Use of Cancer Tests*. Conducted by the Gallup Organization, analyzed by Lieberman Research, Inc.

———. 1990. *Cancer Facts and Figures–1990*. New York: American Cancer Society.

American Medical Association. 1989. Council on Scientific Affairs. "Mammographic Screening in Asymptomatic Women Aged 40 Years and Older." *Journal of the American Medical Association* 261(17):2535–42.

Andersen, R. M. et al. 1981. "Access to Medical Care among the Hispanic Population of the Southwestern United States." *Journal of Health and Social Behavior* 22:78–89.

Anstett, P. 1991. "Breast Cancer Rate Likely to Fall by Year 2000, Conference Is Told." *Arizona Daily Star*, March 29.

Bishop, Jerry E. 1988. "Mammographs for Women Aged 40–49 Would Cut Cancer Risks—at High Cost." *Wall Street Journal*, March 11.

Brown, Martin L., Larry G. Kessler, and Fred G. Rueter. 1990. "Is the Supply of Mammography Machines Outstripping Need and Demand?" *Annals of Internal Medicine* 113(7):547–52.

Byrd, R. 1989. "Breast Cancer Death Rate is Rising, US Researchers Say." *Arizona Daily Star*, August 25.

Chao, A., A. Paganini-Hill, R. K. Ross, and B. E. Henderson. 1987. "Use of Preventive Care by the Elderly." *Preventive Medicine* 16:710–22.

Clark, Margaret. 1970. *Health in the Mexican-American Culture*. Berkeley: University of California Press.

Cohen, David, Benjamin Littenberg, Cheryl Wetzel, and Duncan Neuhauser. 1982. "Improving Physician Compliance with Preventive Medicine Guidelines." *Medical Care* 20:1040–45.

Crooks, Catherine E. and Steven D. Jones. 1989. "Educating Women about the Importance of Breast Screening: The Nurse's Role." *Cancer Nursing* 12:161–64.

Cubillos, Hermina L. with Margarita M. Prieto. 1987. *The Hispanic Elderly: A Demographic Profile*. Washington, DC: National Council of La Raza.

Dodd, G. D. 1987. "The History and Present Status of Radiographic Screening for Breast Carcinoma." *Cancer* 50(7):1671–74.

Eng, Eugenia, John Hatch, and Ann Callan. 1985. "Institutionalizing Social Support through the Church and Into the Community." *Health Education Quarterly* 12:81–92.

Farley, Thomas A. and John T. Flannery. 1989. "Late-Stage Diagnosis of Breast Cancer in Women of Lower Socio-Economic Status: Public Health Implications." *American Journal of Public Health* 79:1508–12.

Fernandez, L. et al. 1986. "Risk Factors in Mass Screening for Breast Cancer: Multivariate Analysis of Data from the Cuban Diagnosis Pilot Study." *Neoplasma* 33:535–41.

Fox, Sarah, Dennis Klos, and Carole Tsou. 1988. "Underuse of Screening Mammography by Family Physicians." *Radiology* 166:431–33.

Funch, Donna P. 1986. "Socioeconomic Status and Survival for Breast and Cervical Cancer." *Women & Health* 11:37–54.

Giachello, A. 1985. "Hispanics and Health Care." In *Hispanics in the United States: A New Social Agenda*, P. Cafferty and W. McCready, eds. New Brunswick, NJ: Transaction Books.

Gilbert, F., Jr. and G. Low. 1986. "What Have We Learned from the Breast Cancer Detection Demonstration Project?" *Hawaii Medical Journal* 41(5):15–55.

Gottlieb, Benjamin H. 1985. "Social Networks and Social Support: An Overview of Research, Practice and Policy Implications." *Health Education Quarterly* 12:5–22.

Grady, Kathleen, Stephen Kegeles, Adrian Lund, Claudia Wolk, and Neil Farber. 1983. "Who Volunteers for a Breast Self-Examination Program? Evaluating the Bases for Self-Selection." *Health Education Quarterly* 10:74–94.

Horm, John W. and Edward J. Sondik. 1989. "Person-Years of Life Lost Due to Cancer in the United States, 1970 and 1984." *American Journal of Public Health* 79:1490–93.

Israel, Barbara A. 1985. "Social Networks and Social Support: Implications for Natural Helper and Community Level Interventions." *Health Education Quarterly* 12:65–80.

Kagawa-Singer, Marjorie. 1987. "Ethnic Perspectives of Cancer Nursing: Hispanics and Japanese-Americans." *Oncology Nursing Forum* 14:59–65.

Keith, Pat M. 1987. "Postponement of Health Care by Unmarried Older Women." *Women & Health* 12(1):47–60.

Kosko, Debra A. and Jacquelyn H. Flaskerud. 1987. "Mexican-American, Nurse

Practitioner, and Lay Control Group Beliefs about Cause and Treatment of Chest Pain." *Nursing Research* 36:226–31.
Lee, Isaiah C. 1976. *Medical Care in a Mexican-American Community.* Los Alamitos, CA: Hwong Publishing.
Leslie, L. and Swider, S. 1986. "Changing Factors and Changing Needs in Women's Health Care." *Nursing Clinics of North America* 21(1):111–23.
Lurie, N. et al. 1987. "Preventive Care: Do We Practice What We Preach?" *American Journal of Public Health* 77:801–4.
Markides, K., J. S. Boldt, and L. A. Ray. 1986. "Sources of Helping and Intergenerational Solidarity: A Three-Generation Study of Mexican-Americans." *Journal of Gerontology* 41(4):506–11.
Marks, Gary, Julia Solis, Jean L. Richardson, Linda M. Collins, Lourdes Birba, and John C. Hisserich. 1987. "Health Behaviors of Elderly Hispanic Women: Does Cultural Assimilation Make a Difference?" *American Journal of Public Health* 77:1315–19.
McCall, N., T. Rice, and J. Sangl. 1986. "Consumer Knowledge of Medicare and Supplemental Health Insurance Benefits." *Health Services Research* 20(6):633–57, Part 1.
Menninger, J. 1986. "Sex Differences Associated with the Use of Medical Care and Alternative Illness Behaviors." *Social Science and Medicine* 22:285–92.
Meyerowitz, Beth E. and Shelly Chaiken. 1987. "The Effect of Message Framing on Breast Self-Examination Attitudes, Intentions, and Behavior." *Journal of Personality and Psychology* 52:500–10.
Moskowitz, M. 1986. "Breast Cancer: Age Specific Growth Rates and Screening Strategies." *Radiology* 161(1):37–41.
National Women's Health Resource Center. 1990. "Breast Cancer Research: More Funding and Coordination." *National Women's Health Report* 13(2):2.
Neale A. et al. 1986. "Marital Status, Delay in Seeking Treatment and Survival from Breast Cancer." *Social Science and Medicine* 23:305–12.
Newell, Guy R. and Paul K. Mills. 1986. "Low Cancer Rates in Hispanic Women Related to Social and Economic Factors." *Women & Health* 11:23–36.
O'Malley, R. and S. Fletcher. 1987. "Screening for Breast Cancer with Breast Self-Examination: A Critical Review." *Journal of the American Medical Association* 257(16):2197–2203.
Rathbone-McCuan, E. 1985. "Health Needs and Social Policy." *Women & Health* 10(3):17–27.
Richardson, Jean, Gary Marks, Julia Solis, Linda Collins, Lourdes Birba, and John Hisserich. 1987. "Frequency and Adequacy of Breast Cancer Screening among Elderly Hispanic Women." *Preventive Medicine* 16:761–74.
Rimer, Barbara, Sharon Davis, Paul Engstrom, Ronald Myers, Jay Rosan, Laurie Fox, and Robert McLaughlin. 1988. "An Examination of Compliance and Noncompliance in an HMO Cancer Screening Program," in *Advances in Cancer Control V: Cancer Program Product Line Management,* Program for Clinical Biological Research 278:21–30.
Rybolt, Ann H. and Larry Waterbury. 1989. "Breast Cancer in Older Women: Trends in Diagnosis." *Geriatrics* 44(6):69–82.
Saint-Germain, M. A. and Alice J. Longman. 1990. "Older Women and Preventive

Health Care: Final Report." Submitted to the AARP/Andrus Foundation, February 28.

Sheley, J. and G. Lessan. 1986. "Limited Impact of the Breast Self-Examination Movement: A Latin American Illustration." *Social Science and Medicine* 23(9):905–10.

Shingleton, W. and K. S. McCarty, Jr. 1987. "Breast Carcinoma: An Overview." *Gynecologic Oncology* 26:271–83.

Sidel, Ruth. 1986. *Women and Children Last*. New York: Penguin.

Solis, Julie, Jean Richardson, John C. Hisserich, Fernando Torres-Gil, Gary Marks, Lourdes Birba, and Norma Alicia Pino. 1985. "Cancer Screening Behavior Among Elderly Hispanic Women." Keynote address at the Second International Conference on Cancer and Hispanics, Nogales, Arizona, November 21–22.

Taplin, Stephen, Carolyn Anderman, and Louis Grothaus. 1989. "Breast Cancer Risk and Participation in Mammographic Screening." *American Journal of Public Health* 79:1494–98.

Texidor del Portillo, Carlota. 1987. "Poverty, Self-Concept, and Health: Experience of Latinas." *Women & Health* 12:229–42.

Thompson, Grey B., Larry G. Kessler, and Leslie P. Boss. 1989. "Breast Cancer Screening Legislation in the United States: A Commentary." *American Journal of Public Health* 79(11):1541–43.

U.S. Preventive Services Task Force. 1989. *Guide to Clinical Preventive Services*. Baltimore: Williams & Wilkins.

Walker, A. P., L. Neal, R. K. Ausman, J. Whipple, and B. Doherty. 1989. "Per Capita Income in Breast Cancer Patients." *Journal of the National Medical Association* 81(10):1065–68.

Welch-McCaffrey, Deborah and Jan Dodge. 1988. "Planning Breast Self-Examination Programs for Elderly Women." *Oncology Nursing Forum* 15:811–14.

Zavella, Patricia. 1985. "Abnormal Intimacy: The Varying Work Networks of Chicana Cannery Workers." *Feminist Studies* 11:541–57.

12

Who's Afraid of Being Sued: The Medical Malpractice Insurance Controversy

Edward J. Miller

Among the problems facing the states, the medical malpractice insurance crisis has impacted all. States in their capacity to license and discipline physicians, to regulate insurance companies, and to determine the rules of the game for civil suits (torts) find that they are the first-line actors in the problems and controversies over medical malpractice. All states within the last decade have taken actions to deal with the problem. This chapter focuses on delineating the problem and reviewing the policies that have been adopted or are being considered by the states.

THE MEDICAL MALPRACTICE CRISIS

The word "crisis" is overused today. We have a crisis in the environment, in education, in urban areas, and so forth. The overuse of the word reduces our sensitivities to problems that may truly be in "crisis"—a decisive moment that if corrective action is not taken a disaster impends. By a more strict definition, it is doubtful that the medical system is in crisis or has as serious problems as physician groups would suggest. Nonetheless, the changed medical malpractice environment in which physicians practice has altered the delivery of medical care. State governments, concerned with the health, safety, and welfare of the community, must monitor these changes and take action if necessary.

Medical malpractice is defined as "avoidable adverse outcomes in which a health care provider fails to adhere to the current standards of medical care and the patient is harmed as a result" (U.S. Department of Health and

Table 12.1
Average Incidence of Malpractice Claims by Specialty

	1985	1981-1984	Prior to 1981
All Physicians*	10.1	8.2	3.2
Specialties			
Obst./Gynecology	26.6	20.6	7.1
Surgery	16.5	11.9	4.1
Radiology	12.9	7.1	2.4
Pediatrics	7.6	4.4	2.3
Anesthesiology	6.5	7.2	3.0
Internal Med.	6.3	6.4	1.9
Gen./Family Prac.	5.5	6.1	3.3

*Includes physicians in specialties not listed separately.
Source: American Medical Association (1986), p. 13.

Table 12.2
Total Compensation Paid by Insurers for Medical Malpractice Claims, 1979–85

Year	$000	Growth (%)
1979	391,582	--
1980	521,849	33.3
1981	662,252	26.8
1983	1,064,447	26.7
1984	1,197,088	12.5
1985	1,544,563	29.0

Source: ʼ. ᵔ. Department of Health and Human Services (1987), p. 167.

Human Services, 1987:6). Finding of malpractice is judicially determined in the United States, with the victim being compensated monetarily. Physicians, hospitals, and other health care providers protect themselves against such monetary awards by carrying insurance. Malpractice is to be differentiated from unavoidable adverse outcomes, a consequence of lack of medical knowledge, the course of a disease, or patient reaction to the treatment but where the physician delivered care in accordance with the current standards of medical care (U.S. Department of Health and Human Services, 1987:7).

What has happened in the United States is that the frequency of claims, the severity of claims (the amount awarded), and the consequent malpractice insurance costs have significantly increased. From 1967 to 1975, claims filed against physicians more than doubled. After a leveling-off period from 1975 to 1978, claims resumed their upward spiral, followed by a decline in 1987. Variation by specialties is great, with high-risk specialties such as surgery and obstetrics/gynecology leading the list. Tables 12.1 and 12.2 document the increased frequency and severity of claims and Table 12.3 provides the average cost per claim.

St. Paul Fire and Marine Insurance, the largest insurer of hospitals, re-

Table 12.3
Average Medical Malpractice Allocated Loss Adjustment Expenses (ALAE) Paid
Per Claim by Insurers

Year	ALAE In Dollars
1982	9,121
1983	10,257
1984	11,360
1985	14,715

Source: U.S. Department of Health and Human Services (1987), p. 168.

Table 12.4
Physicians' Average Premiums by Specialty (Dollars in Thousands)

Specialties	1982	1983	1984	1985	% Increase 1982-1985
Ob/Gyn	$10.9	$14.1	$18.8	$23.3	113%
Surgery	9.9	10.9	13.4	16.6	67
Family Prac.	3.5	4.4	4.9	6.7	91
Intern.Med.	3.7	4.4	4.9	5.8	56
Pediatrics	3.7	4.4	4.9	5.8	66
All Physicians	5.8	7.1	8.4	10.5	81

Source: American Medical Association, Socioeconomic Monitoring System Surveys. Reprinted
in U.S. Department of Health and Human Services, 1987, p. 170.

ported that there was a decline in claims in 1987 to 15.4 claims per 100
physicians from 17 in 1986. The average cost per reported claim, which
includes all claims filed, increased to $17,330 in 1987 fro $13,966 in 1986
(Blum, 1989:1). The inverse relationship between claim frequency and average cost per reported claim is not surprising considering the possibility
that the dropoff in claims is due to fewer frivolous claims.

Along with the increased awards, insurance companies have increased
their premiums to physicians and other health care providers. The increases,
as shown in Table 12.4, have been large, especially for high-risk specialties,
and vary considerably from state to state with premiums being the highest
in Florida, Illinois, Michigan, New York, and Washington, D.C.

Taken at face value, the premiums appear large with significant increases.
But as a percent of physicians' gross incomes, it remains a small percent,
increasing on the average from 3.1 percent in 1982 to 4.6 percent in 1985.
Similarly as a percent of total expenses, cost of malpractice insurance remains relatively small, being 10 percent in 1985. For the highest cost specialty, obstetrics/gynecology, malpractice insurance is a more significant 18
percent of average total expenses in 1985. Even here it remains a small cost
of doing business (U.S. Department of Health and Human Services, 1987:13,
172). Despite continual warnings by physicians of dire consequences of the

availability of health care due to the cost increases in malpractice insurance, studies have failed to document an impact on availability (Zukerman, Koller, and Bovbjerg, 1986:92), and 75 percent of the premium increases have been recovered in increased fees charged (Zukerman et al., 1986:107).

Questions have been raised regarding the justification of the premium increases. Insurance companies obviously have argued that they are needed to cover underwriting losses. But others disagree. A. M. Best, a firm that reports national data regarding insurance firms, shows that malpractice-writing firms have actually been making six times more in premiums than paid out in claims from the period studied from 1978 to 1983 (U.S. Congress, House Hearings, 1986:145). Zukerman et al. (1986), after reviewing the insurance data, state that malpractice insurance returns less of the premium dollar in payouts than either workers' compensation (paying 55 to 70 percent) or first-party health insurance (85 to 90 percent).

Losses reported by insurance companies in malpractice may be a consequence of their bookkeeping conventions. First, investment income is typically omitted from the calculations of profit. Second and most significantly is that they include a reserve fund for *possible* claims that may have occurred in that year that eventually will have to be paid out. The reserve fund is estimated at a level exceeding true claim experience and thus the bottom line reported, upon which rate-making is premised, makes the firms appear in worse shape than they really are (U.S. Congress, House Hearings, 1986:145). Not only are these numbers used for rate-making, but they are used in arguments before state legislatures to change the rules of the game, making it harder for people to file suits against their insured physicians and hospitals.

CAUSES OF THE INCREASED MALPRACTICE CLAIMS

This chapter is not focused on a review of the causes of the rise in malpractice claims. But as the causes suggested here imply, most of the alternative policies to deal with the malpractice insurance situation do not address the true causes—therefore, it is not surprising that their impact is small. This is true of tort reforms as detailed in a later section.

I would argue that increase in general litigiousness in society is responsible for part of the growth in malpractice suits, but it fails to explain a large percentage of the growth of malpractice cases. Nor are attorneys "shopping" for malpractice causes (Danzon, 1986a). Rather, changes in medicine and the way it is practiced have influenced the change.

With increased knowledge and procedures in medicine, the expectations, many times unrealistic expectations, that patients have of their physicians have increased. The increasing gap between expectations and delivery is bound to advance malpractice charges. Further, the complexity of the procedures themselves are bound to lead to unintentional error. There are more

possibilities of failures in technology, in application of skills, and in knowledge with rapidly advancing complexity. These technologies not only have
the possibility of error in their application but by now undertaking surgery
that previously wasn't done, and by using newly developed invasive diagnostic procedures, more severe adverse outcomes are possible as a result of
these medical interventions. Thus, a state's surgery rate and the ratio of
surgeons to medical specialists in a state were found to be associated with
increased claim severity (Danzon, 1986a:79).

The increasingly impersonal way that medicine is practiced leads to more
malpractice suits. Many years ago if the family doctor made an error, it
was an unfortunate situation but not one that would precipitate a suit. The
physician knew the family well, having taken care of several generations,
making a house call when someone was ill. Today, physicians know their
patients far less well, practicing in impersonalized, sterile atmospheres. Increased specialization finds physicians concerned with a particular "diseased
system" rather than the whole patient. Both the decline in the personalized
nature of medical care, more pronounced in urban centers, and more
tertiary facilities in urban areas explain Danzon's (1985:82–83; 1986a:
69, 72) findings that urbanization is the single most important factor that
interprets interstate differences in both frequency and severity of malpractice
claims.

THE POLITICS OF REFORM: THE ACTORS

Senator Howard Metzenbaum, reflecting on the actors in the malpractice
policymaking system, states: "I cannot remember an issue with so many
important professional interests at stake. You've got the doctors, the lawyers, the hospitals, and the insurance industry. The medical malpractice/
product liability issue has become the superbowl of high powered lobbying"
(U.S. Congress, Senate Hearings, 1986:4).

The medical marketplace has at least four sets of actors: health providers
(especially physicians and hospitals), insurance firms for the health providers, patients, and patients' insurance companies (or government in the case
of the elderly and poor), which pay a considerable part of the cost of
treatment. Each of these groups has a significant impact on the treatment
provided. One could argue that although each has a monetary goal—physicians and insurance companies are in the business to make money and the
patient wants to minimize out-of-pocket costs—each also would like to see
adequate care in meeting the illness.

Among the many difficulties that this marketplace faces is when something
goes wrong. If there is the belief that the adverse medical outcome was a
consequence of an error of omission or commission, the patient may file a
malpractice suit. These suits are governed by the rules of the game for suits—
tort law as determined by the state. Thus it is to the benefit of some actors

(especially physicians and their insurance companies) to restrict the considerations under which suits are filed while other patients would want to maintain a tort system advantageous to them in the event of a mishap.

Medical providers are advantaged in the battle over tort reform. They see their plight as immediate—more suits being filed and more cost of malpractice insurance. They threaten that if "something is not done," access to medical care in the community will be reduced. Extensive lobbying and much use of campaign contributions are the rule in most states. Nationally, the American Medical Association remains among the top-spending Political Action Committees (PACs).

Patients who may have a future case are obviously not stimulated to enter the policy dispute. Typically, the side opposing the alternation of the tort rules of the game are the lawyers—the plaintiff's bar. William Falsgraf, president of the American Bar Association (ABA), in testimony before a House Subcommittee, presented the plaintiff attorney's position:

It is the ABA's belief that the rights of injured persons to recover fully for injuries caused by the wrongful acts of others must be protected. We are concerned that those who seek major changes in the way tort law system deals with causes of medical malpractice show a willingness to trade away the rights of all individuals in the hope of easing a perceived burden on some. No single group in society should receive such special treatment. (U.S. Congress, House Hearings, 1986:95)

Insurance firms, allied with the medical providers, are also powerful actors. They are needed to underwrite the medical system. Their power emanates from their monopoly or at least oligopoly positions. Few states have more than two malpractice insurers, and they are constantly threatening to quit writing policies in the state unless reform takes place. Because malpractice insurance is only a small segment of their business, they are believed. The one "stick" that insurance commissions have is that if they stop writing medical malpractice insurance, they may have difficulties with other insurance lines in the state.

TORT REFORMS IN THE STATES

This section will review the changes in the tort system that have been enacted in a number of states.

Cap on Awards

One reform is to limit the damages that can be covered. Indiana, for example, limited the total recovery from any hospital and/or group providers to $500,000, with liability against any single provider limited to no more than $100,000. Other states have limited elements of the awards. For example, noneconomic awards—which include payment for physical impairment, disfigurement, and pain and suffering—may be limited. Alaska has a limitation of $500,000 per claim, but it exempts disfigurement and severe physical impairment from the limitation. Wisconsin had a $1 million limitation to be adjusted for inflation, which was not renewed by the legislature. Unsuccessful pressure on the legislature had tried to reduce the limitation to $250,000. Currently, a move is under way to restore the $1 million cap.

New limitations on damage awards frequently focus on punitive damages, seemingly easier to enact that limitation on "real" losses. Alaska permits punitive damages only in unusual circumstances if the evidence is clear and convincing. Iowa now allows them only when the defendant engaged in behavior that was "willful and wanton disregard for the rights and safety of another," a difficult finding in a medical malpractice case. Florida takes a less restricted punitive damages approach by simply limiting punitive damages to three times compensatory damages.

Periodic payment is a reform that limits how much is paid per year. Insurance firms would rather pay out a damage award over several years than have to make a lump-sum payment. South Dakota and Rhode Island are two states now permiting periodic payment for awards exceeding $100,000.

According to research under the Ford Foundation by Patricia Danzon, caps on awards do not impact the frequency of claims but do affect severity. But its impact is restricted to the very few large cases, where presumably the situation was worse than most cases (Danzon, 1986a:77).

Collateral Source Rule

Physicians and medical providers and their insurance companies want to see the elimination of the collateral source rule. This rule disallows the consideration in awards payment received by the patient for medical costs by the patient's private medical insurance and worker's compensation (U.S. Congress, Senate Hearings, 1986:717). Defendants want the damage award to be reduced by the amount received from other sources. This is what has been done in Florida. A compromise is to permit the jury to receive information regarding other compensation but not require the reduction. Both California and Massachusetts have taken this approach.

Among tort reform, Danzon (1986a) in her study found that changes in the collateral sources rule had the greatest impact among tort reforms. It affects both claim frequency (p. 72) and claim severity (p. 77).

Statute of Limitations

Traditionally in tort actions, as in many criminal matters, a statute of limitations governs. But in the medical malpractice area, a person may not discover the problem until several years later. This is most notable with a baby and thus states have given extended time to initiate suits here. Obstetricians therefore may be exposed to suits for 20 years or more after the birth of a baby. By this time witnesses will probably not remember what happened even if they are still around.

To reduce suit exposure but allow sufficient time to initiate suits, states have reduced their time limits for suits. California, for example, imposed a three-year statute of limitations on most actions, with minors allowed to sue either during the three-year period or up to their eighth birthday, whichever is longer. Maine requires that for minors, suits commence within six years of the cause or three years of maturity, whichever comes first.

The Ford study did find that reduced statute of limitations had an impact. A one-year reduction appeared to reduce frequency of suits by about 8 percent (Danzon, 1986a:78).

Merit Requirements for Suits

Some states have instituted policies attempting to rid the system of frivolous suits. One method has been the requirement that a certificate of merit, filed by the plaintiff's attorney in consultation with a physician knowledgeable about the issues involved, be included in any malpractice suit. California in 1978 and Wyoming in 1986 instituted such a requirement. It is highly doubtful that this kind of requirement will have a significant impact. Since most malpractice suits are accepted by attorneys on a contingency fee basis, few attorneys will take the financial risk of filing suit unless they have either consulted with a physician to determine that there is a basis for the suit or have a strong reasonable belief based upon experience that the suit is viable. Further, although in former days (and still in some communities) it was difficult to find a physician to testify against other physicians, the situation has changed with the "wall of silence" being penetrated, and in many communities, especially larger communities, where it is not too difficult to find "plaintiff physicians."

Although most states do not require a certification of merit to be filed with the suit, legislation has been enacted in many states permitting the court to penalize a party for filing a baseless claim. In federal court, Rule 11 of the Federal Rules of Civil Procedure allows penalties to be assessed against the party filing the claim and the party's attorney (U.S. Department of Health and Human Services, 1987:135).

Questions regarding expert testimony for plaintiffs have arisen along similar lines. For many years, states limited expert witnesses to physicians who practice in the community. The argument was that medicine as practiced differs from community to community, thus testimony should be restricted to physicians who are familiar with the standards of the community in which the suit is filed. The problem, often noted, is that a "wall of silence" developed with physicians unwilling to testify against their peers when they must practice in the same community. Therefore, it was very difficult to sustain a malpractice suit because plaintiffs were unable to secure expert testimony.

Some states have changed the rules allowing testimony from experts from other areas under the suppositions that medicine is far more nationally uniform today (although studies continue to show significant differences in practice among communities) and that unless outside physicians are allowed to testify, the reluctance of local physicians to testify against one of their own will result in the continuing practice of incompetent practitioners. Despite the laudable goals of this policy change, a impact has been the development of physicians who are professional witnesses, who testify for plaintiffs all across the nation.

Particular concern has been expressed in cases in which these professional witnesses are paid a percent of the plaintiff's award. Such a payment scheme reduces the credibility of their testimony. A new business has emerged of medical brokers who receive a contingency fee of 20 to 30 percent to provide medical testimony. The physician in this case receives a flat fee. Medical-Legal Consultants of Bethesda, Maryland, states that it has 600 physicians on call for witness duty (Richards, 1988:B1). Not only is the American Medical Association concerned about this method of securing expert witnesses, but a committee of the American Bar Association in November 1987, in an advisory opinion, found "substantial ethical problems" with the brokering of physician witnesses (Richards, 1988:B1).

Further, physicians who are not specialists in the area of the malpractice suit may be called upon to testify. Tort changes in Kansas and Michigan have tightened rules of admission of expert witnesses to assure that they are very familiar with the medical questions in the case, by requiring them to practice specialties that the case concerns.

Arbitration Panels

To reduce backlogs in the court system, alternative modes of conflict resolution have been developed. In medical malpractice, arbitration panel systems—typically composed of lawyers, physicians, and public (lay) members—hear the case and make a judgment. Arguments favoring this approach include the following: experts who consider a number of malpractice cases hear the case; the rules of evidence can be relaxed, getting at the basis of the case more rapidly; and the panels can weed out unworthy cases, saving not only court time but physicians' time, money, and anguish over unworthy suits (U.S. Senate Hearings, 1986:344).

Maryland has a mandatory arbitration panel system, with each panel composed of three people—an attorney chairman, a health care provider, and a consumer. The panel, using informal rules, determines the merit of the action and the amount of the award. If the losing party appeals to the court, which happened only 14 percent of the time from 1977 to 1983 (from 1984 to 1991, 6 percent were waived to court from the arbitration system), then the losing party has the burden of proof to show that the decision of the panel was in error (U.S. Congress, Senate Hearings, 1986:377). While many states are considering this approach, Wisconsin has abandoned the use of its Patient Compensation Panels on the recommendation of physicians.

Danzon's review of arbitration panels showed that these panels actually increased the number of claims filed by encouraging more small claims, most likely a consequence of the simplified procedures. Severity is reduced by 20 percent, but according to Danzon (1986a:77) overall cost is not reduced since the reduced severity is offset by increased frequency.

Attorneys' Contingency Fees

Attorneys have historically used the contingency fee approach in civil tort suits. Typically receiving one-third of the settlement, an attorney takes a risk in accepting a case (Corsi, 1984:216–18). Traditionally, attorneys have argued that such a compensation scheme allows clients too poor to pay an attorney to bring a case against a party that has wronged them. Attorneys maintain that a contingency fee compensation system limits frivolous suits, because the financial risk that attorneys must take provides an incentive to be selective in case acceptance.

Physicians, on the other hand, frequently argue that plaintiff attorneys solicit cases with the contingency fee system being an incentive to the client to bring a case. If the client loses the action, he doesn't have to worry about attorney fees. Additionally, physicians argue that contingency fees increase severity as attorneys benefit in direct proportion to the damages recovered.

Several states have considered contingency fee limitations in medical malpractice as currently exist in some other areas such as workers' compensation. California, for example, has instituted a sliding scale, allowing attorneys to collect 40 percent from the first $50,000; 33–1/3 percent from the next $50,000; 25 percent from the next $100,000; and 10 percent from any amount exceeding $200,000.

Danzon and Lillard (1983) found a small impact of contingency fee limitations on the size of settlements and the number of cases dropped. But in a more extensive study, Danzon stated that the contingency fee limitations did not appear to have any systematic impact on either the frequency or size of awards (Danzon, 1986b).

DISCIPLINARY ACTION AS AN APPROACH TO
STEM MALPRACTICE

Data reveal that malpractice cases are disproportionately distributed among physicians. By disciplining the small percentage of physicians in a

Table 12.5
Disciplinary Actions Taken Against Physicians in the States, 1985

Type of Action	Number
License Revoked	606
License Suspended	235
Probation	491
Other Penalties	975

Source: Brinkley, (1986).

community who have incurred the larger proportion of malpractice claims, including removing licenses and restricting practices, the amount of malpractice will be reduced and hence claims frequency. Table 12.5 presents data on disciplinary actions in 1985. Incompetent physicians increase insurance rates for all in their specialties, for insurance firms charge what is known as a "community rating" rather than an "experience rating," whereby the insurance costs would increase if the physician is successfully sued.

There has been an increase in the number of disciplinary actions taken in many states. But large backlogs remain (U.S. Department of Health and Human Services, 1986:i). Of the disciplinary actions taken, only a small percent relates to incompetence with more than three-fourths involving drug or alcohol abuse by the physician or inappropriate prescribing of drugs. Concerning the lack of action for incompetence, the Department of Health and Human Services Report (1986:14) stated:

The minimal response in the area of physician incompetence is placing boards in an increasingly untenable position as the incidence of malpractice cases and public concern about the implications of these cases increase.... Boards, it is increasingly felt, can and should do something about this situation.

Reasons for inaction cited in the Report include that alleged malpractice disciplinary cases are complex and long, even when a tort malpractice action has been rendered; that the brunt of proof requiring "clear and convincing" evidence rather than the "preponderance of evidence" makes judgments difficult; and that there remains considerable variation among acceptable practice (p. 14). Responding to this problem, Wisconsin in 1985 changed its law to allow admission of a court finding of physician negligence in patent care to serve as conclusive evidence that negligence in treatment occurred. Another Wisconsin change is the adoption of the lesser evidence standard of "preponderance of the evidence" for "clear and convincing evidence" (U.S. Department of Health and Human Services, 1986:14–15).

The number of disciplinary actions in a state is unrelated either to the population of the state or the number of physicians in the state. Correlations using 1985 data on discipline reveal a nonsignificant correlation of $-.102$ between population and disciplinary actions and $-.151$ between the number of physicians in a state and the number of disciplinary actions. Therefore either the quality of physicians differs remarkably among the states or the regulatory environment significantly differs to explain the differential number of actions. Although the first probably does explain some of the variance, the probability is that the latter explains considerably more. For example, Connecticut and Arizona had about the same population in 1985 but Connecticut had 2,602 more physicians. Despite the greater number of physicians and therefore the greater possibility of malpractice situations, Connecticut brought only four actions against physicians with no license revocations while Arizona brought 115 with 11 licenses being revoked (Brinkley, 1986:14).

The federal government in 1991 established a national data base containing physician malpractice records, which previously were not available. Access to this data base will assist states in the licensing activity by informing licensing boards and hospital committees in states to which a physician might move of previous disciplinary actions; provide peer review actions, such as professional review by a hospital or health maintenance organization peer review committee; and enable legal suits against physicians. Patients will not have access to the reports on individual physicians. Use of the material will be restricted to licensing boards and staffing committees.

INSURANCE REFORMS

In addition to tort reforms and enhanced enforcement, another major approach to the malpractice issue concerns reforms to the insurance system.

Patient Compensation Funds

The patient compensation fund is a reinsurance concept whereby the carrier's liability is limited to a specified sum per claim and per year for physicians insured. The excess is paid out of a state-operated fund, financed by fees levied on all health care providers and in some state funds from general revenue. The purpose of such funds is to insure the availability of malpractice insurance in the state by limiting the liability of insurance carriers. Fifteen states have developed state patient compensation funds (U.S. Department of Health and Human Services, 1987:134–35). The problem encountered by the funds, similar to that encountered by individual insurers, is solvency, with states finding that they must increase fees, thereby triggering dollar levels.

Insurance companies frequently use private reinsurance such as Lloyds of London. But with many reinsurers either withdrawing from malpractice insurance liability or substantially increasing rates, which are then passed along by the first-part insurer, reinsurers have contributed to the problem. Whether the state as reinsurer can do a better job is the question in developing state patient compensation funds. At minimum, the state funds will not withdraw as private reinsurers have, and we will have a better understanding of the true financial picture. Reinsurers, who are mostly international, are not regulated.

Experience Rating

A further insurance reform is to adopt experience rating in place of community rating. Rather than charge each physician in a particular specialization category the same rate, insurance premiums should depend on the claims experience of the individual physician. Therefore, physicians who do not have any or few malpractice suits filed against them will pay substantially less than those with many suits. Since data show that a small percent of physicians are responsible for a disproportionate percent of malpractice suits, this reform would end subsidization and lower premiums for a large number of practitioners. In 1986 Massachusetts enacted a law requiring the use of merit rating. Although it is frequently argued that merit rating would also serve as a deterrent to physicians incurring malpractice suits, it would seem that the often-discussed stress and time commitments on the part of physicians who are sued are now a deterrent, with little being added by the threat of having insurance premiums go up.

Class Rating

To establish rates, physicians are divided into classes based upon the frequency and severity of malpractice suits in that class. Thus, obstetricians and neurosurgeons pay significantly more in malpractice premiums, both in dollar terms and in percent of income, than family practitioners who do not deliver babies. The result, it is argued, is that physicians are reluctant to go into specializations that are associated with both greater malpractice risks and greater insurance costs. Even physicians practicing higher risk specialties are said to be giving up high-risk procedures to lower malpractice insurance rates. For example, 12.3 percent of obstetricians/gynecologists (surveyed in 1985) are restricting their practice to gynecology and many family practitioners are no longer delivering babies, a procedure that would put them in a higher class for malpractice premiums (see Needham Porter Nevelli Report reprinted in U.S. Congress, Senate Hearings, 1986:78–140, especially Table 28).

One approach is to reduce the number of premium classes and reduce the rates of the higher premium specialists. To compensate, the rates would have to increase for those in the lower class categories. Two justifications for this subsidization can be given. First, we need to maintain physicians practicing in the higher rate categories, and lowering their premiums is one step in that direction. Second, the lower rate category physicians are now paying a lower percent of their income in malpractice insurance than specialists. Their practice benefits from having available for referral the higher insurance category specialists.

CONCLUSIONS

Two key concerns of medical malpractice in the United States are the functioning of the tort system and the governmental regulatory system for disciplining physicians. Concerning the regulatory system, professional regulation in the medical area is no different than that existing in other professional areas—inadequate review of physicians and imposition of disciplinary actions where appropriate. (For a discussion of professional regulation of attorneys see E. J. Miller [1988].) With increasing public criticism of medical discipline (Department of Health and Human Services, 1986:12) and an increasing concern among physicians that a few among them are responsible for a large number of malpractice suits, examination of physician competence has improved in many states. There is general agreement though that discipline remains inadequate.

As for the tort system, physicians and insurance firms have pushed for change. They claim that the present tort system magnifies malpractice actions and has put such an economic burden on the system that the delivery of health care in the United States is being adversely affected.

Others would disagree. The purpose of the tort system is to act as a deterrent to practitioners who might commit malpractice (Danzon, 1985:4; U.S. Congress, House Hearings, 1986:96). With medicine being a case of market failure as patients are unable to judge the worth or risks of treatment, physicians (the suppliers in the market) make the determination. The tort system fundamentally states that if physicians are negligently wrong, they must bear the financial risk. Therefore, it says to physicians that there is a penalty if you do not stay up with current treatment, order unnecessary risky procedures, do procedures that you are inadequately trained for, or simply provide insufficient attention to or follow up of a patient resulting in injury.

Physicians, being risk adverse, make a side payment to insurance companies to bear the risk. This third-party payment financially insulates physicians from the deterrent impact of the tort system (Danzon, 1985:5), although not from the time and psychological impacts of suits filed against them. The financial insulation could be reduced if the insurance system charged physicians on the experience basis (number of malpractice claims made against them) rather than on the community rating basis (Daly, 1977:29).

Is the tort system at variance with incidence of true malpractice? Surely some of the claims filed are not justified. But a quantitative evaluation suggests that of the studies of occurrence of malpractice, the frequency of suits represents only a small percent (Danzon, 1985:20–25; U.S. Congress, Senate Hearings, 1986:2). Although there is an increasing number of large settlements, these occur in only severe cases. It is a matter of judgment how much compensation severely injured people are entitled to beyond the payment for medical expenses and economic losses. For a majority of suits the physician wins and no compensation is awarded. The average dollar amount awarded in a finding of negligence is modest (Blum, 1989).

Some reforms of the tort system do seem prudent. A statute of limitations, longer for minors, seems justified to put more certainty into the system. The admission into evidence of collateral benefits has shown an impact in reducing claim frequency and severity and seems justified. Additionally, an initial arbitration system whose impact is to reduce the significant litigation costs of the system should also be considered. But overall, given the purposes of the tort system to compensate victims of malpractice and to deter its commission, it should be essentially allowed to work as a regulator in the medical care market.

REFERENCES

American Medical Association. 1986. *Socioeconomic Characteristics of Medical Practice. 1986.* Chicago: American Medical Association.

Blum, A. 1989. "Malpractice: Claims Down, Costs Up." *National Law Journal,* January, 1.

Brinkley, J. 1986. "State Medical Boards Disciplined Record Number of Doctors in '85." *New York Times,* November 19:1.

Corsi, J. 1984. *Judicial Politics.* Englewood Cliffs, NJ: Prentice-Hall.

Daly, J. C. 1977. *The Medical Malpractice Dilemma.* Washington, DC: American Enterprise Institute for Public Policy Research.

Danzon, P. M. 1985. *Medical Malpractice: Theory, Evidence, and Public Policy.* Cambridge, MA: Harvard University Press.

———. 1986a. "The Frequency and Severity of Medical Malpractice Claims: New Evidence." *Law and Contemporary Problems* 49:57–84.

———. 1986b. "Medical Malpractice Claims: New Evidence." *Medical Malpractice* 28.

———. 1986c. *New Evidence in the Frequency and Severity of Medical Malpractice Claims.* Santa Monica, CA: Rand Corporation.

Danzon, P. M. and L. A. Lillard. 1983. "Settlement Out of Court: The Disposition of Medical Malpractice Claims." *Journal of Legal Studies* 12:345–77.

Miller, E. J. 1988. "Public Members on Professional Regulatory Boards: The Case of Lawyers in Wisconsin." *Administration and Society* 20:369–90.

Richards, B. 1988. "Doctors Seek Crack Down on Colleagues Paid for Testimony on Malpractice Suits." *Wall Street Journal,* November 7:B1.

U.S. Congress. House Hearings. 1986. Hearings before the Subcommittee on Health and the Environment of the Committee on Energy and Commerce. *Medical Malpractice,* hearing no. 99–152.

U.S. Congress. Senate Hearings. 1986. Hearings before the Committee on Labor and Human Resources. *Federal Incentives for State Health Care Professional Liability Reform Act of 1985.* Hrg. 99–920.

U.S. Department of Health and Human Services, Regional Inspector General. 1986. *Medical License and Discipline: An Overview.* June (Xerox).

U.S. Department of Health and Human Services. 1987. *Task Force on Medical Liability and Malpractice.* August.

Zuckerman, S., C. F. Koller, and R. R. Bovbjerg. 1986. "Information on Malpractice: A Review of Empirical Research on Major Policy Issues." *Law and Contemporary Problems* 49:85–111.

Selected Bibliography

HEALTH POLICY IMPACTS

Aaron, Henry J. and William B. Schwartz. 1984. *The Painful Prescription: Rationing Hospital Care*. Washington, DC: The Brookings Institution.

Arrow, K. 1963. "Uncertainty and the Welfare Economics of Medical Care." *American Economic Review* 53:941.

Blank, Robert H. 1986. *Rationing Medicine*. New York: Columbia University Press.

Boles, K. 1989. "Implications of the Method of Capital Cost Payment on the Weighted Average Cost of Capital." *Health Services Review* 21:189.

Broyles, R. and M. Rosko. 1990. *Fiscal Management of Healthcare Institutions*. Owings Mills, MD: National Health Publishing.

Dardanoni, V. and A. Wagstarr. 1987. "Uncertainty and Inequalities in Health and the Demand for Health." *Journal of Health Economics* 6:283.

Derthick, Martha and Paul J. Quirk. 1985. *The Politics of Deregulation*. Washington, DC: Brookings Institution.

Fein, Rashi. 1986. *Medical Costs: The Search for a Health Insurance Policy*. Cambridge, MA: Harvard University Press.

Fuchs, Victor R. 1986. *The Health Economy*. Cambridge, MA: Harvard University Press.

Lowi, Theodore J. 1963. "American Business, Public Policy, Case-Studies and Political Theory." *World Politics* 16:766–815.

Manga, P., R. Broyles, and D. Angus. 1987. "The Determinants of Hospital Utilization Under a Universal Public Insurance Program in Canada." *Medical Care* 27:658.

Marmor, Theodore R. 1983. *Political Analysis and American Medical Care: Essays*. New York: Cambridge University Press.

Rosko, J. 1989. "Impact of the New Jersey All-Payer Rate Setting System: An Analysis of Financial Ratios." *Hospital and Health Services Administration.* 34:53.

Russell, Louise B. 1986. *Is Prevention Better Than Cure?* Washington, DC: The Brookings Institution.

Wilensky, G. and L. Rossiter. 1986. "Alternative Units of Payment for Physician Services." *Medical Care Review* 43:133.

HEALTH CARE PROVISION FOR THE NEEDY

Ansberry, C. 1988. "Dumping the Poor: Despite Federal Law, Hospitals Still Reject Sick Who Can't Pay." *Wall Street Journal,* November 29: A1, A10.

Bookheimer, S. 1989. "Uncompensated Care and the Hospital: A Political-Economic Perspective." *Journal of Health and Human Resources Administration* 11:328–40.

Buss, Terry F. and F. Stevens Redburn. 1983. *Shutdown in Youngstown: Public Policy for Mass Unemployment.* New York: State University of New York Press.

Gold, A. R. 1989. "The Struggle to Make Do Without Health Insurance." *New York Times,* July 30:1, 11.

Hadley, J. 1982. *More Medical Care, Better Health.* Washington, DC: The Urban Institute.

Hollingsworth, J. R. and E. Hollingsworth. 1986. "A Comparison of Non-Profit and For-Profit Hospitals in the United States: 1935 to the Present." Program on Non-Profit Organizations. Institution for Social and Policy Studies, Yale University (PONPO Working Paper No. 113, June).

Hopkins, B. 1979. *The Law of Tax-Exempt Organizations.* New York: John Wiley.

Hopkins, Kevin R. 1987. *Welfare Dependency.* Washington, DC: U.S. Department of Health and Human Services, September.

Kellerman, A. L. and B. B. Hackman. 1988. "Emergency Department 'Patient Dumping': An Analysis of Interhospital Transfers to the Regional Medical Center at Memphis, Tennessee." *American Journal of Public Health* 78:1287–92.

Moyer, M. E. 1989. "A Revised Look at the Number of Uninsured Americans." *Health Affairs* 8:102–10.

Powell, W. W. 1987. *The Nonprofit Sector: A Research Notebook.* New Haven, CT: Yale University Press.

Rice, M. F. 1989. "Medical Indigency and Inner-City Hospital Care: Patient Dumping, Emergency Care and Public Policy." *Journal of Health and Social Policy* 1:1–29

IMPLEMENTING HEALTH INSURANCE

Berk, Marc and Gail Wilensky. 1987. "Health Coverage of the Working Poor." *Social Science and Medicine* 25(11):1183–87.

Brandon, W. P. 1991. "Two Kinds of Conservatism in U.S. Health Policy: The Reagan Record." In *From Rhetoric to Reality: Comparative Health Policy and the New Right,* C. Altenstetter and S. C. Haywood, eds. London: Macmillan.

Davidson, S. M. and T. R. Marmor. 1980. *The Cost of Living Longer: National Health Insurance and the Elderly.* Lexington, MA: Lexington Books.

DeJong, Gerben. 1989. "America's Neglected Minority: Working-Age Persons with Disabilities." *The Milbank Quarterly* 76:311–51, Supplement 2, Part 2.

Fox, Daniel. 1989. "Policy and Epidemiology: Financing Health Services for the Chronically Ill and Disabled, 1930–1990." *The Milbank Quarterly* 67:257–287, Supplement 2, Part 2.

Ginzberg, E. 1984. "The Monetarization of Medical Care." *New England Journal of Medicine* 310(18):1162–65.

Grimaldi, P. J. and J. A. Micheletti. 1982. *Diagnosis Related Groups: A Practitioner's Guide.* Chicago: Pluribus Press.

Jones, Gareth R. and Charles W. L. Hill. 1988. "Transaction Cost Analysis of Strategy-Structure Choice." *Strategic Management Journal,* 9:159–72.

Kane, R. L. and R. A. Kane. 1991. "A Nursing Home in Your Future?" *New England Journal of Medicine* 324:627–29.

Kemper, P. and C. M. Murtaugh. 1991. "Lifetime Use of Nursing Home Care." *New England Journal of Medicine* 324:595–600.

Levitan, Sar A., Garth L. Mangum, and Ray Marshall. 1981. *Human Resources and Labor Markets.* New York: Harper & Row.

Rivlin, M. R. and J. M. Wiener. 1988. *Caring for the Disabled Elderly: Who Will Pay?* Washington, DC: The Brookings Institution.

PREVENTION AND RISK FACTORS

Chao, A., A. Paganini-Hill, R. K. Ross, and B. E. Henderson. 1987. "Use of Preventive Care by the Elderly." *Preventive Medicine* 16:710–22.

Crooks, Catherine E. and Steven D. Jones. 1989. "Educating Women about the Importance of Breast Screening: The Nurse's Role." *Cancer Nursing* 12:161–64.

Daly, J. C. 1976. *The Medical Malpractice Dilemma.* Washington, DC: American Enterprise Institute for Public Policy Research.

Danzon, P. M. 1985. *Medical Malpractice: Theory, Evidence, and Public Policy.* Cambridge, MA: Harvard University Press.

Farley, Thomas A. and John T. Flannery. 1989. "Late-Stage Diagnosis of Breast Cancer in Women of Lower Socio-Economic Status: Public Health Implications." *American Journal of Public Health* 79:1508–12.

Kagawa-Singer, Marjorie. 1987. "Ethnic Perspectives of Cancer Nursing: Hispanics and Japanese-Americans." *Oncology Nursing Forum* 14:59–65.

Sidel, Ruth. 1986. *Women and Children Last.* New York: Penguin.

Sloan, F. A. 1985. "State Responses to the Malpractice Insurance 'Crisis' of the 1970s: An Empirical Assessment." *Journal of Health Politics, Policy and Law* 9:4–20.

Zuckerman, S., C. F. Koller, and R. R. Bovbjerg. 1986. "Information on Malpractice: A Review of Empirical Research on Major Policy Issues." *Law and Contemporary Problems* 49:85–111.

Name Index

Garfinkel, I., 121
Garfinkel, Steven, 150
Gass, J., 21
Georgopolous, Basil, xxi
Giachello, A., 189
Gilbert, F., 189
Ginsberg, P., xxi, 21
Gold, A., xxi, 84
Goldberg, D., 57
Goldberg, G., 22
Goldman, Harry, 150
Goodman, J., 84
Gottlieb, Benjamin, 189
Graddy, E., 100
Grady, Kathleen, 189
Greenberg, W., 21
Greenlick, M., 21
Greensberg, D., 84
Grossman, Steven, 121
Grothaus, Louis, 191
Guffey, Teddylen, 136

Hackaman, B., 84
Hadley, J., 21, 72
Hall, J., 57
Hammons, G., 21
Handler, E., 22
Harnley, M., 84
Hatch, John, 189
Havighurst, C., 21
Hayward, R., 120
Haywood, S., 120
Heagy, Thomas, 48
Hellinger, Fred, 150
Helms, C., 22
Henderson, B., 188
Henderson, Mary, 150
Herbert, F., 48
Hess, J., 121
Hill, Charles, 136
Hillman, Diane, 136
Himmelstein, D., 21, 84, 121
Hisserich, John, 190, 191
Hoadley, John, 48
Hollingsworth, E., 100
Hollingsworth, J., 100
Holthaus, D., 84
Homer, M., 20

Hopkins, B., 100Hopkins, Kevin, 72
Horm, John, 189
Hornbrook, M., 21
Horrigan, Michael, 72
Horvath, Francis, 72
Hsaio, W., 21
Hughes, K., 168

Idris, A., 84
Iglehart, J., 21
Israel, Barbara A., 189

Jacobs, Philip, 168
Jacobson, Carol, 136
Jazairi, N., 57
Jensen, G., 21
Jensen, Gail, 150, 151
Jones, D., 84
Jones, Gareth, 136
Jones, Steven, 189

Kagawa-Singer, Marjorie, 189
Kamberg, C., 21
Kane, R., 121
Kasper, J., 72
Kass, Nancy, 150
Kegeles, Stephen, 189
Keith, Pat, 189
Kellerman, A., 84
Kemper, P., 121
Kerschner, Paul, 150
Kessler, Larry, 188, 191
King, Martha, 72
Kirkman-Liff, Bradford, 136
Kirkman-Liff, Tracy, 136
Kissick, W., 49
Klos, Dennis, 189
Koller, C., 208
Kosko, Debra, 189
Kovar, M., 121
Kramon, Glen, 168

Langwell, K., 21
Lee, E., 169
Lee, Isaiah, 190
Lee, P., 21
Lee, Philip, xxi
Lee, Robert, 151

Subject Index

About the Contributors

ANONA F. ARMSTRONG is Managing Director of Evaluation Training and Services, Australia Pty. Ltd. and an Associate of the Department of Psychology at the University of Melbourne, as well as a Fellow of the Australian Psychological Society and Past President of the Australasian Evaluation Society. She is a management consultant specializing in evaluation.

ROBERT H. BLANK is professor of political science and associate director of the Program for Biosocial Research at Northern Illinois University and at the University of Canterbury, Christchurch, New Zealand. Among his recent books are *The Political Implications of Human Genetic Technology, Redefining Human Life, Reproductive Technologies and Social Policy, Rationing Medicine, Regulating Reproduction,* and *Life, Death, and Public Policy.*

WILLIAM BRANDON is professor of political science and codirector of the Health Policy and Finance Research Institute at Seton-Hall University, specializing in health politics and policy. His recent work has been included in *From Rhetoric to Reality: Comparative Health Policy and the New Right* and *Health Politics and Policy.*

ROBERT W. BROYLES is a professor in the College of Health Related Professions at the Medical University of South Carolina. In addition to nine books, his articles have been published in *Medical Care, Social Science and Medicine, Inquiry,* and *Medical Care Review,* among others.

TERRY F. BUSS is professor and director of the doctoral program in urban studies at the University of Akron and director of research at St. Elizabeth Hospital Medical Center. He has published more than 150 articles and 8 books on numerous public policy issues including poverty, health, unemployment, and plant closings.

BETTE S. HILL is associate professor of political science at the University of Akron. Dr. Hill's major research interests are health and aging politics and she has published in gerontology and policy journals. She and Katherine Hinckley are currently researching the politics of Medicare and health interests groups.

KATHERINE A. HINCKLEY is associate professor of political science at the University of Akron. Her major research interests are Congress and interest groups. Dr. Hinckley has published in American politics and policy journals.

CAROL K. JACOBSON is an assistant professor at Arizona State University. Her primary research interest is the impact of the strategic positioning of health care organizations on performance, as measured by efficiency as well as financial measures.

WALTER J. JONES is associate professor of Health Services Administration at the Medical University of South Carolina. His primary research interests are in the areas of health policy and politics, and he has published research dealing with a wide variety of health policy issues.

WOODROW JONES is Associate Dean and professor of political science at Texas A & M University. He is co-author of *Black American Health* (Greenwood Press, 1987) and *Health of Black Americans from Post Reconstruction to Integration, 1871–1960* (Greenwood Press, 1990).

JAMES LARSON is associate professor of public administration at the University of Arkansas, Little Rock. He is the author of *The Measurement of Health: Concepts and Indicators* (Greenwood, 1991) and has published articles in the areas of health administration and policy.

ALICE J. LONGMAN is a professor at the University of Arizona College of Nursing, Tucson. Her major field of interest is oncology nursing and she teaches undergraduate as well as graduate students.

EDWARD J. MILLER is professor of political science and codirector of the Center for the Small City at the University of Wisconsin–Stevens Point. He is joint editor of the nine-volume *The Small City and Regional Community:*

Proceedings and author for articles on health policy, legislative process, and state and urban governments.

MIRIAM K. MILLS was professor of organizational science at The New Jersey Institute of Technology. She was coeditor of *Biomedical Technology and Public Policy* (Greenwood, 1989), and coauthor of *Multi-Criteria Methods in Alternative Dispute Resolution* (Greenwood, 1990), and *Evaluation Analysis with Microcomputers.* Dr. Mills also wrote extensively on conflict resolution, public policy, and social impacts of technology.

BERNARD J. REILLY is professor of management at Widener University. He has published or presented over 100 articles at national conferences and his articles appear in such journals as *Health Politics, Law and Review, Hospital and Health Services Administration, Inquiry,* and *Business Economics.*

MITCHELL F. RICE is professor of public administration and political science at Louisiana State University, Baton Rouge. He is coeditor of *Health Care Issues in Black America* (Greenwood Press, 1987) and co-author of *Blacks and American Government: Politics, Policy and Social Change.*

MICHELLE A. SAINT-GERMAIN is a research associate at the Southwest Institute for Research on Women. Her research focuses on public policy, especially in relation to women. She is currently conducting research on older Hispanic women and preventive health care, the Arizona state legislature, and elected women in Central American republics.

SUSAN M. SANDERS is assistant professor, Graduate Program in Public Services, DePaul University. In addition to researching aspects of tax-exemption policy, she studies the economic and organizational aspects of nonprofit organizations, and serves as a consultant to a variety of religious organizations that sponsor hospitals, nursing homes, and housing projects for the elderly.

ROGER S. VAUGHAN is an economic consultant, specializing in human resource issues, based in Santa Fe, New Mexico. He is the author of over 100 books and articles on state and local human development and economic development topics.

Policy Studies Organization publications issued with Greenwood Press/Quorum Books

Policy Through Impact Assessment: Institutionalized Analysis as a Policy Strategy
Robert V. Bartlett, editor

Biomedical Technology and Public Policy
Robert H. Blank and Miriam K. Mills, editors

Implementation and the Policy Process: Opening up the Black Box
Dennis J. Palumbo and Donald J. Calista, editors

Policy Theory and Policy Evaluation Concepts, Knowledge, Causes, and Norms
Stuart S. Nagel, editor

Biotechnology: Assessing Social Impacts and Policy Implications
David J. Webber, editor

Public Administration and Decision-Aiding Software: Improving Procedure and Substance
Stuart S. Nagel, editor

Outdoor Recreation Policy: Pleasure and Preservation
John D. Hutcheson, Jr., Francis P. Noe, and Robert E. Snow, editors

Conflict Resolution and Public Policy
Miriam K. Mills, editor

Teaching Public Policy: Theory, Research, and Practice
Peter J. Bergerson, editor

The Reconstruction of Family Policy
Elaine A. Anderson and Richard C. Hula, editors

Gubernatorial Leadership and State Policy
Eric B. Herzik and Brent W. Brown, editors

Public Policy Issues in Wildlife Management
William R. Mangun, editor